ST. <S0-BJH-945>

ST. MARY'S CITY, MARYLAND 2068

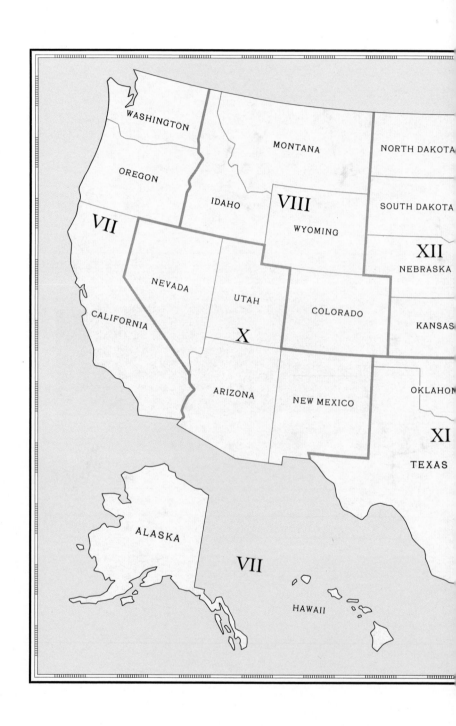

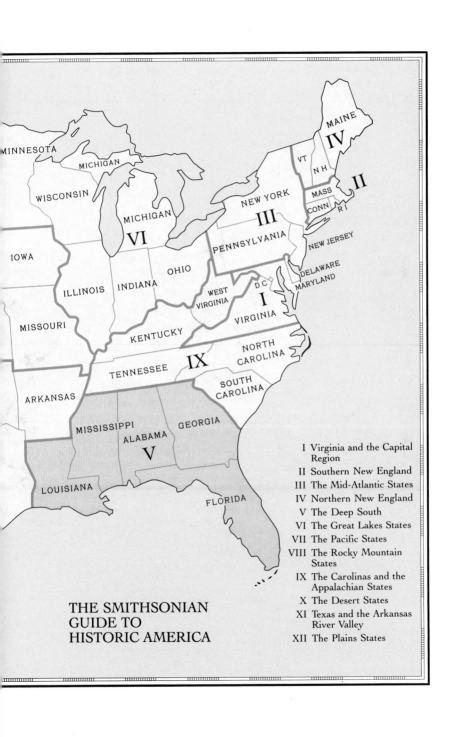

I Virginia and the Capital
  Region
II Southern New England
III The Mid-Atlantic States
IV Northern New England
V The Deep South
VI The Great Lakes States
VII The Pacific States
VIII The Rocky Mountain
  States
IX The Carolinas and the
  Appalachian States
X The Desert States
XI Texas and the Arkansas
  River Valley
XII The Plains States

THE SMITHSONIAN
GUIDE TO
HISTORIC AMERICA

# THE
# SMITHSONIAN
## GUIDE TO
# HISTORIC AMERICA

## THE DEEP SOUTH

TEXT BY
WILLIAM BRYANT LOGAN
VANCE MUSE

EDITORIAL DIRECTOR
ROGER G. KENNEDY
DIRECTOR OF THE NATIONAL MUSEUM
OF AMERICAN HISTORY
OF THE SMITHSONIAN INSTITUTION

Stewart, Tabori & Chang
NEW YORK

Text copyright © 1989 Stewart, Tabori & Chang, Inc.

Due to limitations of space, additional photo credits appear on page 463 and constitute an extension of this page.

All information is accurate as of publication. We suggest contacting the sites prior to a visit to confirm hours of operation.

Published in 1989 by Stewart, Tabori & Chang, Inc., 740 Broadway, New York, NY 10003.

All rights reserved. No part of this book may be reproduced by any means without the written permission of the publisher.

FRONT COVER: Stanton Hall, Natchez, MS.
HALF-TITLE PAGE: Panorama of Savannah, painted by Firmin Cerveau in 1837.
FRONTISPIECE: Castillo de San Marcos, St. Augustine, FL.
BACK COVER: Print House, New Echota State Historic Site, GA.

SERIES EDITOR: HENRY WIENCEK
EDITOR: MARY LUDERS
PHOTO EDITOR: MARY Z. JENKINS
ART DIRECTOR: DIANA M. JONES
ASSOCIATE EDITOR: BRIGID A. MAST
PHOTO ASSISTANT: BARBARA J. SEYDA
EDITORIAL ASSISTANT: MONINA MEDY
DESIGN ASSISTANT: KATHI R. PORTER
CARTOGRAPHIC DESIGN AND PRODUCTION: GUENTER VOLLATH
CARTOGRAPHIC COMPILATION: GEORGE COLBERT
DATA ENTRY: SUSAN KIRBY

LIBRARY OF CONGRESS CATALOGING-IN-PUBLICATION DATA

Logan, William Bryant.
    The Deep South.

    (The Smithsonian guide to historic America)
    Includes index.
    1. Southern States—Description and travel—1981-    —Guide-books.
2. Historic sites—Southern States—Guide-books. 3. Gulf States—Description and travel—Guide-books. 4. Historic sites—Gulf States—Guide-books. I. Muse, Vance, 1949-
II. Kennedy, Roger G. III. Title. IV. Series.
F207.3.L64 1989        917.6'0443        88-33091
ISBN 1-55670-068-7 (pbk.)         ISBN 1-55670-069-5

Distributed by Workman Publishing, 708 Broadway, New York, NY 10003

Printed in Japan

10 9 8 7 6 5 4 3 2 1
First Edition

# CONTENTS

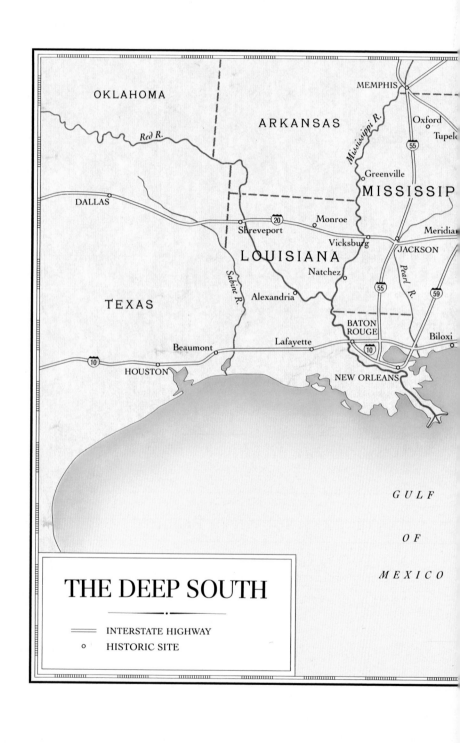

THE DEEP SOUTH

═══ INTERSTATE HIGHWAY
○ HISTORIC SITE

# INTRODUCTION

ROGER G. KENNEDY

In this volume we will try to turn away from the nineteenth-century view of our national history as the domain of New England, as a Thanksgiving Day pageant of Pilgrim Fathers with the *Mayflower* upon the horizon and Olde England not far beyond. This is not New England—a Pilgrims-first approach here would leave too many things unexplained. The wonderful complexity of this region's history is driven home at the magnificent Castillo San Marcos in Saint Augustine, as one stands observing ceremonies in which English, French, Spanish, Mexican, Texan, Confederate, and American flags are hauled up and down, accompanied by national anthems (when available).

Let us start at the most impressive site remaining from the prehistory of the Old South. It is not impressively named—"Poverty Point"—nor is it easy to find—it lies along a back road near the hamlet of Monticello, Louisiana. Its location, however, far from the seaboard, conjures us to look outward from the center of our continent, not inward from any stern and rockbound coast. The site also summons us to be respectful of people whom we do not usually regard as our predecessors.

Poverty Point is not as well known as Stonehenge, but it is equally ancient and equally ambitious. At the same time the English upon Salisbury Plain were laboring slabs of stone into a circle 100 feet in diameter and surrounding them with an earthwork 300 feet wide, the ancient people of Louisiana were moving 30,000,000 fifty-pound loads of earth into a composition of six concentric ridges, the widest of which is 4,000 feet in diameter.

Poverty Point is a magnificent puzzle; eight miles of its rings can still be discerned, still 10 feet high, 75 feet wide and 100 to 150 feet apart. At the time of the spring and fall equinoxes, if one climbs by its earthen ramp to the top of a mound to the west of the rings, one can still have a clear view of the sun rising over the 37-acre central plaza, a view like that at the same conjunctions of earth and moon at Stonehenge. Three thousand winters and spring rains have washed over this achievement; the Bayou Macon has cut deeply into it and left it vulnerable to plows and pillage and to that indifference that arises in the presence of a past we do not feel to be our own. This is one of the monuments to the American past that is beyond restoration but not beyond recognition and respect.

The Old South is even older than Poverty Point. Near Little Salt Springs, in central Florida, archaeologists are exploring the traces of hardy pioneers who hunted giant tortoises, mastodons, giant sloths, and bison 12,000 years ago. Six thousand years later, some southerners had become agriculturists—this was considerably before the people of the British Isles left evidence of doing so in Ireland. About the time the Dorian Greeks invaded the Aegean Basin and conquered Troy, centers of trade and ritual observance like Poverty Point had grown up throughout the lower Mississippi Valley. By A.D. 1300, the Old South had produced large towns.

Later, in the age of Froissart and Boccaccio, of the Hundred Years' War and Giotto, the good citizens of whatever they called Moundville, Alabama (preserved as Mound State Park south of Tuscaloosa) created a 400-acre ceremonial cluster of twenty mounds, some sixty or more feet in height. It is still there, and below the bluffs, the Black Warrior River can still be fished. There are intriguing "barrow-pit" indentations upon the surface of the plateau that were probably fishponds, where the people of Moundville—like the priests and priestesses of Astarte or the monks at Fountains Abbey in Yorkshire—may have kept sacred fish. Around A.D. 1200, there may have been about 3,000 inhabitants at Moundville. It was a metropolis of the Mississippian culture, whose leading city was Cahokia, near Saint Louis. The decline of these large complexes had begun even before European diseases decimated (in the literal sense—cut to a tenth) native populations.

Of the 200,000 to 300,000 inhabitants of the Old South in 1650, only 10,000 or so were European, and few of those 10,000 spoke English. It was the French and Spanish who first established themselves in the region stretching from what is now Georgetown, South Carolina, to the Sabine River in Louisiana. By 1520, Spaniards were wintering in Tennessee, and within twenty years they had crossed Nebraska. Saint Augustine, Florida, was founded initially to contest the region not with the English, who were not much of a threat, but with the French, who were probing the Atlantic and Gulf coasts. British attempts to seize the entryways to the Mississippi and to make a beachhead at Pensacola failed. The Spanish and French languages and architecture were still dominant after Europeans had been at work in the Old South for fully 250 years.

Let us now imagine a winter migrant from Boston to Palm Beach who, believing it all started at Plymouth Rock, might be surprised to chance upon the huge keep of Fort Matanzas, thrusting its arrogant bulk out of the swamp fifteen miles south of Saint Augustine. It was built in 1742, but it looks much older, as if it were one of the now-vanished Spanish forts that once occupied every major strategic point on that coast. In the twilight it has the aspect of an outpost of Aigues Morte, the Crusaders' port in the south of France, or a Moorish fort intended to protect Seville from pirates ascending the meanders of the Guadalquivir.

Let our imaginary Yankee next come to the fulfillment of Spanish military architecture in North America—the Castillo San Marcos, guarding Saint Augustine itself. In 1675, when its walls were nearly complete, it was considerably more impressive than anything the English had managed to erect upon their precarious footholds on this continent. This enormous structure, with its four stone bastions and backward-sloping walls, was built to withstand cannon fire, as it did on three occasions when the British sought to take it and failed. It was the culmination of Spanish technical advances achieved in the process of building nine previous forts upon the site. The first was in place a century before the Pilgrims set foot in America. There was another massive fortress in Pensacola, and the brick citadel of the French at Mobile, Fort Condé, was once as formidable as the Castillo at Saint Augustine. These brooding, baleful crystals of hostility remind us to persist in the reorientation required of our imaginary Yankee: These were outposts of the Caribbean system. In this region the organizing reality of things from the onset of the Europeans until 1820 or so was the Caribbean Sea, not the American landmass.

The earliest European settlements arose from a desire either to attack or to defend the routes taken by Spanish fleets in carrying American treasures. The British and Dutch outposts in the West Indies and on the North American shores were the roosts of state-chartered pirates. The Spanish fortresses were intended to give shelter from their raids. Real pirates as well were there from the beginning, drawn by the opportunity to participate in the transfer of the immense riches of America to Europe. They were distinguished from the captains and admirals licensed by the crowns of England, France, and Holland chiefly by the color of legality given

OPPOSITE: *An oak tree in Alabama, shrouded with Spanish Moss.*

the latter's predations by a slip of paper. Piratical free enterprise entered with the same objectives as reasons of state: the securing of booty previously sweated out of the ground by native laborers and, later, by slaves imported from Africa.

European architecture in the Old South began to become elegant during the next stage in the development of the Caribbean system, when sugar joined silver and gold as a source of great wealth. The French, British, and Dutch could not deprive the Spaniards of their hold upon the lucrative mainland; the mines of San Luis Potosi and of Peru were beyond the reach even of Sir Francis Drake and Sir John Hawkins. So the islands of the West Indies were stripped of their trees and became vast sugar plantations. To supply those plantations with food and draft animals, Barbadian planters shifted capital and younger sons to Georgia, Florida, and the Carolinas and, indeed, organized northern supply points as distant as Shelter Island and Rhode Island. As late as 1803, Napoleon thought of Louisiana primarily as a supplier of foodstuffs to provide for Saint Domingue's sugar plantations and was willing to sell Louisiana to the United States only after it became clear that slave rebellions and wholesale destruction had reduced the value of Saint Domingue's plantations.

The attitudes and outlooks of the West Indies planters were shared throughout the Old South. Slave rebellions in the Caribbean were immediately felt to be threats in Louisiana and the Gulf States. In the decades before the Civil War many Southerners, hemmed in by Northern demands to limit the expansion of slavery on the American continent, looked to the Caribbean—they pressed for the annexation of Cuba and parts of Central America to augment the slave-and-plantation system of the Old South.

The modern visitor can see vestiges of this interaction between the Old South and the Caribbean in the architectural unity of the shores of the Gulf. Everywhere the pirates roamed, everywhere the slave system penetrated, cottages raised on stilts (or posts, or high basements) appeared, from Brazil to Wilmington, North Carolina. Everywhere, after 1730 or so, verandahs were added and, after 1830, given the classical touches that brought the creole cottage within the ambit of what we choose to call, sometimes, "the Greek Revival." Stilts became posts and posts became columns. Verandahs expanded to form houses surrounding houses. Observant travelers on the islands and along the shore, to places such as Barbados, Charleston, Mobile, and even such inland points as Natchez will see the old hip-roofed cottage form with extended eaves and be reminded that they are on the ancient pirate routes and within the Caribbean system.

By 1706, the Spaniards had brought their version of the Renaissance to North America. The classical columns for their Governor's Palace in Saint Augustine were considerably more ambitious than anything in the English colonies. Saint Augustine contains many buildings marking it as Spanish. Its founder, Pedro Menéndez de Avilés, attempted to make it so, and to assure that it would also be Roman Catholic he massacred his French Protestant competitors who had settled near present-day Jacksonville. He also began laying the foundations for the series of missions that lasted until the end of the seventeenth century, when they were destroyed by the English and their allies, the Creek. By 1715, the island missions and eighteen more along the fertile bottomlands of the Apalache and Ocilla Rivers, well into Alabama, were ravaged and abandoned. We are lamentably uninformed of the lives of the friars, free blacks, and "mission Indians"who lived in them. But Saint Augustine and Matanzas can set our imaginations turning.

The earliest views of New Orleans show a village quite different from that we might expect from the surviving buildings there, all of which are from the "Spanish Period," 1763 or later. At the outset there were no signs of piazzas or balconies. The little houses of French New Orleans of about 1725 were of half-timber or palisaded construction, squat, with the walls filled in with brick or mud mixed with straw. We presume that the older French settlements such as Ocean Springs (Old Biloxi, 1699), Fort Louis (near Mobile, 1711), Natchitoches (1714), and Natchez (1716) looked like this too, for New Orleans was a latecomer (1718), and these were the ways Frenchmen had built for generations.

But soon things came to be grander and breezier; the breeziness appeared after 1740 or so with the arrival of the piazza, later called the verandah. The grandeur is more to the point, for it shows the intermingling of imperial French and Spanish influences also evident in the political history of the entire region from Saint Augustine to the Texas border. The recently restored Ursuline Convent in New Orleans (1749-1753) is exceedingly French. The nearby Cabildo (1795), if we remove the mansard roof imposed in the 1850s, is the manifestation of an effort to place a Spanish stamp upon a town that was already committed to the French tradition.

The Cabildo is a Mexican-Spanish building, almost a duplicate of the Casa Reales built in Antiquera a decade earlier.

The Bourbon kings of France and Spain not only built these splendid buildings but also assured the success of our Revolutionary War. From Spanish garrisons in Louisiana came money and supplies for the Americans, with more aid smuggled past the British fleet to assist George Washington in keeping the American army together. And to Valley Forge, in 1779, came the news that the French and Spanish governments had crossed the line from lend-lease to formal declarations of war on Great Britain. Washington was jubilant; he expected "that this formidable junction of the House of Bourbon will not fail of establishing the Independence of America in a short time."

The Spanish forces in the Old South were led by a military hero of Washington's dimensions, Bernardo de Galvez, veteran of wars against the Portuguese, Algerians, and Apaches. As Governor of Louisiana, he had already opened the port of New Orleans to the Americans, had confiscated British shipping there, and had sent supplies to George Rogers Clark, who was campaigning in the Ohio Valley. In the summer of 1779, he assembled an expeditionary force of Spaniards and Canary Islanders, free blacks and Indian recruits, and swept up the Mississippi, collecting British outposts and prisoners as he went: Fort Bute went first, then Baton Rouge, then Fort Pammure in Natchez. One flying column took Thomson's Creek and Amite, farther west, while another settled down for a siege of Pensacola.

The British attempted a counterstroke against Saint Louis but were repulsed, and the Spanish pursued them all the way to capture Saint Joseph, on Lake Michigan. Washington wrote the Spanish that among the beneficial effects "upon the Southern states" was a diversion of British forces that would otherwise combine against him. Galvez sent yet another army of blacks and whites to take Mobile and then to press on against the citadel at Pensacola.

Plaques and earthworks in Yorktown, Virginia, and Pensacola tell us of the two great sieges of 1781. The capture of the British expeditionary force led by General Cornwallis at Yorktown was made possible by the participation of three times as many French fighting men as Americans. At Pensacola, a Spanish force of 4,000 captured another British army of 1,500 men, together with 400 Choctaws and 100 of the faithful Creek. The twin victories of

Yorktown and Pensacola, brilliantly led by Washington and Galvez, drove the British to the conclusion for which Washington had hoped in 1779.

This does not carry us very far into the history of the Old South, but local historical societies and house museums await with full expositions of the nineteenth century and its central event, the War Between the States. It is well to be wary of any preconceptions, as there are many surprises in store for the traveler with curiosity. Perhaps the largest are the persistence of Native American peoples throughout the region and the profusion of dialects among all it people. Then, too, there are the complexities of the Civil War story; we learn that the Confederate flag never flew over Natchez and that the builders of most of the wonderful white-columned houses there were opposed to secession, as were the Yankee merchants who were largely responsible for the construction of the Garden District of New Orleans.

The surprises of natural history are equally great: the great Cohutta wilderness within an hour and a half of Atlanta, with virgin timber and heights one does not expect in Georgia, up to 5,000 feet; the stands of loblollies in the Sipsey Wilderness in Alabama and Bienville Forest in Mississippi; and, everywhere, the brooding presence of great antiquity. Poverty Point and Moundville are merely two examples. Fort Matanzas is another, bringing to mind the buccaneering tradition of the coasts from Amelia Island, where Gregor MacGregor held forth, to Barataria, where Jean Lafitte was wont to distribute to his literate victims the "Corsair" of Lord Byron, in which he had been admiringly depicted. How many poetic pirates can any other region boast? Or for that matter, how many piratic architects? The buccaneer Bartholomy Lafon laid out most of New Orleans's Garden District and the town of Donaldsonville, and was also the designer of Lafitte's "Red House," where he practiced architecture, piracy, and the study of hieroglyphics, to the admiration of his host.

The history of the Old South is the portion of the human experience in that region that has been written in script. A longer and larger tale is told in its architecture. Poverty Point was the first human inscription upon this landscape, to be read by us as best we can. There were people there, doing their best to lead dignified and affectionate lives long before Pedro Menéndez de Avilés came to Saint Augustine and the senior O'Hara created "Tara."

# NEW ORLEANS
## AND THE
# BAYOU
# COUNTRY

OPPOSITE: *The Maddox-Brennan House in New Orleans's Garden District, built in the 1850s by the publisher of the New Orleans* Daily Crescent.

The first European to trek across Louisiana was probably Hernando de Soto, who set out from Florida in 1540 and died here two years later on a futile search for gold. The region was then ignored by Europeans for over 150 years, until the French explorer La Salle made his way down the length of the Mississippi from the Great Lakes. Upon reaching the Gulf of Mexico on April 9, 1682, he claimed the whole of the Mississippi Valley for France and named it Louisiana for his king, Louis XIV.

France envisioned a settlement at the mouth of the Mississippi that would give it complete control of the fur trade of the vast American interior. But it was not until 1718 that New Orleans was established as the seaport for the inland trading posts at Natchez (Mississippi) and Natchitoches. The latter had been established in 1714 at the farthest navigable point on the Red River, which flows into the Mississippi River. From Natchitoches the French hoped to open a trade route with Mexico, but the Spanish, in order to impose a limit on the design, set up a garrison and trading post at Los Adaes, not far from Natchitoches.

Despite the enormous commercial potential of Louisiana, the colony developed slowly. King Louis XIV's officials, distracted by European war and short of cash, turned over development of the colony to a private company in 1712. That effort failed and a Scottish financier, John Law, set up a new company to develop Louisiana in 1717. Law sold shares in the company and energetically promoted the colony, describing the Gulf Coast and the lower Mississippi as a paradise. The coast was in fact a steamy cypress swamp. In far-off France Law's propaganda created a frenzy of stock speculation—the so-called Mississippi Bubble, which burst in 1720, wiping out many French fortunes. War with the Natchez Indians in the late 1720s and early 1730s further hindered the growth of Louisiana. By 1750 there were only about 10,000 European settlers in the entire region. They were not only French, but Spanish, West Indian, German, and Irish, as well. Amidst the oppressive heat and plagues of yellow fever brought by the mosquitoes, the settlers harvested the cypress trees and built cottages and houses by packing bricks and sometimes *bousillage* (a mixture of mud and moss) between the timbers. For the most part these dwellings were inspired by those of the West Indies, designed to catch breezes and protect the inhabitants from rain and sun. Wide, shady porches, called galleries, surrounded the houses.

*An 1806 view of New Orleans from a downriver plantation, by local artist J. L. Bouqueto de Woiseri. An eagle symbolizes the era of prosperity that followed the 1803 American acquisition of Louisiana. The painting also shows the city's long levees and blocks of raised houses.*

Louisiana passed out of French hands in the 1760s: The territory west of the Mississippi was ceded to Spain in 1762, and the lands east of the river were ceded to England in 1763. During the Revolutionary War, New Orleans was a valuable source of supplies and cash to the Americans. Early in the war Spanish officials in the town rendered their aid covertly, but when Spain declared war against England in 1779 Governor Bernardo de Gálvez led expeditions against British posts on the Mississippi and the Gulf Coast.

France's imperial ambitions in America revived in the 1790s, leading to negotiations with Spain for the return of Louisiana. The king of Spain traded Louisiana to Napoleon in exchange for a throne, in Etruria, for his son-in-law, with the condition that the territory never be ceded to another power.

In 1803, when Napoleon was in need of funds, he authorized the sale of the entire French territory to the United States. The Americans had hoped to purchase, for $10 million, only New Orleans and Florida (which they thought belonged to France, when in fact it was still Spanish) or, failing that, shipping rights on the Mississippi. The American ministers, James Monroe and Robert

Livingston, were flabbergasted by the offer, and made the purchase, for $15 million, even though it was trebly illegal—France's agreement with Spain forbade it; Napoleon was supposed to obtain the approval of his legislature for any such sale, and did not; and the U.S. Constitution had no provision for expanding the nation by purchase, a technicality President Jefferson decided to overlook.

Louisiana became a state in 1812 and soon emerged as an important agricultural region and commercial gateway. Via river, bayou, and road came harvests of cotton, indigo, rice, and sugar. The southern cypress swamps and northern pine forests fed a lumber industry. Cattle ranches and dairy farms were established. In 1840 the port of New Orleans was comparable to New York harbor in volume of traffic. The state's plantation agriculture was based upon slavery. The French system of laws in Louisiana's earliest days guaranteed some rights to blacks, and prejudice against blacks was not as rigid as elsewhere in America. According to the geographer D. W. Meinig, "Blacks and mulattoes were laced all through Louisiana society: they were found in all settings—urban, plantation, small farm, backwoods; at many levels—from gang slave to plantation owner, from household servant to prosperous tradesman; and often in intimate, regular association with Europeans, Indians, and mestizos." Interracial marriage was not uncommon. The Spanish civil code expanded the rights of blacks; the Napoleonic Code withdrew some of them; and the American slave system eliminated nearly all of the rest.

In 1861 Louisiana joined other southern states in seceding from the Union. Less than a year later Federal gunboats steamed up the Mississippi and seized New Orleans and Baton Rouge, virtually without gunfire. Though Louisiana did not suffer much direct destruction, it was cut off from its world markets. Confederate general Richard Taylor wrote in 1863: "Louisiana, from Natchitoches to the Gulf, is a howling wilderness and her people are starving." Taylor, with a small force of men based in the bayou country, cherished vain hopes of ousting the Northerners from New Orleans. However, during the 1864 Red River Campaign in northern Louisiana, Taylor defeated a superior Federal army at the Battle of Mansfield.

OVERLEAF:   *On April 24, 1862, amid heavy gunfire, David Farragut leads his fleet past the two forts protecting the approaches to New Orleans. One of his gunners reported "My youthful imagination of hell did not equal the scene about us at this moment."*

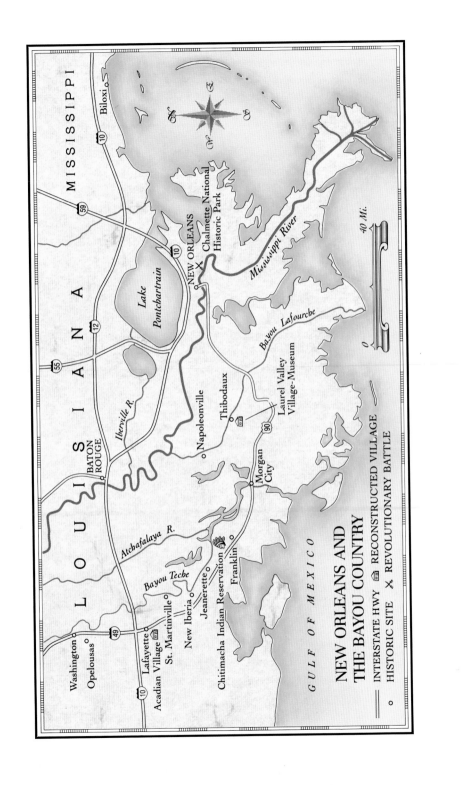

# NEW ORLEANS AND
# THE BAYOU COUNTRY

— INTERSTATE HWY   🏛 RECONSTRUCTED VILLAGE

× HISTORIC SITE   × REVOLUTIONARY BATTLE

○

40 Mi.

MISSISSIPPI

L O U I S I A N A

MISSISSIPPI

Biloxi

BATON ROUGE

Lake Pontchartrain

Iberville R.

NEW ORLEANS

Chalmette National
Historic Park

Mississippi River

Bayou Lafourche

Napoleonville

Thibodaux

Laurel Valley
Village–Museum

Morgan City

Atchafalaya R.

Bayou Teche

Franklin

Chitimacha Indian Reservation

Jeanerette

New Iberia

St. Martinville

Lafayette
Acadian Village

Washington

Opelousas

GULF OF MEXICO

FARRAGUT APRIL 24ᵗʰ 186

The state recovered slowly in the aftermath of the war and the radical transformation of its economy from slave labor to a kind of sharecrop, or wage peonage. As in so many other places, economic depression saved many architectural vestiges of the old order, because there was little reason to tear them down. Restoration has salvaged much of what was beautiful about the state's antebellum period. The Mississippi River is still busy with commercial traffic, particularly with the huge tankers of the petrochemical industry, which roared to life here at the beginning of the twentieth century. Among that traffic are reproductions of two nineteenth-century paddlewheelers, the *Mississippi Queen* and the *Delta Queen,* which steam past long stretches of refineries as well as some riverfront scenes that seem to have changed little in two hundred years.

This chapter, on southern Louisiana, begins with New Orleans and then covers the bayou country to the south and west of the city.

# N    E    W        O    R    L    E    A    N    S

The city of New Orleans has been many things: a thoroughly European settlement yet a quintessentially American boomtown; a hedonistic colonial outpost (named for the depraved duke of Orléans, Louis XV's powerful regent) and a Catholic stronghold; a steamy, tropical badland, twisted and teased into ordered gardens.

From the north in 1543, Spanish explorers sailed the crescent pass of the Mississippi on which New Orleans is situated, as did La Salle's French expedition a century later. But it was Jean-Baptiste Le Moyne, sieur de Bienville (whose brother, Pierre Le Moyne, sieur d'Iberville, claimed Mobile and Biloxi for France in 1699) who, in 1718, had the audacity to push upriver from the Gulf of Mexico nearly 100 miles to the future site of New Orleans.

Surrounded by the frequently overflowing Mississippi River, the bay-sized Lake Pontchartrain, and Bayou Saint John, this was not a likely place to build a city. The first tasks were to raise levees (river control will always be essential to the survival of New Orleans) and to fill the swampy land with oyster shells and cypress pilings. Convicts were brought from French prisons to do the hard labor. Sidewalks, still called banquettes, were raised above the mud. A contingent of clergy came to staff a chapel that preceded Saint Louis Cathedral, and by 1734 the Ursuline Convent sprawled along Chartres Street. France promoted the colony as a get-rich-quick paradise, and young adventurers were followed by shiploads

*Many New Orleans houses include galleries and secluded rear gardens, which function as outdoor rooms in this tropical climate.*

of marriageable orphans, known as the *casette* girls for the small chests that contained their meager dowries.

Somehow, a city was taking shape, much of it built of the abundant native wood. Resistant to rot, cypress was the all-purpose building material of southern Louisiana, used to make houses, to trim them, and to fashion armoires, beds, and other furniture. The indigenous construction in the French Quarter is *briquette-entre-poteaux,* or brick-between-posts. The locally made bricks, too soft to support a structure by themselves, were laid between sturdy cypress timbers, the exterior then smeared with stucco. A few late-eighteenth-century cottages still stand, and the brick-between-post construction can be seen through worn plaster or frame. Typically a narrow porte cochere leads to a lush courtyard and rear entrance. Inside, the foursquare plan could not be simpler. Grander houses of two and three stories repeated the larger ground-floor plan upstairs. *Garçonnières,* accommodating a family's young men and overnight guests, were separate from the main house, often over-looking courtyards. Cast-iron balconies, known locally as galleries, became the ubiquitous street decoration of the city. Galleries were like outdoor rooms, designed to let residents catch the breeze outside as much as the mosquitoes will allow.

When Spain was given control of the Louisiana territory in 1762, New Orleans hardly noticed the change in government. The city's French and Spanish families intermarried for decades, creating a Creole culture. Creoles, those of French and Spanish descent born in the New World, had a strong influence on the cuisine and architecture of the West Indies and southern Louisiana. Cajuns, the French Canadians expelled from Acadia (Nova Scotia) by the British in the mid-eighteenth century, settled mostly in the bayou country. (The word *Cajun* came from a muffled, perhaps drawled, pronunciation of "Acadian.") The 1790s brought refugees from the French Revolution and the West Indian slave rebellions. They were mainly planters and merchants, many of whom had already diversified their investments into Louisiana and were able to purchase some of the city's finer residences and participate in the lively cultural life of its theaters and three opera houses. The Creole culture, unlike the cotton empire throughout most of the South, offered mulattoes and the *gens de couleur libre*, free people of color, an important and recognized role. Many free blacks themselves owned slaves, plantations, and urban real estate.

The Louisiana Purchase of 1803—made after the territory had briefly passed back to France—was not popular with many Creoles,

*Fate Marable's jazz band aboard a Mississippi River steamboat. Marable is the pianist; at his left, holding a cornet, is the young Louis Armstrong, who was born in New Orleans in 1900.*

who grew to resent the Americans pouring into town, as well as the tighter restrictions on blacks. But it also brought New Orleans into the continental system. The city soon became a world-class port, with steamboats and tall sailing ships jamming the Mississippi in both directions—it was linked not only to the eastern seaboard and overseas markets via the Gulf of Mexico, but to burgeoning Midwestern cities along the upper Mississippi and Ohio rivers. Fortunes were made by planters and brokers of indigo, cotton, and sugar, and by merchants, bankers, and shippers. In 1826, a European visitor wrote, "New Orleans, for eighty years the wretched asylum for the outcasts . . . who could not venture one hundred paces beyond its gates without utterly sinking to the breast in mud . . . has become . . . one of the most beautiful cities in the Union, inhabitated by 40,000 persons who trade with half the world."

While Creoles remained in the French Quarter and in *faubourgs* (suburbs) along the Bayou Saint John, Americans created their own world uptown, in the Garden District and other neighborhoods carved out of plantation land. They built houses in the classic antebellum styles, with colonnades and expansive gardens. The commercial pace of the city slowed during the Civil War, when Union troops sealed off the southern end of the Mississippi. New Orleans was occupied, quickly and bloodlessly, at the outset of the war in January 1862. Some Confederate sympathizers were replaced by Union army officers in occupancy of large houses, but the city was fortunate to see no combat or destruction. Certainly New Orleans has endured hard times since, but it has always seemed to value merriment and tolerance. For nearly two centuries, the most anticipated event of the year has been Mardi Gras, heralding the Lenten season. That celebration—an orgy arising from a religious observance—epitomizes this city of paradoxes.

Because of its location on an enormous crescent of the Mississippi River (hence its nickname, the Crescent City), New Orleans is geographically confounding—uptown is south, downtown is north, and the sun rises over the west bank of the river. Directions of the compass mean little here, where the local terms are lakeside (toward Lake Pontchartrain), riverside, uptown, and downtown. The Vieux Carré (literally, old square), more popularly known as the French Quarter, is a grid of sixty-six blocks. Canal Street is the boundary between the French Quarter and the "American" portion of the city built after New Orleans came under the American flag. This section begins at Jackson Square, describes the French Quarter, and then proceeds to the Garden District.

# THE FRENCH QUARTER

The names on the streetposts of the French Quarter reveal its
Gallic origins: Bourbon, Chartres, Toulouse, Dumaine, Burgundy.
The Quarter's basic plan has not changed since 1718, when Bien-
ville established the first successful settlement here. Today in the
French Quarter, where no building is higher than the central spire of
Saint Louis Cathedral, Bienville would still be able to find his way.

## JACKSON SQUARE

At Bienville's landing spot, the bend in the river that forms the base
of the French Quarter, the French laid out a parade ground, the
*Place d'Armes*. Soldiers executed drills on the green under French,
Spanish, Confederate, and U.S. flags, and it has served as a public
promenade and meeting place as well. The Place d'Armes was
landscaped by the Baroness Pontalba in a mostly French fashion,
with parterre beds, neat walkways, and rows of trimmed hedges.
Many tall trees now obscure much of that geometric order. For the
centerpiece, she ordered a bronze equestrian statue of Andrew
Jackson, and when the work was completed in 1856, the old military parade ground was reopened as Jackson Square.

### Saint Louis Cathedral

Facing the square from Chartres Street, the triple-steepled cathedral stands on the site of earlier churches. The first was probably
destroyed by a hurricane in 1722; its successor went up in flames in
1788. Don Almonester y Roxas, a Spaniard who had made a fortune in New Orleans real estate, offered to build a new cathedral
with his own funds, his only stipulation being that the congregation
pray for his soul after his death. The new structure was completed
in 1794, and Don Almonester, who died four years later, is buried
beneath the marble floor. In 1851 significant changes were made
to the cathedral: The interior was enlarged, a classical facade was
added, and steeples were placed atop the central and twin towers.

Flanking the cathedral are the **Cabildo** and the **Presbytère,** nearly
identical buildings that embody both Spanish and French influences. The French had the last say, as the Spanish arcades of both
buildings are topped by mansard roofs.

opposite: *Saint Louis Cathedral towers over Jackson Square, where the ceremonies concluding the Louisiana Purchase took place. A statue of Andrew Jackson is at center.*

The Cabildo, built in 1795, replaced two other Spanish government houses that burned on the same site. The American flag was first flown from its balcony in 1803 to herald the Louisiana Purchase, some negotiations of which were completed by Governor William C. C. Claiborne in an upstairs chamber. Andrew Jackson was cheered here after the Battle of New Orleans in 1815, and when Louisiana seceded from the Union in 1861, the Confederate government established offices in the Cabildo. Severely damaged by fire in 1988, the Cabildo is closed indefinitely for repairs. Its contemporary, the Presbytère, once housed the clergy of Saint Louis Cathedral. It now contains state offices and part of the **Louisiana State Museum** (504–568–6968), displaying collections of firearms, late-nineteenth-century Newcomb pottery made at Tulane University, Indian relics, and a death mask of Napoleon Bonaparte—one of five bronzes cast from the plaster original that was made hours after the exiled emperor died on the island of Saint Helena on May 5, 1821.

## Pontalba Buildings

Facing one another across Jackson Square, the Pontalba Buildings are named for the woman who built them, Micaela Almonester de Pontalba. She was the daughter of Don Almonester y Roxas, the Spaniard who financed the Cabildo, the Presbytère, and Saint Louis Cathedral in the 1790s. Micaela married a French baron's son in 1811 (the wedding was held in Saint Louis Cathedral) and, after a long and unhappy sojourn in France, returned to New Orleans in the 1840s to do something with the fortune her father had left her. Among her properties were dilapidated commercial blocks on the northern and southern sides of the Place d'Armes, which she replaced with two magnificent buildings. She commissioned plans from the city's most renowned architects, James Gallier, Sr., and Henry Howard, and added her own touches. The result is an unlikely but successful New Orleans hybrid: The twin, block-long Pontalba Buildings are Neoclassical in a casual Creole way. The baroness handled all details of the job, from ordering the demolition of the old structures to securing new building permits and ordering materials (including granite and marble from New England quarries). The buildings were ready for occupancy in 1850 and were quickly filled, even with apartments renting for $300 per month, an exorbitant rate at the time. Shops and other commercial enterprises were located on the street level, and apartments occupied second and third stories.

*The 1850 Pontalba buildings were constructed to the exacting standards of their builder, the Baroness de Pontalba, who shocked her contractors by wearing pantaloons "to go up the ladders to examine the work herself."*

## 1850 House

Located on the downriver side of the square in the lower Pontalba Building, the 1850 House is furnished as it was when occupied by several Creole families prior to the Civil War. A narrow porte cochere leads to a staircase at the rear, ascending to an enormous parlor with mid-nineteenth-century New Orleans–made furniture. There are elaborately carved beds, perhaps from the shop of Prudent Mallard, a swan-shaped crib, marble-topped washstands and desks, a shapely harp, and mirrored sideboards next to a huge dining-room table. (Mallard's career as a cabinetmaker is the subject of much research and speculation: He did make some furniture, but by 1850 his store was probably selling furniture by Eastern makers that has been mistakenly attributed to Mallard himself.) Rising from floor to ceiling, "guillotine" windows open onto a gallery; the cast-iron railings throughout both buildings bear an entwined AP monogram, for Almonester and Pontalba.

LOCATION: 523 Saint Ann Street. HOURS: 10–3 Wednesday–Sunday. FEE: Yes. TELEPHONE: 504–568–6968.

# HERMANN-GRIMA HOUSE

This rare example of American architecture in the French Quarter was built in 1831 by Samuel Hermann, a Jewish immigrant from Frankfurt, Germany, who had arrived in Louisiana in 1804. He settled near his fellow countrymen on a stretch of the Mississippi near Baton Rouge known as the German Coast and proceeded to turn a dry-goods business into a vast merchandising, shipping, and credit operation. By the 1820s Hermann was rich and moved his family to New Orleans.

The Georgian house he built resembled no other dwelling in New Orleans but many on the eastern seaboard. Unlike its neighbors with their discreet shuttered French doors and rear porte cochere entrances, Hermann's house faces the street with formal doorways flanked by tall sash windows. Inside, rooms open off a central hallway—Creole houses typically have no hallways, only the porte cochere and rooms opening onto one another. The decoration of Hermann's house is lavish: Corinthian columns separate the parlor and dining room, crystal chandeliers hang from leafy plaster medallions, and some black and gold marble mantels are carved with classical details. Fashionable trompe l'oeil effects include cypress doors grained to resemble mahogany and maple, marble baseboards, and wallpaper painted as drapery. The panic of 1837 badly damaged Hermann's business empire, and he was forced to sell the house. Most of the furniture that fills the house today belonged to subsequent Creole owners, the Felix Grima family.

LOCATION: 820 Saint Louis Street. HOURS: 10–4 Monday–Saturday. FEE: Yes. TELEPHONE: 504–525–5661.

The **Historic New Orleans Collection** (533 Royal Street, 504–532–4662) is a museum and research center that occupies the ca. 1880 townhouse of its founders, General and Mrs. L. Kemper Williams, and the 1792 Merieult House. Special gallery exhibits focus on New Orleans culture and history: cuisine, ethnic groups, Mardi Gras, publishing, and the arts. On view in the Merieult House are documents pertaining to the Louisiana Purchase of 1803 and to the Federal occupation of New Orleans during the Civil War, as well as old maps of the city.

OPPOSITE: *A rosewood bed equipped with a* mosquitaire *is placed to take advantage of every breeze entering the 1850 House, part of the Pontalba buildings.*

## URSULINE CONVENT

France's Ursuline order of nuns arrived in New Orleans early in the city's development, in 1727. To the devout, the nuns arrived just in time, for the outpost city was already on its way to being considered the most dissolute in New France. Dedicated in 1734, the convent may be the oldest European-built structure in the Mississippi River valley and the cross on the front gate may be the region's oldest work of wrought iron. The convent was an enormous construction project at the time—it sprawls over half a city block at Chartres and Ursuline streets. Sold by the nuns in 1824, it later became the archbishop's official residence. Beautifully restored, the convent now serves as headquarters for the archives of the archdiocese of New Orleans. The adjacent **Our Lady of Victory Catholic Church** was built in 1845 as the archbishop's chapel.

LOCATION: Chartres and Ursuline streets. HOURS: By appointment only. FEE: Donation. TELEPHONE: 504–866–1472.

Across Chartres Street on land once owned by the convent is the **Beauregard-Keyes House** (1113 Chartres Street, 504–523–7257), named for two famous occupants, former Confederate general Pierre G. T. Beauregard (1866–1868) and, in the 1940s, the author Frances Parkinson Keyes, who set her best-selling novels in New Orleans. The house, built in 1826, is Neoclassical and contains some furnishings and mementos of Beauregard and Keyes.

**Madame John's Legacy** (632 Dumaine Street) is believed to have been built in 1727 and rebuilt by a French sea captain in 1788, with shuttered French doors, living quarters above the raised basement level, and a wide overhanging roof. The house got its unusual name from the title of an 1879 short story by New Orleans writer George Washington Cable. It is a property of the Louisiana State Museum, not open to the public.

## OLD U.S. MINT

The mint produced coins for nearly twenty-five years prior to the Civil War and again from 1879 to 1920. It is a handsome if hulking three-story building, a veritable fortress of stuccoed brick trimmed with granite, with a graceful Ionic portico facing Esplanade Avenue. Its vaulted interior is an exhibition space for the Louisiana State Museum's jazz and Mardi Gras exhibits, including musical instruments and biographical presentations on such figures as

Bessie Smith and Louis Armstrong, as well as Carnival masks, costumes, party favors, and invitations. Another exhibit describes the operation of the old mint. The site on which the mint stands was the scene of Andrew Jackson's review of his troops before their battle with the British at Chalmette Plantation and of the hanging of a Confederate for desecrating the American flag.

LOCATION: 400 Esplanade Avenue. HOURS: 10–5 Wednesday–Sunday. FEE: Yes. TELEPHONE: 504–568–6968.

The **Old Pharmacy Museum** (514 Chartres Street, 504–524–9077) preserves La Pharmacie Française, which opened in 1823. It contains an array of nineteenth-century medical instruments and manuals and hand-blown medicine bottles and flasks. A mid-nineteenth-century soda fountain of brass and Italian black and rose marble is also in place.

**Lafitte's Blacksmith Shop,** now converted to a bar at 941 Bourbon Street, was owned by the brother of pirate and smuggler Jean Lafitte, who died around 1826. Lafitte was an iron mason, and it is likely that the outlaw Frenchman used the smithy as one of the diversified enterprises in his worldwide operations. Built as a small house around 1770, the *briquette-entre-poteaux* construction is revealed through bare patches of the stucco finish.

According to a New Orleans legend (also claimed by at least four other places in America), **Napoleon House** (500 Chartres Street, private) was to be the refuge of the exiled French emperor. In 1821, in Napoleon's sixth year of exile, a group of admirers in New Orleans plotted to rescue him, but soon after they had purchased a ship for the expedition, he died. Later, one of Napoleon's doctors did come to New Orleans and set up offices in this house; he also brought along a treasured relic, the death mask of Napoleon that is on display in the Presbytère.

## GALLIER HOUSE

James Gallier, Jr., whose father was also a distinguished architect, designed the city's French Opera House (which no longer stands) and Greek Revival houses in the Garden District. For his own family, he chose a narrow townhouse site on the quiet edge of the French Quarter. The exterior is Italianate, its stucco facade stippled and scored to resemble stone, with an overlay of frilly cast iron. Inside, it combines Victorian opulence with up-to-date amenities: built-in closets, a ventilation system, a skylight, and, in the kitchen, hot running water, an iron range, and a floor covering called Kamptulicon, a forerunner of linoleum.

The double parlor, divided by gilded Corinthian columns, is crowded with Rococo Revival furniture. The setting is opulent, with fringed and tasseled damask curtains, floral rugs laid upon more floral rugs, globed gasoliers and classical statuary reflected to infinity in gilded mirrors, and trompe l'oeil wallpaper. Baseboards are marbled to match black marble mantels; plaster shells and flowers trim the ceiling. Upstairs, the master bedroom also is all Rococo; one of the children's bedrooms is cluttered with dolls, toys, and a tea set. The servants' quarters, in a wing facing a small parterre courtyard, are appointed only with the essentials (probably family castoffs)—four-poster beds, armoires, and chests made in Louisiana.

LOCATION: 1118–1132 Royal Street. HOURS: 10–3:45 Monday–Saturday. FEE: Yes. TELEPHONE: 504–523–6722.

*Ironwork on the house of James Gallier, Jr. At left, the cast-iron gates at the front entrance. At right, the second-floor gallery, showing the house's stucco facade scored to resemble granite blocks.* OPPOSITE: *Gallier House's Rococo Revival parlor, above, has a small sofa, called a meridienne, designed for ladies wearing hoopskirts. Two of Gallier's four daughters shared a bedroom, below, shown here prepared for a dolls' tea party.*

Across Governor Nicholls Street from Gallier House is a three-story French Empire "graystone" sometimes called the **Haunted House** (private), built in 1832 by Dr. and Madame Lalaurie, prominent in the social life of the Quarter. As one version of the story goes, on a night when the couple was at the opera, a fire swept through the house. Neighbors heard screams and rushed in to find slaves, emaciated and beaten, shackled to their beds. Most of them were rescued, but others perished, including a young girl. Their extreme mistreatment of their slaves exposed, the Lalauries fled to Mobile, from which they sailed to France. Later occupants, including Union officers during the Civil War, reported strange sights and sounds, including a shrouded visage of a crying girl.

Extending for five blocks at the edge of the French Quarter along Decatur Street is the **French Market,** an institution since the 1790s. Here vendors sold fresh fish, farm produce, herbs, and exotic merchandise such as golden Chinese carp, escargots, Chinese tea, and medicinal powders from Africa. Then as today, the French Market was a place to socialize as well, with musicians adding to the lively scene.

At 915 Royal Street is one of the South's traditional "cornstalk" cast-iron fences. (Uptown, its twin surrounds an Italianate house in the Garden District, at 1448 Fourth Street.) Wrought and cast iron, much of it manufactured initially in Cincinnati and Philadelphia, is the most ubiquitous decoration throughout New Orleans—not just in balcony railings and galleries, but columns and their capitals, door and window grilles, fences and gates, graveyard statues, and courtyard and garden furniture. Some of the wrought iron was made locally by black, German, and Irish artisans working at anvils. By the mid-1800s, New Orleans foundries were producing great quantities of cast iron, fashioned by pouring the molten metal into elaborately carved wooden molds. Among the popular motifs were flowers, fleurs-de-lis, rosettes, hearts, and arrows. Some families commissioned ironwork that bore monograms or crests.

In New Orleans, much of which is below sea level, burial six feet deep was often impractical, especially during plagues of cholera and yellow fever, when hundreds of victims died in a single week (8,000 died in the yellow-fever epidemic of 1853). There are

OPPOSITE: *A servant's room in Gallier House, furnished with Louisiana-made items, including a high-post bed and an armoire.*

*New Orleans's cast iron takes many fanciful shapes. The city has two cornstalk fences—one in the Garden District and one in the French Quarter—which resemble cornfields ready for harvest.*

ghastly legends of floods washing over graveyards and decomposed bodies floating through town. In 1800 Saint Louis Cathedral consecrated the first of three cemeteries where Catholics (mostly Creole merchants) were buried aboveground, in elaborate tombs of marble and granite. The faithful of lesser means were laid to rest in vaults, stacked upon one another like drawers in a morgue. Wandering through New Orleans's cemeteries, especially those near the French Quarter, is not recommended for visitors, or for natives. Though picturesque and seemingly peaceful, these burial grounds are known to shelter many present-day outlaws.

# B U S I N E S S     D I S T R I C T

**Canal Street,** the uptown border of the French Quarter, is one of the widest avenues in the world. Along both sides of the street, where Creoles and Americans mingled to do business, are nineteenth-century commercial buildings. The Civil War interrupted construction of the Egyptian-style **U.S. Custom House** (423 Canal Street, 504–589–6324), begun in 1849 with future Confederate general Pierre G. T. Beauregard the army engineer in charge. (Henry Clay attended the groundbreaking.) Union headquarters during the Civil War, the massive marble-and-iron building required firmer support than swampy New Orleans could offer, and it sits on deeply anchored cypress pilings. Inside, Marble Hall, measuring 125 by 95 feet, is illuminated from a glass ceiling supported by fourteen columns.

Canal Street is the terminus of the **Saint Charles Streetcar,** in operation since 1835. The line runs along Saint Charles Avenue, through the modern business district past Lafayette Square, in the 500 block. Across from it is **Gallier Hall** (545 Saint Charles Avenue, 504–586–4311), considered the finest work of architect James Gallier, Sr. Its Greek Revival colonnade extends ninety feet in length. Mayor's offices inside are furnished with original Rococo Revival tables and chairs. Gallier also was called in to work on **Saint Patrick's** (724 Camp Street), completed in 1841, the major Gothic Revival structure in the city. **Saint Mary's Assumption Church** (2330 Constance) was completed in 1860, just prior to the Civil War. A red-brick building with Italianate elements, it has a 142-foot tower that changes from a square to an octagonal plan at the roof level. The facade is notable for its intricate brick corbelling, and the interior is richly decorated with plaster ornamentation.

Uptown from the business district, Saint Charles Avenue is interrupted by **Lee Circle.** The 1884 bronze statue of Robert E. Lee, standing atop a fluted, sixty-foot column, is the work of New York sculptor Alexander Doyle. Some of the Civil War general's artifacts are a block away in the **Confederate Museum** (929 Camp Street, 504–523–4522), housed in an 1891 reddish sandstone building designed in the Romanesque Revival style by local architect Thomas Sully. The large exhibition hall displays battle flags, weapons, uniforms, and medical instruments as well as many personal effects donated by the soldiers themselves.

# THE GARDEN DISTRICT

From Lee Circle, Saint Charles Avenue leads to neighborhoods settled by Americans after the Louisiana Purchase. The most successful and socially ambitious of the newcomers built their houses in the Garden District. Though these residences were not as grand as some of the plantation homes upriver, they were still imposing, particularly those built in the city's prevailing Greek Revival style, with double rows of columns—Ionic below, Corinthian above, trimmed with cast-iron railings. Instead of the hidden Creole courtyard, Garden District houses boasted extravagant landscaped gardens, dotted with pavilions, statuary, and fountains. The rooms were scaled for entertainment: double parlors, lavishly detailed with plaster, marble, and moldings, open up into ballrooms (in the French Quarter, even the richest Creoles were more discreet about their wealth). These formal houses work with the local climate. High-ceilinged central hallways open at the front and back, providing ventilation, as do tall windows in most rooms that open onto front porches and galleries. A classic example of the local Greek Revival style is the **Strachan House** (1134 First Street, private), where Jefferson Davis died while on a visit in December 1889. The house was built in 1850 by a Kentucky planter. During the Civil War it was occupied by Union general Benjamin Butler.

The raised **cottage** at 2340 Prytania (private) is believed to be the oldest house in the Garden District, built in 1832 by a Philadelphia businessman, Thomas Toby, and his Creole wife. The **Bultman House** (1525 Louisiana Avenue, 504–895–7766) was built in 1860 by James P. Freret, Sr., who owned a cotton press in town. The Freret family held the house until 1880. In 1941 the playwright Tennessee Williams, who later settled in the French Quarter, was a guest in one of its upstairs rooms. Grandly scaled, the rooms contain an eclectic mix of nineteenth-century furniture.

Another excellent example of the Greek Revival is the **Maddox-Brennan House** (2501 Prytania, private). Its colonnades and elaborately framed doorway may be viewed through a cast-iron front gate. The Italianate **townhouse** at 1315 First Street (private), with an exuberant cast-iron facade, was built in 1869 by a Virginia cotton broker, Joseph Carroll. Equally impressive is the 1869 **villa,** also ornamented with iron, at 1331 First Street. Architect Henry

OPPOSITE: *The lush formal garden behind the 1850 Strachan House is designed in the French and Italian styles.*

Howard designed **Colonel Short's Villa** at 1448 Fourth Street (private) for Robert Henry Short of Kentucky. Completed in 1859, the house is known for its cast-iron cornstalk fence.

The Gothic Revival **Trinity Episcopal Church** (1329 Jackson Avenue) was built in 1853. One of Trinity's bishops was Leonidas Polk, the "fighting bishop" of the Confederacy, who died in battle at Pine Mountain. Businesswoman Clara Hagan built the Crescent City Skating Rink in 1884 as a city attraction during the Centennial Cotton Exposition. Known today as the **Rink,** the renovated wooden edifice at Prytania and Washington, is used for retail and other commercial purposes.

Founded in 1833, **Lafayette Cemetery Number 1** (1428 Washington Avenue) is the burial ground of some prominent Garden District families. It is filled with elaborate tombs but also lined with rows of vaults where less affluent citizens were laid to rest. Among those who lie here are some of the 8,000 victims of the yellow-fever epidemic of 1853. The cemetery is enclosed by a high wall that, like most of the tombs, is made of brick covered with stucco.

# AUDUBON PARK AREA

The Byzantine-style **Touro Synagogue** (4328 Saint Charles Avenue) was built in 1907 and named for Judah Touro, a prominent Jewish philanthropist, whose father was the rabbi at Touro Synagogue in Newport, Rhode Island, the oldest surviving synagogue in the United States.

The institutional ensemble on Saint Charles Avenue includes the Jesuit **Loyola University,** established in 1912. Many buildings on Loyola's campus were designed along Tudor-Gothic lines.

**Tulane University** grew out of the 1834 Medical College of Louisiana and the University of Louisiana (established in 1847). Named for benefactor Paul Tulane in 1884, it occupies a handsome campus across from Audubon Park in the 6800 block of Saint Charles Avenue. Tulane University's **Middle American Research Institute** (504–865–5110) has a significant collection of Central American, Mexican, and pre-Columbian artifacts and archaeological items including some of the most famous examples of marble

OPPOSITE: *A house in New Orleans's Garden District, where, according to Mark Twain, "No houses could well be in better harmony with their surroundings, or more pleasing to the eye, or more home-like and comfortable looking. . . ."*

vases from Honduras dating from the classical period of A.D. 750 to 1000, and a fine collection of Guatemalan textiles from the 1930s. Part of Tulane, **Sophie Newcomb College** was established in 1886 for women. Benefactor Josephine Louise LeMonnier Newcomb gave more than $3 million to the school in memory of her only daughter, Harriet Sophie Newcomb, for whom the college is named. The college's art school produced a local arts-and-crafts ceramic known as Newcomb pottery, examples of which are on display in the Newcomb Art Gallery and in the Presbytère on Jackson Square. **Audubon Park,** which extends to the Mississippi levee, was developed in the 1870s from a sugar plantation and was the site of the Centennial Cotton Exposition, celebrating the 100th anniversary of Louisiana's international cotton exports. In the park is a statue of its namesake, the artist John James Audubon.

At the uptown end of Saint Charles, the streetcar enters **Carrollton,** once part of the Macarty Plantation. As a separate municipality, the town of Carrollton was the seat of Jefferson County; Henry Howard designed its 1855 Neoclassical **courthouse** at 719 South Carrollton Avenue. A mélange of nineteenth-century buildings lines Carrollton's Oak Street. In 1874 the town was annexed by the city of New Orleans.

*Edgar Degas painted this scene of a typical workday in his uncle's cotton brokerage in 1872, showing family members doing the various tasks involved in their trade.*

# OUTER NEW ORLEANS

## NEW ORLEANS MUSEUM OF ART

Formerly named the Delgado Museum, for Isaac Delgado, the sugar broker who founded it in 1911, the museum's collections of art from North, Central, and South America range from the pre-Columbian period to the present. Also outstanding are the eighteenth- and nineteenth-century furniture, displayed in period rooms, and works by the French Impressionist Edgar Degas, who visited relatives in New Orleans from 1871 to 1872. The artist's brothers, Achille and René, lived and worked at the New Orleans Cotton Exchange. Maternal relatives, the Mussons, lived on Esplanade Avenue not far from the museum. Though he cursed the "impossible light" of his working conditions, Degas enjoyed his stay in New Orleans: "Everything attracts me here," he wrote. Among the works he painted here are a number of family portraits and a well-known afternoon scene at the Cotton Exchange.

LOCATION: City Park. HOURS: 10–5 Tuesday–Sunday. FEE: Yes. TELEPHONE: 504–488–2631.

Across Bayou Saint John from City Park is **Saint Louis Cemetery Number 3** (3421 Esplanade Avenue), where there is a monument designed by James Gallier, Jr., in memory of his parents, who were lost at sea. **Metairie Cemetery** (Pontchartrain Boulevard and Metairie Road) was formerly a racetrack. The grounds were landscaped and consecrated for burial in the 1870s and now are filled with extraordinary memorial architecture and statues. General Pierre G. T. Beauregard was buried here, and there is a monument to Stonewall Jackson. Other prominent Confederates are also buried here.

## PITOT HOUSE

In the late 1700s Bayou Saint John, snaking into New Orleans from Lake Pontchartrain, was lined with French settlers' plantation houses. One of them, Pitot House, would be at home on a Caribbean island. Its architecture was dictated by the climate: The brick-floored basement not only was cooling but could survive flooding; the steeply pitched, overhanging roof protected against rain and sun; the wide galleries upstairs and downstairs opened to the shady outdoors.

Pitot House already existed when James Pitot arrived in New Orleans in the 1790s from Saint Domingue (now Haiti). Pitot, a Frenchman from Normandy (he changed his name from Jacques), and his wife were refugees from the West Indian slave rebellions. In New Orleans, he was able to resume his import-export business. "[Here in] a territory almost as vast as Europe," he wrote, "one's mind can run wild thinking . . . about the future." Pitot ran an international trade in French wines, English pewter and silver, Chinese porcelain, South American coffee, and Louisiana-grown cotton, sugar, and indigo. In 1803 he became the first elected mayor of New Orleans.

Except for the formal Federal-style salon, Pitot House is similar to a simple West Indian island cottage. It is furnished with pieces of the kind that Pitot often sold himself, such as cypress armoires and rush-bottomed chairs made by local artisans. Original paint colors have been duplicated, including the soft red known as *grand rouge* that Creoles created by mixing brick dust with buttermilk.

LOCATION: 1440 Moss Street. HOURS: 10–3 Wednesday–Saturday. FEE: Yes. TELEPHONE: 504–482–0312.

## CHALMETTE NATIONAL HISTORICAL PARK

The final battle of the War of 1812 was fought on Chalmette Plantation, about six miles south of New Orleans, on January 8, 1815. As it turned out, the men who died there might have been saved—the treaty ending the war had been signed on December 24, but word of the treaty had not yet reached the British in the United States. The battle at Chalmette made a final, decisive statement in the U.S. struggle with Great Britain over westward expansion. Guaranteeing the security of the city and the lower Mississippi River valley, it made a hero of Andrew Jackson.

Until late 1814 the war had been largely waged in the North; the British had captured and burned the American capital but had failed to capture Albany or Baltimore, while a series of American invasions of Canada had failed. The British hoped to seize New Orleans, gateway to the Gulf of Mexico and the Mississippi River. Hearing of the enemy advance, General Andrew Jackson arrived in the city on December 2 to meet the British head on. By the 23rd,

OPPOSITE: *Pitot House, a West Indian-style residence built in the 1790s, was acquired by New Orleans's first elected mayor, James Pitot, in 1809.*

about 2,000 British troops were camped on the levee below Chalmette. That evening Jackson's men—some 1,800 regular soldiers, a black regiment, a few Choctaw Indians, and recruits from New Orleans including Jean Lafitte and other corsairs—made an unsuccessful assault on the British encampment. The combat was fierce, hand-to-hand, and inconclusive. Jackson fell back the next day to Chalmette Plantation, where he put up a defensive line of earth, wood planking, and empty powder kegs. On January 8 the British, their numbers increased to approximately 8,900, attacked the Americans, who mustered about 5,400, across open ground and took terrible losses: Jackson's men inflicted 2,000 casualties and suffered only 13.

A point on Jackson's defensive line is marked by a 100-foot marble obelisk in the 141-acre battlefield park. Details of the battle, Jackson's strategy, and other information on the war are the focus of exhibits in the visitor center. Also on the site is **Beauregard House,** an 1830s Greek Revival plantation house designed by James Gallier, Sr. Opposite it is the **Chalmette National Cemetery.**

LOCATION: 8606 West Saint Bernard Highway. HOURS: June through August: 8:30–6 Daily; September through May: 8:30–5 Daily. FEE: None. TELEPHONE: 504–589–4428.

# B A Y O U      C O U N T R Y

West of the Mississippi River is the legendary and romantic landscape of the bayous, such as Teche, Atchafalaya, and Vermilion. Here centuries–old mossy trees cast their shadows over waters teeming with alligators and water moccasins. The bayous are famous as the home of Louisiana's Cajuns, descendants of French Acadians expelled by the British in the 1750s from their homes in Canada. Some Acadians were forcibly resettled in New England, Maryland, and Virginia; some were shipped to England; but several thousand made their way south to the Louisiana bayous.

Henry Wadsworth Longfellow immortalized their tragic wanderings in his 1847 narrative poem *Evangeline*. In the poem two young Acadian lovers, Gabriel and Evangeline, are separated in the dispersion from Acadia. Many years later they meet again in Louisiana, where Gabriel dies in the care of his Evangeline, an aged

OPPOSITE: *Beauregard House, one room deep with generous galleries on both sides, was built in 1840 on Chalmette Battlefield, scene of General Andrew Jackson's great victory in the War of 1812.*

*Visiting French painter Alfred Boisseau painted this Choctaw Indian family walking in the wilderness of Bayou Saint John, near New Orleans, in 1847.*

nun. Although Longfellow never visited Louisiana, his evocative descriptions of the bayou country are accurate: a region of perpetual summer and a "maze of sluggish and devious waters." Like the Creoles, with their ties to the Caribbean, Cajuns brought a rich element to the mix of Louisiana culture. In many bayou towns, both English and French are spoken (though the French is a dialect that a visitor from France might find hard to understand).

Until the Civil War, when Federal gunboats patrolled the bayous and interrupted commerce in the area, livelihoods came from rice and sugar growing and pecan harvests. Some planters were as successful as their counterparts on the Mississippi and built great manor houses along the bayous. The green pastureland lying between the waters encouraged dairy farming and also cattle raising, which some pursued on a Texas-sized scale, driving enormous herds to New Orleans markets. Cypress trees grew thick and tall in the swamps, and lumber towns grew up around sawmills. Many made their living by hunting alligators (sold for their hide and meat); others brought in enormous catches of catfish and of the tiny "lobster of the bayou," crayfish.

This tour of the bayou country begins with Thibodaux, takes a short detour north to Napoleonville, then follows Routes 90 and 49 from Morgan City to Washington.

# THIBODAUX

Fifty-five miles southwest of New Orleans, Thibodaux grew in the early 1800s as a trading center on the Bayou Lafourche. To the city it sent Chitimacha baskets, timber, and sugar; goods from New Orleans included furniture, coffee, and books. The seat of Lafourche Parish since 1807, the town has beautifully maintained its **courthouse** (Third and Green streets), designed in 1861 by Henry Howard. **Saint John's Episcopal Church** (718 Jackson Street), consecrated in 1845, is the oldest Episcopal church in the state, and one of the oldest west of the Mississippi.

According to one of the ubiquitous "escape legends," Queen María Luisa Teresa of Spain, fearing her country's defeat in the Napoleonic wars of the early 1800s, was prepared to flee to Louisiana and made arrangements for a house to be built. As it turned out **Rienzi** (Route 308, private), the raised cottage alleged to have been reserved for the queen's exile, was never occupied by royalty.

Two miles south of Thibodaux on Route 308 is the **Laurel Valley Village-Museum** (504–446–1187). Formerly the site of a 5,000-acre sugar plantation, the village consists of a complex of 1840s structures including a manor house, barns, slave cabins, smithy, sheds, general store, schoolhouse, and ruins of the sugar mill. A working town into the twentieth century, Laurel Valley is a rare example of an intact, self-contained plantation village.

# NAPOLEONVILLE

In 1863, as Confederate general Richard Taylor sought to oust the Yankees from southern Louisiana and New Orleans, the town of Napoleonville was occupied by Northern soldiers. Local stories say that **Christ Episcopal Church** (Routes 10 and 1) was used as a stable by Federal soldiers, who also reportedly shot out the original stained-glass windows for target practice. The **courthouse** on Levee Street was built in 1896.

## Madewood

This magnificent Palladian plantation house on the Bayou Lafourche belonged to Colonel Thomas Pugh, one of a family of North Carolinians who grew rich in Louisiana. The Pughs owned

OVERLEAF: *The sugar mill at Olivier Plantation on Bayou Teche painted in 1861 by the French artist Marie Adrien Persac. The fashionable figures that people his landscape were cut from magazines and pasted on the painting's surface—an early form of collage.*

some twenty plantations in southern Louisiana. New Orleans architect Henry Howard designed Madewood on a typically palatial
scale—some ceilings are twenty-five feet high, and it was said that
everyone in the parish could fit into the ballroom. Its brick walls
are three-and-a-half feet thick. Construction lasted eight years,
ending in 1848. Many furnishings in the recently restored house
are from Pugh's day.

LOCATION: Route 308. HOURS: 10–5 Daily. FEE: Yes. TELEPHONE:
504–369–7151.

## MORGAN CITY

A railroad town that came into being in the mid-1800s (as Brashear
City), Morgan City was fortified during the Civil War by the Confederates, but all of their forts have vanished. The **Turn of the
Century House** (715 Second Street, 504–385–6159) shows how a
well-to-do family lived in 1906, when the house was built. Oak and
mahogany furniture fill the paneled rooms. Earlier items—toys,
clothing, bottles, baskets—are part of the house's collection. A
Mardi Gras collection of costumes, headpieces, masks, and other
trappings from Morgan City's celebrations are on the second floor.

## FRANKLIN

Several plantation houses are located in and around Franklin,
founded in 1808. Restored by the Louisiana Landmarks Society,
the 1853 **Grevemberg House** plantation (Sterling Road, 318–828–
2092) contains mid-nineteenth-century furnishings and Civil War
memorabilia. The center of a large sugar plantation, **Oaklawn
Manor** (Irish Bend Road, 318–828–0434) was the home of Alexander Porter, an Irish merchant who became a U.S. senator.
Among his guests here was Henry Clay. The bricks in the three-
story Greek Revival house were made from clay and dirt on the
property.

Near **Baldwin** is a 283-acre reservation of the Chitimacha Indians,
now a unit of the Jean Lafitte National Park. The **Chitimacha
Tribe of Louisiana Preservation Museum** (off Route 326, 318–
923–7215) displays their craft work, such as baskets woven with
strands of cane gathered from swamps and woodlands. The colorful designs are still made with natural dyes: black from black-
walnut leaves, yellow from powac roots, and red from berries.

# JEANERETTE

Settled by Cajuns in the 1790s, Jeanerette lies mostly along the south bank of Bayou Teche. One of its earliest houses, a raised cottage called **Alice** (Route 87, private), was floated up the bayou from Baldwin. The slender columns of such Creole-style galleries became stout in the Greek Revival style, as seen in **Bayside,** built in 1830 on Jeanerette's largest sugar plantation (Route 87, private).

Three commercial buildings, all on West Main, are notable: **LeJune's Bakery** (Number 1510), which has been in operation since 1884; the old **Jeanerette Opera House** (Number 1334), a deep, two-story building (now an office building) sporting a white cast-iron balcony; and the **Jeanerette Lumber and Shingle Company** (Number 1440), once headquarters of the city's thriving lumber business. Pictorial histories of over 200 years of southern Louisiana's sugar and lumber industries are among exhibits at the **Jeanerette Museum** (500 East Main, 318–276–4293).

# NEW IBERIA

Located in a thicket of oak, cypress, and pecan trees on Bayou Teche, New Iberia first attracted settlers from the Canary Islands in the late eighteenth century. Joined by Cajuns, their settlement grew briskly, mostly from cattle raising and sugar growing. They also produced the spices and peppers essential to the hot sauces used in the regional cuisine. Tabasco sauce has been made by the McIlhenny family for four generations at their factory (318–365–8173), on nearby **Avery Island.**

The **Church of the Epiphany** (303 West Main Street) was used as a hospital during the Civil War. Episcopal bishop Leonidas Polk consecrated the church in 1848. A 1912 rice mill, **Konriko** (309 Ann Street, 318–364–7242), offers tours and an audio-visual presentation on the history of rice harvesting and milling.

The oldest house in New Iberia, **Broussard House** (1400 East Main Street, 318–364–6210) was built in 1790 by Armand Broussard, the son of one of the first Acadians to arrive on the bayou. No nails were used in the pegged-cypress construction, and the walls contain the original *bousillage* (mud and moss). Slightly raised on brick piers, the house has a steeply pitched overhanging roof shading a deep gallery. Four pairs of wide French doors lead inside. Sharing its three-acre site is **Mintmere Plantation House.** Built in 1857 on a 480-acre sugarcane plantation, the spacious raised cottage has Greek Revival detailing.

## Shadows-on-the-Teche

Sugarcane planter David Weeks, who inherited and purchased thousands of acres of rich farmland in southwestern Louisiana, commenced work on this beautiful plantation house in 1830. The coral-colored brick house, with eight white columns, stands on a slight elevation above Bayou Teche. It is known as Shadows-on-the-Teche for the shady live oaks that surround it.

Weeks, though of English stock, built his house in the French colonial manner, with French doors, an outside staircase, and wide galleries front and back. Rising from one end of the porch, the outside stairs are nearly concealed by a roof-high screen of louvers and latticework. The Weeks family furnished the house in the latest style, American Empire. The furniture of the first-floor rooms dates mostly to the 1830s and 1840s; the second-floor living quarters have been restored to reflect the tastes of the 1850s.

*Shadows-on-the-Teche, a modest but exceedingly charming house overlooking a bayou, was built in the 1830s by planter David Weeks. The surrounding live oaks were planted by Mary Clara Weeks soon after the house was built.*

David Weeks never actually lived in the house. In June 1834 while he was seeking medical attention at Yale Medical College in Connecticut, his wife, Mary Clara, moved into the house with their six children. Weeks died that August and his widow subsequently married Judge John Moore. In October 1863 Union general William B. Franklin used the house as a headquarters when he was on his way to the Red River Campaign and a portion of the army occupied the house until January 1864. During this time, when the Moores were living on the third floor, Mary Clara died.

Shadows-on-the-Teche fell into disrepair until the 1920s, when David Weeks's great-grandson began its restoration. He bequeathed it to the National Trust for Historic Preservation upon his death in 1958.

LOCATION: 317 East Main Street. HOURS: 9–4:30 Daily. FEE: Yes. TELEPHONE: 318–369–6446.

## SAINT MARTINVILLE

This bayou town was the meeting place of Gabriel and Evangeline in Longfellow's poem. The **Evangeline Oak,** where they met, still thrives on Port Street at the Bayou Teche landing. A statue of Evangeline stands next to **Saint Martin de Tours Catholic Church,** established in 1765. The present church, built by slaves in 1832, contains some furnishings from the first structure on the site, including the original box pews and altar, and a marble baptismal font that may have been a gift from Louis XVI—among the area's eighteenth-century arrivals were a number of royalists who fled the French Revolution. The town's **courthouse,** faced with four tall Ionic columns, was built in the 1850s. The **Longfellow-Evangeline State Commemorative Area** (1200 North Main Street, 318–394–3754) contains a raised Creole cottage, typical of the French and Creole plantation-type dwellings of the nineteenth century in southern Louisiana.

## LAFAYETTE

Having attracted more Acadian refugees than any other spot in southern Louisiana, Lafayette is the unofficial capital of bayou country. Settled in the 1770s, it was known for over a century as Vermilionville, after the neighboring bayou named by the French for its reddish color. The livelihoods here, beef and dairy farming

*The Acadian Village (opposite and above) in Lafayette, the Cajun capital of Louisiana.*

and fishing, were also those of its many sister towns in the area. Cash crops included sugar, yams, and rice. In the 1880s the New Orleans–Houston railroad came through, and Vermilionville grew into a sizable town; in 1884 it was rechristened Lafayette.

Alexander Mouton, a member of one of the town's founding families, served as U.S. senator from Louisiana from 1837 to 1842 and as governor from 1843 to 1846. His first home, a double-galleried townhouse built in 1800, is now the **Lafayette Museum** (1122 Lafayette Street, 318–234–2208). Among its collections are nineteenth-century issues of *L'Impartial,* the town's French and English newspaper.

At Lee and Jefferson avenues is a **memorial** to Alfred Mouton. A brigadier general in the Civil War, he was wounded at the Battle of Shiloh in Tennessee and killed at Mansfield, Louisiana. Charles Mouton built the square-pillared, gable-roofed **Charles Mouton House** (338 North Sterling Street, 318–233–7816) about 1820.

All the elements of a typical Cajun bayou settlement of the nineteenth century have been reproduced from vintage structures and accoutrements in **Acadian Village,** a folk-life museum (south of Route 342, 318–981–2364). Clustered along a small winding bayou are simple cypress cottages, a chapel, village store, sheds, and barns. Most are authentic nineteenth-century buildings, and all contain furnishings, tools, and fabrics from the early to mid-1800s. Cajun crafts and cooking are demonstrated.

## CHRETIEN POINT PLANTATION

This elegant Greek Revival house stands upon land acquired by Hypolite Chretien, a cotton planter, in about 1776. His son, Hypolite II, married a Spanish woman, Felicité Neda, and in 1831 they moved into this house. Hypolite died of yellow fever soon after, and Felicité took over the running of the plantation, assisted later by her son Hypolite III. Though outbuildings were destroyed during the Civil War, the house remained in the family. Jules Chretien, great-grandson of the plantation's founder, was one of the first cotton planters in the area to switch to rice. He dammed the bayou to irrigate his fields, but his neighbors broke the dam so that they could get water for their cattle. Jules's farm failed and the house went into decline, serving as a hay barn at one point. It has now been completely restored and furnished with nineteenth-century pieces and portraits.

LOCATION: Off Route 10, west of Grand Coteau. HOURS: 10–5 Daily. FEE: Yes. TELEPHONE: 318–233–7050.

## GRAND COTEAU

Known for oak-alley landscapes and raised Creole cottages, Grand Coteau is the location of the **Academy of the Sacred Heart** (1821 Academy Road, 318–622–5275), built as a girls' school in 1821. The main building, dating from the early 1830s, is one of the largest pre–Civil War buildings in Louisiana; it is faced with a three-story, twenty-two-bay cast-iron colonnade.

## OPELOUSAS

Originally a bayou trading post of the Opelousa Indians, this fertile area attracted Frenchmen and Spaniards in the 1720s. The rich soil and pastureland encouraged diverse agricultural activity: Farmers raised corn, rice, sweet potatoes, and cattle. In the early years of the

OPPOSITE: *A shrimp trawler passing fishing camps in Terrebonne Parrish, near the Gulf of Mexico in the heart of Louisiana bayou country.*

settlement the route to New Orleans was convoluted—from Bayou Courtableau to Bayou Teche to the Atchafalaya to the Gulf, then up the Mississippi to the city. But in the 1760s the Spanish began blazing a series of east–west roads. By the end of the century, the Old Spanish Trail was the chief route of commercial traffic, including cattle drives from Opelousas to New Orleans. The town was incorporated in 1821, and it became one of the most prosperous in the state, with cotton added to the roster of cash crops. During the Civil War, when Federals occupied Baton Rouge, Opelousas briefly served as state capital and Governor Thomas O. Moore set up his office in a two-room house on Market and Landry streets (private).

The **Jim Bowie Museum** (Route 190, 318–948–6263) commemorates the life of adventurer Jim Bowie, who was born in Kentucky and came to the bayou country in 1802 as a boy. His father built a house on what is now the museum lawn. Bowie left home as a teenager, did well as a Louisiana sugar planter, and was elected to the state legislature. In 1827 he was wounded—but killed his opponent—in a duel outside the town of Vidalia in eastern Louisiana. A historic marker has been placed at the scene of Bowie's "Sand Bar Fight" at Vidalia's Mississippi River bridge. Attracted to opportunities in frontier Texas, he moved west in the late 1820s and married the daughter of the territory's Mexican governor. When Mexico announced a prohibition on further Anglo settlement, however, Bowie joined forces with William B. Travis, Davy Crockett, and other Texas revolutionaries. In 1836 he died at the Alamo. Popular wisdom credits Bowie with the invention of the bowie knife, but it was actually patented by his brother; Jim is believed to have added a guard to the design. His career is the focus of exhibits in the Opelousas museum .

The **Estorge House** (427 Market Street, 318–948–4592), built as early as 1827, signaled flush times in Opelousas that would last until the Civil War. Most of the windows contain original, now-iridescent glass panes. Among the eighteenth-century furnishings is a spool-post, Gothic Revival bed. Ceilings are painted in dramatic trompe l'oeil.

# WASHINGTON

In the small hills just north of Opelousas, Washington is situated between two bayous, Courtableau and Carron. Incorporated in

1835, the town prospered because the waterways here were deep and wide enough for steamboats. Farmers and planters could readily dispatch cotton, sugar, and livestock down the Courtableau to the Mississippi. The town came to a standstill during its occupation by Federal troops, and it suffered a second blow in 1883, when it was bypassed by the railroad. The **Washington Museum and Tourist Information Center** (Main and Dejean streets, 318–826–3626) provides free guidance to sites.

The oldest residence in town is **Hinckley House** (405 East Dejean Street, 318–826–3906), built in the early 1800s. Collections include family heirlooms and steamboat memorabilia. Also on the property is an 1803 graveyard.

The **Nicholson House of History** (Main and Vine streets, 318–826–3670) is the early 1800s residence of the town's first mayor, Gerard Carrier. Used as a fort and a hospital during the Civil War, it bears marks of both: Guns were fired from portholes cut beneath the house, and bloodstains mar the floorboards of an upstairs bedroom.

Both Union and Confederate officers occupied **Magnolia Ridge** (private) at different times during the war. The proprietor of the 1830 Greek Revival mansion was Judge John Moore, who later married the widow of David Weeks of Shadows-on-the-Teche. The heart-of-pine flooring throughout the house ranks with the finest in Louisiana.

The slate-roofed **Steamboat House** (private), located at a wide path where the unwieldy boats could turn around, was a popular inn. One of the largest plantation houses in bayou country is the three-story brick **Arlington House** (Route 103, 318–826–3298), built for Amos Webb in 1829. Webb, who became a major in the Confederate army, is buried with other family members in the adjacent graveyard. The house called **Starvation Point** originally was a trading post and stage stop for overland travelers. In the steamboat era, boatmen stayed here. Built in 1790, the Creole-style house has been restored and is open by appointment.

About five miles north of Washington is **Homeplace** (Route 182, 318–826–7558), a pleasant raised Creole cottage. The 1826 house was built on land that had been part of a large Spanish grant in the 1790s. All of the furnishings are from the early nineteenth century. The grave of an unknown Confederate soldier is marked on the grounds.

# THE
# RIVER ROAD
## AND
# NORTHERN
# LOUISIANA

OPPOSITE: *Nottoway's Italianate white ballroom, one of sixty-four rooms in the largest plantation house in the South.*

Between New Orleans and Baton Rouge, the roads on the east and west banks of the Mississippi River are known as the River Road. (The River Road actually extends to Natchez, Mississippi, though the term most often refers to this eighty-mile dual route off Interstate 10 that connects the two cities.) Plantations once abutted each other on both sides of the river—planters could load bales of cotton or bags of sugar onto boats docked virtually at their front doors. They were very much tied to New Orleans, center of their commerce, and some planters kept lavish pieds-à-terre in the city.

Several River Road houses survive as restaurants or inns. Others have been restored and furnished to their periods by private owners, the River Road Historical Society, and other preservation groups. The route today is a winding one, following the quick lefts and rights of the levee. Flat green land fans out from the river, where former cotton and cane fields now sprout petroleum refineries. Unless otherwise noted, all of the following sites are on the east bank heading north from New Orleans to Baton Rouge. Next, the chapter covers Feliciana Parish, a plantation area north of Baton Rouge settled by the English. The final section describes the valleys of the Red and Cane rivers, and northeastern Louisiana.

# THE     RIVER     ROAD
## DESTREHAN

Three tiny dormer windows and slender twin chimneys peeking from the wide hip roof make this 1787 house, built for a Creole planter, seem enormous. Eight columns stretch across the front, which is flanked by matching *garçonnières*. Predating Pitot House in New Orleans and Magnolia Mound in Baton Rouge, it may be the oldest plantation house in the lower Mississippi Valley. Louisiana armoires and beds are among the period furnishings.

LOCATION: 9999 River Road, Route 48, Destrehan. HOURS: 10–4 Daily. FEE: Yes. TELEPHONE: 504–764–9315.

OPPOSITE: *Evergreen, with guest quarters surrounding its formal garden, is one of the few Louisiana plantations with intact outbuildings.*

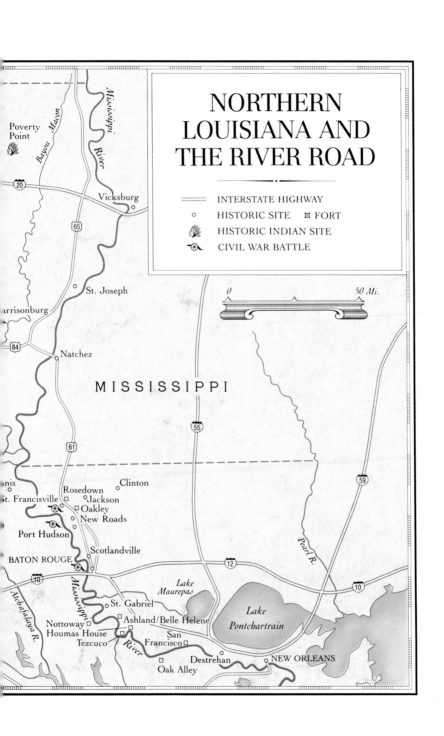

# NORTHERN
# LOUISIANA AND
# THE RIVER ROAD

———— INTERSTATE HIGHWAY

○ HISTORIC SITE    ⊠ FORT

HISTORIC INDIAN SITE

CIVIL WAR BATTLE

0                               50 Mi.

Poverty
Point

Mississippi River

Bayou Macon

20

Vicksburg

65

St. Joseph

arrisonburg

84

Natchez

MISSISSIPPI

55

61

nis

St. Francisville

Rosedown

Clinton

Jackson

Oakley

New Roads

59

Port Hudson

Scotlandville

BATON ROUGE

12

10

10

Mississippi River

Atchafalaya R.

St. Gabriel

Nottoway

Houmas House

Tezcuco

Ashland/Belle Helene

San Francisco

Lake
Maurepas

Lake
Pontchartrain

Pearl R.

Destrehan

NEW ORLEANS

Oak Alley

# SAN FRANCISCO

The most conspicuous house on the River Road is San Francisco, an 1854 triumph of the festive "Steamboat Gothic" style. Built with extravagant decoration, the house apparently cost a fortune—its name, evolved from the French slang *sans frusquin* (without a cent), is a joking reference to the expense. It was constructed by Edmond Bozonier Marmillion, whose family inventories were later consulted for the restoration. Though the exuberant exterior attracts immediate attention, San Francisco is also famous for its High Victorian furniture, beautifully marbleized and grained cypress moldings, and, particularly, five giant ceiling medallions of painted wood.

LOCATION: River Road, Route 44, Garyville. HOURS: 10–4 Daily. FEE: Yes. TELEPHONE: 504–535–2341.

*San Francisco's builder, Edmond Bozonier Marmillion, hoped to create the light and festive ambience of a steamboat in his country house. A fanciful cistern is at left.*

*Oak Alley's twenty-eight massive live oak trees are echoed in the Greek Revival house's twenty-eight Doric columns.*

## OAK ALLEY

When sugar planter Jacques Telesphore Roman bought this site as a home for his bride in 1837, he acquired magnificent century-old landscaping. Sometime in the eighteenth century a French settler had built a small house here and planted an allée of oaks—fourteen trees on each side—leading to the river's edge. The romantic quarter-mile canopy of oaks is one of the enduring romantic settings of the antebellum South, almost upstaging the house at the end of it. The columned Creole-Greek synthesis has carved doorways on the ground and gallery levels rivaling those of Rosedown in Saint Francisville.

LOCATION: Route 18, along the River Road (west bank), Vacherie. HOURS: March through October: 9–5:30 Daily; November through February: 9–5 Daily. FEE: Yes. TELEPHONE: 504–523–4351.

# TEZCUCO

Its name an Aztec word for respite, Tezcuco is a raised cottage in the comfortable Creole style, complete with wrought-iron railings and a side gallery made entirely of cast iron. The planter who built it in 1850, Benjamin Turead, supplied his own building materials—bricks fired in his kilns and timber from his cypress thickets. Louisiana-made furniture fills the airy rooms (ceilings are sixteen feet high) and there are collections of nineteenth-century silver, crystal, and pottery.

> LOCATION: River Road, Route 44, Darrow. HOURS: 10–5 Daily. FEE: Yes. TELEPHONE: 504–562–3929.

Designed with two dozen stout columns, **L'Hermitage** (River Road, Darrow, 504–891–8493) was an 1812 wedding present from planter Marius Pons Bringier to his son Michel, who would soon serve under Andrew Jackson in the Battle of New Orleans.

# HOUMAS HOUSE

Now attached to the rear of Houmas House, the original structure on this former sugar plantation was built by a French planter who bought the land from the Houmas Indians in the late eighteenth century. The early structure was built in the style of a French country house with Spanish influence. In 1812 the house was bought by South Carolina's Wade Hampton, a Revolutionary War general. It was later purchased by his son-in-law, John Smith Preston, who remodeled it to incorporate Greek Revival elements. On either side of the chief residence he added an octagonal *garçonnière*. Preston, who grew sugarcane on the surrounding 12,000 acres, owned Houmas House for some twenty years before selling it to John Burnside, an Irishman. When Union officers tried to take the house at the start of the Civil War, Burnside refused, claiming that as a British subject he was exempt from such confiscation—and he won his argument.

> LOCATION: 942 River Road, Burnside. HOURS: February through October: 10–5 Daily; November through January: 10–4 Daily. FEE: Yes. TELEPHONE: 504–522–2262.

OPPOSITE: *Houmas House, above, originally built in the late eighteenth century and remodeled in the 1840s. It was restored in the 1940s and furnished with pieces made by early Louisiana artisans. Below, the working kitchen.* OVERLEAF: *Nottoway, built in 1859 in the Italianate style.*

# ASHLAND/BELLE HELENE

About sixty miles north of New Orleans is Ashland, surrounded by thirty-foot-tall columns. Its scale is remarkable, even in this land of very big houses. It was built by Duncan Kenner, a statesman, planter, and horse breeder who had a track on the grounds of his plantation so he could watch the races from his gallery. It is probable that Kenner called on James Gallier, Sr., to design the house, which was completed in 1841. A cypress swamp, like the one harvested to build the house, continues to thrive here. In the 1880s, Ashland was sold to a German sugar planter who renamed it after his granddaughter Helene.

LOCATION: 7497 Ashland Road, off the River Road, 5 miles north of Darrow. HOURS: 9–5 Daily. FEE: Yes. TELEPHONE: 504–473–1328.

# NOTTOWAY

Designed by Henry Howard, James Gallier, Sr.'s rival as a society architect, Nottoway was called the White Castle when it went up in 1859. Howard, a master of eclectic styles, produced an Italianate fantasy for his client, John Randolph, whose cane fields covered 7,000 acres. The 64-room Nottoway may be the largest plantation house surviving in the South. It is now a restaurant and inn.

LOCATION: Route 1 (west bank), 2 miles north of White Castle. HOURS: 9–5 Daily. FEE: Yes. TELEPHONE: 504–545–2730.

# SAINT GABRIEL

This town on the east bank of the Mississippi, fifteen miles south of Baton Rouge, is the site of **Saint Gabriel** (River Road, Route 141), believed to be one of the oldest surviving Catholic churches in the Louisiana Purchase territory. Originally built in 1769 by Acadian refugees who settled on Bayou Manchac, it was dismantled and moved downriver in 1772. Made of cypress, the simple structure has a square bell tower rising above a steep roof. Colorful stencil work and turned columns and balustrades enliven the interior.

One of the oldest family-owned sugar plantations on the Mississippi, **Saint Louis** (River Road, south of Plaquemine, private) was established in 1807. In scale and sophistication this house, built in 1858, recalls Greek Revival houses in New Orleans.

# MOUNT HOPE

Built in 1817 by German planter Joseph Sharp, Mount Hope originally stood on 400 riverfront acres. The property is now smaller, and the river has changed course, but the house and handsome outbuildings remain much as Sharp left them. The front and rear galleries of the main house are shaded by an over-hanging shingled roof. The house contains Civil War artifacts in addition to nineteenth-century furnishings.

LOCATION: 8151 Highland Road, Baton Rouge. HOURS: 9–4 Monday–Saturday. FEE: Yes. TELEPHONE: 504–766–8600.

# BATON ROUGE

According to legend, when Pierre le Moyne, sieur d'Iberville, made his way up the Mississippi River in 1699, he came upon an unusual landmark on the bluffs about 230 miles upriver. The two Indian tribes sharing the area, the Houmas and the Bayougoulas, had staked off their separate hunting grounds by smearing a tall cypress pole with the blood of animals. Soon afterward, the place turned up on the Frenchman's map as Baton Rouge, meaning "red stick." What is believed to be the site of the cypress pole is marked by a sculpture at Southern University in the town of Scotlandville, about five miles north of Baton Rouge.

Even after Britain was ceded the area as West Florida in 1763, Baton Rouge remained resolutely French in character. Among the few buildings standing from the city's French days are the **Lafayette buildings** (private), located on the street of the same name at numbers 342 and 348. Built in the 1760s, the near twins sport cast-iron galleries typical of New Orleans's French Quarter. While touring the United States in 1825 the Marquis de Lafayette stayed in number 342.

In September 1779 the Spanish captured the chief British fortification—a star-shaped earthen mound—in a skirmish known as the First Battle of Baton Rouge. For almost twenty years the Spanish flag flew over the region, which would again pass to the French in the secret treaty that preceded the Louisiana Purchase of 1803. In 1810, when the Spanish still insisted that the area was theirs and was thus exempt from the Louisiana Purchase, a group of Americans stormed the old Spanish fort. Known as the Second Battle of Baton Rouge, this conflict ended Spanish claims.

## Old State Capitol

In 1861 the state voted to secede from the Union in the second-floor chambers of this building. It was constructed of cast iron and brick in 1849, to designs by James Dakin. The crenelated exterior is as indestructible as it looks; however, an 1862 fire gutted the interior while Federal forces were using it as a barracks and prison. Now restored, the interior is dominated by a huge circular iron staircase spiraling toward the stained-glass rotunda. The iron fence surrounding the building was cast in 1852 by a local foundry.

LOCATION: 150 North Boulevard. HOURS: 9–4:30 Tuesday–Saturday. FEE: None. TELEPHONE: 504–342–8211.

*Baton Rouge's Old State Capitol was designed in 1847 by James Dakin, who submitted the winning designs just five days after the Louisiana Building Commission announced the competition.*

## Louisiana State Capitol

In 1932 Huey P. Long, Louisiana's controversial populist former
governor, built a new capitol. The thirty-four-story (450-foot) Art
Deco skyscraper that went up in 1932 was the tallest building in the
South at the time. The depression-era construction project required an enormous and spirited output of labor and skill. Murals
and bas-reliefs throughout the three main chambers—Memorial
Hall, Senate, and House—are fine examples of heroic, allegorical
Works Project Administration (WPA) art, representing the state's
history and nature, industry and agriculture, science and art. In
1935 Long—by then a U.S. senator—was assassinated in the capitol. A **monument** to him stands over his grave in the capitol
gardens. The capitol's observation deck affords a panoramic view
of the surrounding area.

LOCATION: State Capitol Drive. HOURS: 8–4:30 Daily. *Observation
Deck:* 8–4 Daily. FEE: None. TELEPHONE: 504–342–7317.

Begun in 1819, the **Pentagon Barracks** (State Capitol Drive at the
River Road, 504–342–1866) stand on the site of an eighteenth-
century British fortification. For five years soldiers performed
most of the construction, cutting cypress from nearby swamps and
making bricks from clay and silt collected from the riverbank. Four
of the original buildings are still standing; the fifth was razed in
1820 because it had been poorly constructed of inferior material.
The barracks contain the lieutenant governor's office, apartments
for legislators, and the **Capitol Complex Visitor Center** (504–342–
1866). The buildings are uniform—two stories, red brick, faced
with columns—and enclose a parade ground. General Zachary
Taylor was headquartered here when U.S. troops were dispatched
to the Mexican War in 1845, and it was here that he received news
that he had won the 1848 presidential election. At the time, postage
to Louisiana was paid by the recipient rather than the sender, and
legend has it that the letter announcing Taylor's victory sat at the
post office for several days until, finally, soldiers were dispatched
to pay the fee and deliver the election tidings to Taylor. At various
times during the Civil War both Union and Confederate soldiers
occupied the barracks.

The **Old Arsenal** (capitol grounds), built by the U.S. government in the 1830s, still seems impregnable behind its ten-foot-high
brick wall. The military post was discontinued in 1879 and in 1886

it became the site for Louisiana State University, which moved
from this location in 1925. The arsenal building served as cadet
barracks until 1932. On adjacent grounds are two cannon commemorating the 1779 Battle of Baton Rouge. The guns sit on a
thousand-year-old Indian ceremonial mound, also used as a burial
ground for Union soldiers. Another cannon, a local curiosity, is
located at Riverside Mall and Laurel Street, where it is buried
muzzle down in the sidewalk.

East of the capitol is the forty-room **Governor's Mansion**
(1001 Baton Rouge Expressway, 504–342–0926). Built in 1962, it
recalls a sprawling plantation house, with twenty-one Doric columns along the front and sides. The **Old Governor's Mansion** (502
North Boulevard, 504–344–9463) was built during Huey Long's
administration. Its design resembles the White House, perhaps to
give the ambitious Long a feel for the real thing. It is now operated
by the **Louisiana Arts and Science Center** as a historic house
museum, furnished to reflect the times of the nine governors who
occupied it. The **Zeiss Planetarium** is located behind the house.

Also behind the Old Governor's Mansion is **Beauregard Town,**
laid out as a European-style town in 1806 by planter-turned-devel-
oper Elias Beauregard. The original plan called for the houses and
cottages to be surrounded by a college, convent, theater, meeting
hall, and other public and private buildings. The streets in Beauregard Town are named for European kings and lined with early-
nineteenth-century residences, some embellished in the Victorian
manner later in the century.

Built as the Yazoo and Mississippi Valley Railroad Depot in
1925, the **Louisiana Arts and Science Center Riverside Museum**
(100 South River Road, 504–344–9463) contains changing exhibits
on the fine arts, a children's gallery, and an Egyptian tomb exhibit.

## Louisiana State University

Established as a land grant college in January 1860, the Louisiana
State Seminary of Learning and Military Academy was first head-
quartered in Pineville, in central Louisiana. Its first president was
William Tecumseh Sherman, who would soon lead Northern ar-
mies across much of the South. Known as the "Old War Skule
[School]," it was closed during the war and reopened in 1865. After
a fire destroyed much of it four years later, the school moved to
Baton Rouge, where it became Louisiana State University and

*The salon of the Mississippi River steamboat Princess, painted in 1861 by Marie Adrien Persac and now in the Anglo-American Art Museum at Louisiana State University. It is the earliest known view of a Mississippi steamboat interior.*

Agricultural and Mechanical College. In the 1880s the university occupied the Pentagon Barracks and surrounding area. In 1925 it moved to its present location south of town, near ancient Indian ceremonial mounds. Exhibits in the **L.S.U. Museum of Geoscience** include artifacts of Indian life. Standing at the entrance to the **School of Aerospace Studies and Military Science** are two of the cannon that fired the first shots of the Civil War upon Fort Sumter—a gift to the university from General Sherman.

Collections in the **Anglo-American Art Museum** (504–388–4003), located in L.S.U.'s Memorial Tower, are meant to demonstrate the relationship between the United States and Great Britain, particularly the cultural influence British people have had on Americans. Period rooms represent English and American living, furniture styles, and decorative arts from the early seventeenth through the mid-nineteenth centuries. In addition, the museum holds important collections of New Orleans–made silver, Newcomb crafts, and other Louisiana arts and crafts.

The **L.S.U.** **Rural Life Museum** (6200 Burden Lane, 504–765–2437) is divided into three exhibit areas. The barn contains hundreds of artifacts of everyday rural life from prehistoric times to the early twentieth century. The working plantation consists of a complex of buildings—commissary, overseer's house, kitchen, slave cabins, sick house, schoolhouse, blacksmith shop, sugarhouse, and gristmill. Louisiana folk architecture is exemplified in seven buildings, including a church, pioneer's cabin and corncrib, potato house, shotgun house, Acadian house, and dogtrot house.

### Magnolia Mound

Irish immigrant, merchant, and indigo planter John Joyce built Magnolia Mound in the 1790s. Named for its location, the house sits in a slightly raised magnolia grove that once extended to the river's edge, where Joyce could choose merchandise from northbound and southbound boats. One of the earliest buildings in the area, the house is Creole in form, raised on brick piers and shaded by an overhanging roof, with windows and doors opening onto front and back galleries. The building materials were available on the spot—cypress, cedar, and, for insulation, mud and moss. Joyce drowned in 1798, and in 1802 his widow, Constance, married a Frenchman named Armand Duplantier. Duplantier rotated the plantation's indigo with cotton and sugarcane and updated the house in the fashionable Federal style, adding a dining room and an L-shaped office. He converted the plain foyer into a fancy cove-ceilinged parlor, with mantels, moldings, wallpapers, and fabrics bearing the patriotic emblems of the Federal and First Empire styles. Magnolia Mound appears as it did in Duplantier's day, full of elegant appointments that came to Baton Rouge on the River Road: English silver, Philadelphia and New York furniture, and French porcelain. There are also large Louisiana-made armoires. The sixteen-acre site has a working garden, open-hearth kitchen, and *pigeonnier*.

LOCATION: 2161 Nicholson Drive. HOURS: 10–4 Tuesday–Saturday, 1–4 Sunday. FEE: Yes. TELEPHONE: 504–343–4955.

Most of Baton Rouge's historic sites are within a short distance of the state capitol, which stands at the northern border of the down-

OPPOSITE: *The L.S.U. Rural Life Museum, a village settlement of modest buildings and a working plantation. The museum re-creates the life of Louisiana's common folk in this area better known for grand plantations.*

*Magnolia Mound, built as a simple cottage and remodeled in the early 1800s to suit the more refined tastes of French planter Armand Duplantier.*

town area. The downtown district is bounded by Government Street to the south and the Mississippi River to the west.

Northwest of Baton Rouge, on the west bank of the Mississippi, is **New Roads,** seat of Pointe Coupee Parish and the location of **Saint Francis Catholic Church** (Route 420), established in 1728. The present building, dating from 1760, was dismantled and moved to high ground in the 1890s when the river threatened to wash it away. The church bell is dated 1719. The red brick Romanesque Revival **Pointe Coupee Courthouse** (Main Street), with a solid square clock tower, was built in 1902.

## PARLANGE PLANTATION HOUSE

This brick and cypress plantation house near New Roads was built in 1750 by the Marquis Vincent de Ternant, who planted indigo and then sugar cane on his property. When the Marquis died in 1757 the plantation passed to his son, Claude, whose wife filled the spacious house with furniture from Europe, and then to his grandson, also named Claude. After the younger Claude died, his widow married into the Parlange family of France. The house and the plantation (still in operation) have remained in the family for more than 225 years. Many original furnishings are preserved.

LOCATION: Route 1, 6 miles south of New Roads. HOURS: 9–5 Daily. FEE: Yes. TELEPHONE: 504–638–8410.

*The restored Magnolia Mound master bedroom, with a prie-dieu, a kneeler, by the bed.*

## PORT HUDSON STATE COMMEMORATIVE AREA

Once Union troops occupied New Orleans in May 1862, Confederates set about fortifying the area just above and below Port Hudson, between East Feliciana and Baton Rouge. Located on the highest river bluffs south of Vicksburg, Port Hudson had immediate strategic importance to the lower end of the Mississippi. By the end of the year, observation towers and cannon were in place and soldiers could easily fire upon Union ships forced to maneuver slowly through a bend in the river at Port Hudson. But when Union forces attacked by land on May 23, 1863, the Confederates, under General Franklin Gardner, found themselves outnumbered about three to one. On the Union side were some of the first black troops enrolled in regimental form in the war. The fighting dragged on for forty-eight days, the bloodiest taking place at Fort Desperate (named by the dwindling number of Confederates defending it—they subsisted on rats during the siege). Finally, on July 9 word of the Vicksburg surrender reached General Gardner, who tendered his own. A trail and boardwalks lead to breastworks on the battlefield and to a viewing tower at Fort Desperate, and in the museum exhibits interpret the siege.

LOCATION: Route 61, 15 miles north of Baton Rouge. HOURS: 9–5 Wednesday–Sunday. FEE: Yes. TELEPHONE: 504–654–3775.

# F    E    L    I    C    I    A    N    A

North of Baton Rouge, Route 61 begins to rise and fall through green hills and rolling fields. Abundant rainfall and loessial soil assured agricultural success here—cotton and indigo grew easily in the parish known as Feliciana, divided into eastern and western halves in 1824. (The parish name is believed to honor the wife of Bernardo de Gálvez, Felicité.) Bayou Sara (now extinct) and other ports along this stretch of the Mississippi River were the most prosperous towns between New Orleans and Natchez, Mississippi.

## SAINT FRANCISVILLE

This town grew up around a 1720 French fort, though when Feliciana became part of England's West Florida, English settlers—including Tories from the eastern United States—began to outnumber the French and Creoles. The parish became resolutely Anglo-Saxon in character, and the Felicianas are still referred to as "English Louisiana." Responding to the persistent Spanish claims on the area, in 1810 a group of planters revolted and formed a tiny republic, flying a lone star flag for seventy-six days, until October 27, when President James Madison declared that the area did indeed belong to the United States.

The center of Saint Francisville is a concise few blocks of houses, offices, courthouse, banks, and churches. The 1903 Neoclassic **courthouse** (107 Prosperity Street) stands on the site of its 1855 predecessor, which was damaged by Federal gunboats stationed on the Mississippi. Just behind the courthouse, also on Prosperity Street, are law offices that have been in use since 1842. Among the historic private buildings that line Royal Street are the 1819 **Barrow House** (number 524), embellished with iron grillwork; the Spanish Colonial **Propinquity** (number 523), built as a store in 1809; **Virginia** (number 447), a stately Greek Revival townhouse; and the 1819 **Market Hall** (number 429).

**Grace Episcopal Church** (494 Ferdinand Street) was begun in 1858 to replace an earlier church built when the congregation was organized in 1828. The exterior of the present church is severe, unadorned Gothic, with an off-center bell tower. The interior is more Baroque, with fine plaster moldings and medallions, a bronze chandelier donated by the owners of Rosedown, early American stained glass, and double-rowed pews carved and false-grained by the builder. The 1861 Pilcher organ is the oldest two-manual tracker organ in use today. When Federal gunboats opened fire on Saint Francisville in 1863, shells badly damaged the church. The commander of one of the gunboats was buried in the churchyard during a brief truce. Waving a white flag, Union soldiers brought ashore the body of Lieutenant John E. Hart, a Mason who had requested a fraternal burial. Though Confederates, his fellow Masons in Feliciana agreed, and Hart was interred behind the church. A marble slab, carved with the Masonic emblem, marks his grave.

A trove of documents, maps, and various exhibits at the **West Feliciana Historical Society Museum** (364 Ferdinand Street, 504–635–6330) illustrate the eighteenth- and nineteenth-century settlement of Feliciana. Thick with live oak, cypress, magnolia, and pine trees, Feliciana lies on the Mississippi Valley "flyway," the migratory route of birds from Canada to Mexico. In the 1820s New Orleans artist John James Audubon, famed for his bird paintings, worked in the area. Some eighty of his paintings are on display in the **Audubon Art Gallery** (in the Best Western–Saint Francisville Hotel on Route 61, 504–635–3821).

## OAKLEY

John James Audubon was employed as a tutor at Oakley, an airy West Indies–style plantation house built in the early 1800s in the Feliciana wilderness, which was rich in bird life. Mr. and Mrs. James Pirrie had hired the artist to teach drawing to their daughter Eliza. Audubon was paid a monthly fee of sixty dollars, and room and board were provided for him and his talented young apprentice, Joseph Mason. Audubon spent half of each day making his own paintings, from specimens he and Mason collected from the nearby woods. Audubon was delighted by what he encountered. "The rich magnolias covered with fragrant blossoms," he wrote in his journal, "the holly, the beech, the yellow poplar, the hilly ground and even the red clay, all excited my admiration. [It] seems . . . almost supernatural, and surrounded by numberless warblers and thrushes I enjoyed the scene."

Restored to the time of Audubon's residency, Oakley is furnished with Federal-style furniture. Compared to many of its antebellum neighbors, Oakley is disarmingly simple—Adam mantels are among the few adornments—and the practicality of its design has endured. It is hard to imagine a more comfortable spot in the parish than the jalousied upper galleries at Oakley—breezy, shady, and safe from sun and rain. A weaving and laundry room opens off the kitchen in the back; the barn contains early carpentry and farm tools and equipment.

LOCATION: Route 965, off Route 61, in the Audubon State Commemorative Area. HOURS: 9–5 Wednesday–Sunday. FEE: Yes. TELEPHONE: 504–635–3739.

Among the arrivals to the Felicianas after 1800 were enterprising planters from the Carolinas, Virginia, and Georgia who had exhausted their soil and came to start anew in the rich Mississippi Valley. One of those families, the Barrows of North Carolina, came to West Feliciana in 1801 and their descendants built some of the finest plantation houses in the state—Greenwood, Afton Villa, and Rosedown. These and others lie on either side of Route 61. **The Myrtles** (Route 61, north of Saint Francisville, 504–635–6277) began as a simple cottage and was enlarged in 1834. The long front gallery was embellished with lacy cast iron in the 1850s. Inside, the plaster moldings and ceiling medallions are examples of the opulence of the antebellum decade. West of Route 61 is **Live Oak Plantation** (504–655–4682), a two-story brick Creole cottage built in 1808. Its architectural integrity has been preserved in a meticulous adaptive restoration.

At **Greenwood** (off Route 1, 504–655–4475), one of the Barrows's cotton and sugar plantations, twenty-eight columns surround the massive Creole-Greek house built in 1830 and nearly destroyed by fire in 1960. Now reconstructed, the house appears much as it did before the damage. Inside are many objects rescued from the fire, including family portraits, silver hardware from doors and cabinets, and some eighteenth-century furniture. Another victim of fire was **Afton Villa** (Route 61, 504–635–6773), a Gothic Revival mansion built by the Barrows in 1848. The ruins are surrounded by a formal garden and park planted with seasonal bloom. Just north is **Catalpa** (Route 61, 504–635–3372), a late Victorian cottage built on the site of an early 1800s plantation house. Still in the family of the original owner, cotton planter William J. Fort, the house is full of nineteenth-century furniture, portraits, porcelain, and silver. The oaks surrounding the house were planted in 1814.

OPPOSITE: *Rosedown's blue and gold Music Room, where Turnbull descendants entertained plantation visitors.*

Catalpa's neighbor, **The Cottage** (Route 61, 504–635–3674), was built on a 1795 Spanish land grant. Grand as far as cottages go, the main house is about a hundred feet long, with dormer windows above the gallery. Around the house are various original dependencies—kitchen, milk house, carriage house, smokehouse, and the plantation's one-room school.

# ROSEDOWN

The 1828 marriage of Martha Hilliard Barrow and Daniel Turnbull was a dynastic one, a merger of hefty West Feliciana plantation fortunes. (She grew up in the Federal-style plantation house **Highland,** a private residence on Route 69.) Following their wedding Martha and Daniel left on a European honeymoon. Throughout the grand tour of palaces, great houses, and gardens of Europe, they collected ideas for Rosedown and its grounds. On their return in 1835, a local carpenter-builder commenced construction of a small central house, to which they added two Creole-Greek wings in 1844 and more rooms at the back in 1858. Though not desiring a monumental house, they did demand a fine one; an agreement with one of the contractors concluded, "The workmanship and style [are] not to be surpassed in the state."

The Turnbulls merged their lands into a 3,500-acre estate around their home. The 30-acre gardens were the special domain of Martha, an accomplished horticulturist. An allée of 200-year-old oaks shades the long avenue leading up to the house. On either side of it, paths wind past statues and fountains and around beds of azaleas and camellias—Rosedown was among the first plantations in Louisiana to grow Oriental species successfully. Martha's garden was one of color and fragrance, with hundreds of sweet olive trees, gardenias, and hydrangeas; neat rows of dwarf boxwood framing parterres filled with roses; and, near the house, herb gardens, a hothouse, and handsome tool and planting sheds.

Slaves and free blacks performed the labor, from harvesting cypress and cedar from swamps on the property to cutting it by hand and in the Turnbull sawmill. (Some wood was imported; among Turnbull's papers is an invoice for 555 feet of West Indian mahogany used in the staircase.) Local carpenters molded, carved, and fluted timbers used for columns and for millwork throughout the house.

OPPOSITE: *All the furniture in the Rosedown nursery is original, including some family toys.*

As soon as the work was completed in 1838, Rosedown became the scene of lavish dinners, hunting parties, balls, and weddings. Daniel Turnbull died in 1861. During the Civil War Martha sometimes had to share the house with both Confederate and Federal troops. She died in 1896, at the age of 87. The house stayed in the family until the 1950s, when a Texan bought and restored it.

Certainly the most monumental furniture at Rosedown is the Gothic bedroom suite, originally intended as a victory gift for Henry Clay in the event that he won the presidential election of 1844. Clay lost, and the set came to Rosedown rather than to the White House. Turnbull added a northern wing to the house to accommodate it and, to balance the design, an identical wing was added to the southern end. Built as a library, it features a fireplace flanked by bookcases made by Prudent Mallard.

LOCATION: Route 10 at Route 61. HOURS: March through October: 9–5 Daily; November through February: 10–4 Daily. FEE: Yes. TELEPHONE: 504–635–3332.

## CLINTON

Established as the seat of East Feliciana Parish in 1824, Clinton grew during its first century as a legal and educational center. Among the town's outstanding buildings are the 1841 **East Feliciana Parish Courthouse** (Courthouse Square and Saint Helena Street), its twenty-eight columns and octagonal cupola rising above the town square, and, facing it, the Greek Revival **Lawyers' Row,** five cottages that were originally the offices of a dozen lawyers.

## JACKSON

The original seat of Feliciana Parish, Jackson was named for Andrew Jackson after the Battle of New Orleans. Among the buildings constructed during the town's busy pre–Civil War period are the 1850 **Audubon Public Library** (Bank Street), the ca. 1816 **Old Feliciana Parish Courthouse** (High Street), and the 1852 **Jackson Presbyterian Church** (Bank Street). The small-scale Greek Revival **Asphodel Plantation House** (Route 68) was built in 1833 by planter Benjamin Kendrick as a gift to his wife. It is now an inn.

Later in the century a railroad running north from Baton Rouge connected Clinton and Jackson to Victorian towns that grew with the train commerce: **Slaughter, Wilson,** and **Norwood,** all settled in the 1880s.

# THE   RED   RIVER   VALLEY

Spilling down from Texas, the Red River creates a southeasterly divide across Louisiana. To the south is bayou country, alternately flat and slightly rolling, in all places verdant. To the north are hills, some rising dramatically, pine belts, and open spaces. The French established a trading post on the Red River at Natchitoches, prompting the Spanish to set up a garrison at Los Adaes. The latter is now but a few traces on the ground, while Natchitoches remains as a handsome remnant of the French colonial period. After the Louisiana Purchase, American settlers arrived in the region from Tennessee and the Carolinas. Development of the region was impeded by the "Red River Raft," an immense jam of logs and other natural debris that blocked passage at Natchitoches. The federal government appropriated $1 million to remove the raft, placing the project in the hands of Captain Henry Miller Shreve. Between 1833 and 1839 Shreve's engineers succeeded in removing the obstruction and opening the territory to development.

During the Civil War, Union General Nathaniel P. Banks led an army up the Red River, intent on seizing the Confederate stronghold at Shreveport. The Red River Campaign of April and May 1864 turned into an ignominious defeat for Banks's grand force, which included ironclads to patrol the Red. After making his first base at Alexandria, Banks drove north along the river until he confronted entrenched Confederates at Mansfield under General Richard Taylor. Though outnumbered, the Southerners sent Banks scurrying in retreat. The Federals repulsed Taylor's pursuers at Point Pleasant but continued their retreat to Alexandria, which they burned before making their escape across the swollen Atchafalaya. The crossing of the Atchafalaya, on an improvised bridge, was one of two engineering successes that salvaged some glory for the Northerners. The other was Colonel Joseph Bailey's damming of the Red River, an extraordinary feat that raised the water level enough to allow Federal gunboats to navigate rapids at Alexandria and escape the approaching rebels.

This tour of the Red River region begins southeast of Alexandria and follows the river to Natchitoches and Shreveport, detouring briefly along the Cane River. The section ends in the northeastern corner of the state at an ancient Indian site, Poverty Point.

Near **Innis** is the slate-roofed **Saint Stephen's Episcopal Church** (off Route 1), consecrated by Bishop Leonidas Polk in 1859, the year after its construction. Its Gothic Revival design was the work of New York architect J. A. Wills.

The 1852 **Edwin Epps House** (Route 71 in the town of Bunkie), the modest frame home of a small-time planter, commemorates the life of the slave Solomon Northup, author of the memoir *Twelve Years A Slave*. Born in New York as a free man, Northup was kidnapped in Washington, DC and sold into slavery in the South. After ten years as Epps's slave he was freed and returned to New York. Illiterate, he dictated the stories that went into his book. The small museum contains furnishings from Epps's and Northup's occupancies, as well as documents about Northup's life.

## MARKSVILLE STATE COMMEMORATIVE AREA

This state park preserves a group of earth mounds, some in the form of truncated pyramids, and village sites occupied by Indians from A.D. 100 to 400. Their culture apparently was closely related to the Hopewell culture in Ohio. Exhibits in a **museum** interpret the natural history of the area and the architecture of the villages as well as displaying local archaeological finds: pottery shards, stone tools, pipes, and animal and human bones.

LOCATION: 700 Allen Street, Marksville. HOURS: 8:30–5 Daily. FEE: Yes. TELEPHONE: 318–253–9546.

## ALEXANDRIA

In the early 1790s two traders from Philadelphia, hearing of lively French, Spanish, and Indian trade at the southeastern end of the Red River, came to establish a permanent settlement on the south bank. One of them, Alexander Fulton, named a town Alexandria for his daughter. On the site of the Fulton and Miller trading post is the **Alexandria Museum of Art** (933 Main Street, 318–443–3458). Among its collections are examples of Louisiana folk art and contemporary Southern art.

As a port on the increasingly busy river, the settlement grew quickly. Cotton and sugarcane were harvested, and forests were cut for a burgeoning lumber industry. The major market for Alexandria and neighboring **Pineville** was New Orleans. Both were wealthy towns in 1864 when General Nathaniel Banks pushed up from the bayous and began his Red River Campaign, and both were occupied virtually without violence. During the Federal retreat from the Battle of Mansfield, however, the Federals torched Alexandria, destroying churches, houses, and public buildings. Some of Banks's soldiers may have taken shelter in Pineville's **Mount Olivet Church** (335 Main Street), built in 1857 with a simple two-columned portico. More than 1,500 unknown Federal soldiers are buried in the **National Cemetery** (209 Shamrock Street), founded in 1867. Spaniards and Frenchmen who manned an eighteenth-century fort on the river rapids are buried in **Rapides Cemetery** (Main Street, Pineville).

Just south of Alexandria is the **Rosalie Sugar Mill** (Rosalie Road and Bayou Robert, 318–443–2420), which survived the Civil War raids. Also surviving from the war is **Kent House** (3601 Bayou Rapides Road, 318–487–5998), built as a two-room cottage about 1800 and enlarged fifty years later. The house resembles others along the lower Mississippi—it is raised on brick piers and has a high-pitched overhanging roof, cypress frame and flooring, and *bousillage* walls. Furnishings include Louisiana-made cabinets and Federal, Sheraton, and Empire pieces. On the grounds are a detached kitchen, slave cabins, and herb garden.

## CHENEYVILLE

With its nineteenth-century houses and the 1853 **Trinity Episcopal Church** (Parish Road 14), the town of Cheneyville maintains an antebellum profile. One of the oldest houses in the area is **Walnut Grove** (Bayou Boeuf, three miles south of Cheneyville, 318–279–2203), built in the early 1800s. The house is large—it accommodated the owner's thirteen children—and was more formal than most of its contemporaries. The doorways and casement windows, precisely placed between pillars, recall the Georgian style. Its fine walnut woodwork was executed by slave and free black artisans.

## CLOUTIERVILLE

Between Alexandria and Natchitoches is the small plantation village of Cloutierville. What is now known as the **Little Eva Plantation** (Route 1, five miles south of Cloutierville, 318–379–2382) may have been the inspiration for Harriet Beecher Stowe's setting of *Uncle Tom's Cabin,* which takes place on the Red River.

The town grew from the plantation of Alexis Cloutier, who secured a large Spanish land grant in the late 1700s. His plantation lay on both sides of the river. In 1822 the town was incorporated and named in his honor. The **Bayou Folk Museum** (Route 1) is located in a house Cloutier built between 1805 and 1813. His wife died while the house was under construction, and it is believed that he never lived there. Restored to Cloutier's time, it was built in the indigenous fashion, with front and back exterior stairways leading from the ground floor to the main living level, made of cypress and pine. Most of the furnishings were made by nineteenth-century Louisiana artisans. The four fireplaces in the house share a common chimney. An accurately furnished and equipped nineteenth-century plantation doctor's office also is on the property. From 1879 to 1884 the house was the residence of the writer Kate Chopin. *Bayou Folk,* a collection of stories set on the Cane River, was published in 1894. Many of the original Cane River settlers are buried in the graveyard of **Saint Augustine Church** (Route 484), built about 1806.

# CANE RIVER PLANTATIONS

## MELROSE

This plantation complex was begun in 1794 by Marie Therese Coincoin, a freed black woman in her fifties, and several of her sons. They raised cotton, indigo, tobacco, and pecans on 6,000 acres. Coincoin had borne fourteen children, four of them fathered by a slave and ten by a French plantation owner named Metoyer. Metoyer freed those ten, who joined their mother in working the plantation, which grew, in the 1830s, to encompass some 12,000 acres. The family used slave labor. Among the nine buildings still standing are the 1796 **Yucca House,** a simple cottage of cypress and *bousillage,* and the 1800 **African House,** actually in the Norman-French style. There are also cabins, an 1833 house, a barn, and a weaving house.

LOCATION: Routes 119 and 494. HOURS: 12–4 Daily. FEE: Yes. TELEPHONE: 318–379–0055.

OPPOSITE: *Two views of life at Melrose Plantation, painted by the twentieth-century artist Clementine Hunter, who worked at Melrose.*

*The ca. 1800 African House at Melrose. Its distinctive overhanging roof is often said to have been derived from the architecture of the Congo, but the style probably has a French origin.*

Also on the Cane River is **Oaklawn** (Route 494, 318–357–9491), an 1830s plantation house that displays all the practicality of the Creole plan and the excellence of black workmanship. Raised on eight-foot brick piers, the front gallery extends more than eighty feet. Between the cypress posts used in construction is a *bousillage* of mud, moss, and deer hair. The many French doors positioned around the house contain original hand-blown glass. Original molding trims the rooms, which contain furniture mostly from the 1840s, including many examples of Louisiana cabinetry. There also are sets of nineteenth-century silver and porcelain.

    **Oakland** (Route 494, private) has been in the Prud'homme family since it was built in 1821. It is an extraordinary complex of manor house (a raised, Louisiana-style cottage) and twenty-seven outbuildings, including the original plantation post office, store, barns, and *pigeonnier*. The "French bottle garden" has parterre beds created by inverted, half-buried French wine bottles—it was the custom to put empty bottles to such use. **Cherokee** (Route 119, private), named for the species of roses growing on the grounds, remains largely unchanged since it was built—before 1839—of

*A desk at Oaklawn displaying the ledger books of stores that sold items to sharecroppers on credit, charging thirty percent interest.*

cypress and *bousillage*. It is surrounded by original stables and slave cabins.

The house at **Beau Fort** (Route 119, ten miles south of Natchitoches, 318–352–5340), a working cotton plantation, stands at the end of an oak allée. Every room of the raised cottage opens onto the generous galleries. Built in the early 1800s of rough-hewn cypress and *bousillage,* the house is furnished with pieces from the nineteenth century.

Eight brick slave cabins stand on **Magnolia Plantation** (Route 119, Derry, 318–379–2221), where cotton and soybeans still are grown. The land has been in the LeComte family since 1753. The manor house dates from the early 1830s, and behind its eighteen-inch-thick brick walls are rooms of Louisiana-made furniture. Burned by Nathaniel Banks's troops during their retreat from Alexandria, the house was restored in 1896. Also on the property are an overseer's house, store, blacksmith shop, *pigeonnier,* and a rare architectural and mechanical treasure—an enormous mule-drawn cotton press, once used to press cotton from nearby fields into bales.

# NORTHERN    LOUISIANA

## NATCHITOCHES

The "New Orleans of the North," Natchitoches is actually a few years older than that city to the south. First explored in 1700 by Sieur de Bienville and French Canadian Louis Juchereau de St. Denis, Natchitoches is the oldest permanent European settlement in the territory of the Louisiana Purchase. The French traded with the Natchitoches Indians and by 1715 had built **Fort Saint Jean Baptiste** (Mill and Jefferson streets, 318–357–3101) on the north bank of the Red River. The wooden fortification, with its chapel rising above pointed fence posts, has been reconstructed on the riverfront. St. Denis's widow is among those buried in the adjacent **American Cemetery.** A riverfront marker for **El Camino Real** indicates the beginning of the highway St. Denis blazed to Texas and Mexico. Though relations between the French and the Spaniards in the area, and some Indians, were strained at times, trade flourished along the abundant roads and waterways.

After the Louisiana Purchase of 1803, Americans began rolling into town by the wagonload, and along with the French and Spanish built a pretty town. **Front Street,** in downtown Natchitoches, recalls the French Quarter in New Orleans, with iron galleries of floral and geometric patterns. Perhaps the city's most famous display of cast iron is the ornate French-made spiral staircase in the courtyard of the 1843 **Luckey's Store** on the 700 block of Front Street. Neighbors in the nineteenth-century commercial block are the **Durcourneau** and **La Coste** buildings, each with a carriageway leading to rear courtyards.

The Civil War interrupted construction of **Trinity Parish Church** (Second and Trudeau streets), noted for its bell tower. Leonidas K. Polk, a Louisiana bishop turned Confederate general, laid the cornerstone in 1857. Dating to the same year is the domed and spired **Immaculate Conception Catholic Church** (Second and Church streets), lit by French crystal chandeliers. The wooden spiral staircase was also shipped from France. A clock tower identifies the 1896 **Courthouse** (Church and Second streets), standing on the site of the original parish headquarters. Inside, a spiral staircase leads into the copper-lined clock tower.

OPPOSITE: *Cherokee, a raised cottage typical of the plantation architecture of the Cane River region.*

Generally, houses in Natchitoches were of the indigenous Creole kind, built for hot-weather comfort. Shady galleries elevated on brick piers were often used as alfresco parlors, catching breezes. Most of the town's historic houses are private but may be toured during an October festival, headquartered at **Lemee House** (310 Jefferson Street, 318–352–4411). Built in 1837, it is the former residence of descendants of one of the town's first families. **Roque House,** built perhaps as early as 1796, faces Cane River Lake as it runs along Front Street. Others include the 1776 **Wells House** (607 Williams Avenue); **Magnolia House** (902 Washington), built in 1806; and the **Tante Huppé House** (424 Jefferson Street), dated to the 1820s. The 1820 **Ackel-Dranquet House** (146 Jefferson Street) may have been the first brick structure in Natchitoches.

West of Natchitoches on Route 485 is **Los Adaes Historic Park** (318–472–9449), site of a Spanish fort and mission established in 1717 and abandoned as the Spanish retreated west after clashing with the French. In 1721 the Spanish returned to the mission and built a hexagon-shaped fort to protect against French encroachment. Los Adaes served as the capital of Spanish Texas until 1773, when it was moved to San Antonio. Artifacts unearthed from the site—arrowheads, eating utensils, bottles—are among the exhibits in the small visitor center at the park's entrance.

In the hills slightly to the south is **Fort Jessup** (Route 6, 318–256–5480), established by Zachary Taylor in 1822. Abandoned after the Mexican War, it is now a state commemorative area, marked by stone pillars, a restored log cabin, and a museum exhibiting documents relevant to the fort's history.

Below Fort Jessup on Route 171 is **Fisher,** a prosperous turn-of-the-century lumber village that appears much as it did in 1899—simple, whitewashed houses surrounded by picket fences, a sawmill and commissary, an opera house, depot, and church. An annual sawmill festival is held every May.

Route 171 leads north to **Mansfield,** scene of the bloodiest and virtually the last major battle of the Civil War fought on Louisiana soil. After a series of Confederate defeats along the Mississippi, Union forces under General Nathaniel Banks marched northward in the summer of 1863, paralleling the Red River. Trailing some 300 wagons, their progress was slow and they were periodically ambushed by the Confederate units of generals Richard Taylor (son of Zachary), Edmund Kirby-Smith, and Alfred Mouton. On

April 8, 1864, at Mansfield, the Federals met an army of half their number—and lost. One of Banks's staff wrote that the Confederate attack was "as sudden as though a thunder bolt had fallen upon us and set the pines on fire . . . we found ourselves . . . in a hissing, seething, bubbling whirlpool of agitated men." The Union soldiers retreated. The next day's battle at **Pleasant Hill** was a draw, and the Federals continued to retreat toward Baton Rouge, which was under Union control. Choosing not to pursue them, generals Taylor and Kirby-Smith hung back to protect Shreveport. Along the way, the Federals burned Alexandria. Monuments to the Confederate principals stand in **Mansfield Battle Park** (Route 175, four miles south of Mansfield, 318–872–1474). The forty-four-acre site also has a museum exhibiting weapons, uniforms, and other artifacts of the Civil War. Defeated in later battles, Kirby-Smith surrendered his remaining forces in Texas and Taylor surrendered in Alabama in the late spring of 1865.

## SHREVEPORT

Following the failure of Banks's campaign, Shreveport served as Louisiana's capital after headquarters had been moved from Baton Rouge and Opelousas. The town had much to lose, as cotton was as much king here as along the Mississippi. The wealth of local planters is abundantly evident on Shreveport's streets. Had General Banks's northward march not been so disastrous, he might have taken the town. Rebels' "Quaker guns"—charred tree stumps positioned around an empty fort to resemble cannon—are on display in a recreation area known as **Fort Humbug** (Stone Avenue and Youree Drive, 318–222–9391).

Fanned out along the southern bank of the Red River, the town would not have grown without the arrival of Henry Miller Shreve, a New Jersey–born veteran of the Battle of New Orleans and a steamboat builder. In 1832 the U.S. government summoned Shreve to an enormous engineering task—to break up a 160-mile log jam that made the Red River above Natchitoches unnavigable. Over a period of more than six years, Shreve knocked away at the obstacle with powerful steam-driven vessels of his own design. In 1835 he completed clearing the log jam as far as the bluff where Shreve Town was to be laid out.

After his success, the United States proceeded to secure much of northwestern Louisiana from the Caddo Indians, whose home this was, in a treaty tilted in the government's favor. (The Caddo received only $80,000 and were to leave the United States and "nevermore to return.") The town grew from a financial venture by a group who formed a partnership in 1836 to purchase the site, lay out lots, and facilitate settlement of the town, which was named Shreve Town in honor of Henry Shreve. (The name was changed to Shreveport the following year.) A rival group planning to establish a town three miles downriver on Coates Bluff was eliminated as competition in 1837 by Shreve, who cut through a bend in the Red River and left Coates Bluff on a shallow backwater instead.

In 1865 the Caddo Parish Courthouse (since replaced) was the last Confederate capitol of Louisiana and the Courthouse Square the last campground of the soldiers of the last major command of the Confederate Army to surrender. Although remnants of resistance remained, when Federal troops arrived to occupy the city on June 6, 1865, the lowering of the Confederate flag marked the official end of the conflict. A thirty-foot marble monument was erected on the square in 1905 to commemorate the event.

*A turn-of-the-century Mardi Gras parade, Shreveport. This demure pageant, less raucous than that of New Orleans, featured proper young ladies in carriages decked with flowers.*

On the Shreveport campus of **Louisiana State University** is the **Pioneer Heritage Center** (8515 Youree Drive, 318–797–5332), a complex of six plantation structures. Representing the frontier period from the 1830s through the Civil War, a plantation manor house, kitchen, blacksmith shop, log dogtrot house, doctor's office, and plantation commissary from the turn of the century are all authentically equipped and furnished to demonstrate the folk life of northwest Louisiana and the Red River region during the nineteenth century.

Much of Shreveport's past in artifacts, maps, clothing, and documents is on display at the **Spring Street Museum** (525 Spring Street, 318–424–0964), housed in an 1866 bank building. A statewide perspective on native industry, wildlife and natural resources, history, and society is on view at the **State Exhibit Museum** (3015 Greenwood Road, 318–227–5196). Exhibits include a 1,500-year-old dugout canoe; Indian basketry, pottery, and stone points; and a diorama of 2,000-year-old earthworks at Poverty Point in northeast Louisiana, along with stone and clay artifacts.

East of Shreveport and northeast of Minden was the home of a religious commune established in 1835 by Germans and abandoned in 1870. The **Germantown Colony and Museum** (Parish Road 110, 318–377–1875) has exhibits installed in the group's original cabins and meeting hall. In **Minden,** the brick Greek Revival **Claiborne Parish Courthouse** (Courthouse Square) was dedicated in 1861. The town's **Ford Museum** (519 Main Street, 318–927–3271) has mounted exhibits that explore the influence of African-American and Scotch-Irish cultures in this region.

## MONROE

First explored by Hernando de Soto in 1541, and more than a century later by Bienville and St. Denis, the riverbank was originally home to the Ouachita Indians, who left the ceremonial **Pargoud Mound** (Pargoud Boulevard). As an outpost against the Indians during the 1780s, the Spanish built **Fort Miro** on a site indicated by a plaque at 424 South Grand Street. The Ouachita River, which brought prosperity to cotton-growing Monroe when the first steamship arrived in 1819, also allowed Federal gunboats, forty-one years later, to destroy the courthouse and other buildings in the town named for that 1819 steamship, the *James Monroe.*

# POVERTY POINT STATE COMMEMORATIVE AREA

Forty miles out of Monroe, toward the northeastern corner of the state, is one of the most significant archaeological sites in North America, the earthen ruins of perhaps the earliest culture known in the Mississippi Valley. Built between 1700 and 700 B.C. by highly advanced Indians, the former village consists of concentric ridges that apparently were foundations for dwellings. Arranged around the ridges are four ceremonial and burial mounds—the largest, called Poverty Point, is shaped roughly like a great bird, 700 by 800 feet at its base and 72 feet high. Archaeologists have determined that some artifacts in the village came from as far away as the Ohio River valley and Appalachia. Among the treasures sifted from the earth at Poverty Point are stone figures in various shapes, arrowheads and stone blades, and round clay balls used to cook in ovens. The artifacts are displayed in the visitor center museum, and a lookout tower provides a panorama of the entire complex.

LOCATION: Route 577, 15 miles north of Delhi. HOURS: 9–5 Wednesday–Sunday. FEE: Yes. TELEPHONE: 318–926–5492.

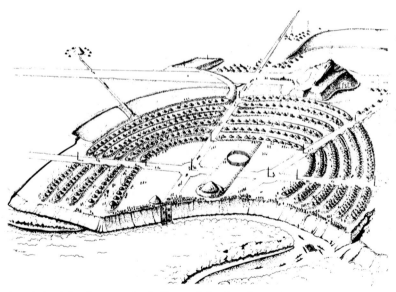

*A conjectural drawing re-creates the Poverty Point site, where a thirty-seven-acre plaza was enclosed by the earthen rings.*

*An aerial photograph of Poverty Point reveals the massive earthen ridges constructed three or four millennia ago.*

## HARRISONBURG

Sitting above the Ouachita River, the major steamboat artery of northeastern Louisiana, Harrisonburg became a lively commercial center linked to Natchez and New Orleans. **Sargeant House** (Catahoula Street, private), once popular with well-heeled steamboat passengers, was built in the 1850s. Because of its position on the river bluffs, Harrisonburg took on strategic importance during the Civil War, for the Federals had every intention of controlling the Ouachita. Confederates erected **Fort Beauregard** (Route 124) in 1862, and though it withstood repeated attacks from Federal gunboats as they ascended the river, the fort was finally seized and virtually destroyed. A park commemorates the site. Federal gunfire also damaged Harrisonburg's **Methodist Church** (Route 8), which still bears the bullet holes. Relics of the war and prehistoric Indian artifacts are on display in the **Catahoula Parish Museum of Natural History** (Short Street, 318–744–5435), housed in the town's courthouse. Sixteenth-century Spanish explorers probably visited the **Harrisonburg Indian Mound** (Route 124), a sacred ground of Natchez or Ouachita tribes.

# MISSISSIPPI

OPPOSITE: *The ornate domed chamber of the State Capitol in Jackson, completed in 1903.*
*The seat of government was moved to Jackson from Natchez in 1822.*

Even a quick geographic glance at Mississippi—ribboned by deep rivers running north to south, and almost uniformly green with forests—can convey the appeal of the place to those who first settled here. The state hosts not only one of the most fertile river valleys of the world, the Mississippi, but two that are among the most productive in North America, the Pearl and the Tombigbee. For years many things grew in these valleys, but none so well as cotton. When cotton ruled, between 1830 and 1860, Mississippi was an amazing kingdom indeed. The riches of antebellum Mississippi, most readily evident in the great columned plantation houses, some in ruin, many beautifully restored, are a compelling chapter of American social and economic history, even a century and a half later. But a tour of historic Mississippi takes travelers further back in time than the Civil War and the plantation decades leading up to it.

When the Spanish explorer Hernando de Soto crossed what is now northern Mississippi in 1540, the area was already home to three nations, the Choctaw, the Chickasaw, and the Natchez. Excellent hunters and fishermen, the Choctaw occupied the central part of the present-day state; the Chickasaw, the north; and the Natchez, the southwest. The Spaniards did not linger long on their first excursion through Mississippi—de Soto stayed for only one season and then continued moving west, into Louisiana. The French came much later, in 1699, when Pierre Le Moyne, sieur d'Iberville, arrived on the Gulf Coast near present-day Biloxi. His was the first permanent European settlement in Mississippi, followed some fifteen years later by a second French outpost, Fort Rosalie, on the Mississippi River. The conflicts between encroaching newcomers and the Indians were inevitable, and the French, growing in number in the territory, drove off the Natchez.

After the Revolution the U.S. took possession of the territory north of the 31st parallel; the region south of that line remained part of Spanish West Florida. Mississippi did not attain its modern borders until it was made a state in 1817 (Alabama, which had been part of Mississippi Territory, was split off as a separate territory at that time). The way was opened for large-scale white settlement of central and northern Mississippi when the Choctaw and Chickasaw were forcibly removed in the 1830s to territory west of the Mississippi. Tribal leaders, without the consent of their people, had signed treaties ceding the land—and were liberally paid by the government for doing so. The Indians left peacefully, under the

*An Atakapa Indian with his wives and slaves, depicted in 1735 by French artist Alexandre De Batz.*

supervision of the U.S. army, but they suffered terribly during the migration from disease, lack of food and supplies, and from the depredations of thieves. About six thousand Choctaw still remain in Mississippi, at a reservation near the town of Philadelphia. Northeast of that town is the Nanih Waiya mound, which is revered in Choctaw legend as the birthplace of the tribe. A larger group of Indian mounds, the Winterville site north of Greenville, includes a fifty-five-foot temple mound and ten smaller mounds.

For the whites who took over the old Indian lands and began planting cotton, boom times were at hand. Along roads and rivers, Mississippi cotton poured into the hands of buyers in New Orleans, one of the busiest ports in the world by the 1830s. When railroads arrived in the 1850s, the pace of commerce only quickened. The plantation economy, based on slave labor, was entrenched, and Mississippi had much to lose if that were threatened. When sectionalism led to the Civil War, Mississippi was among the first of the Southern states to secede, and one of its senators, Jefferson Davis, became president of the Confederacy. Two of Mississippi's historic houses belonged to Davis: Rosemont, his boyhood home, and Beauvoir, his final residence.

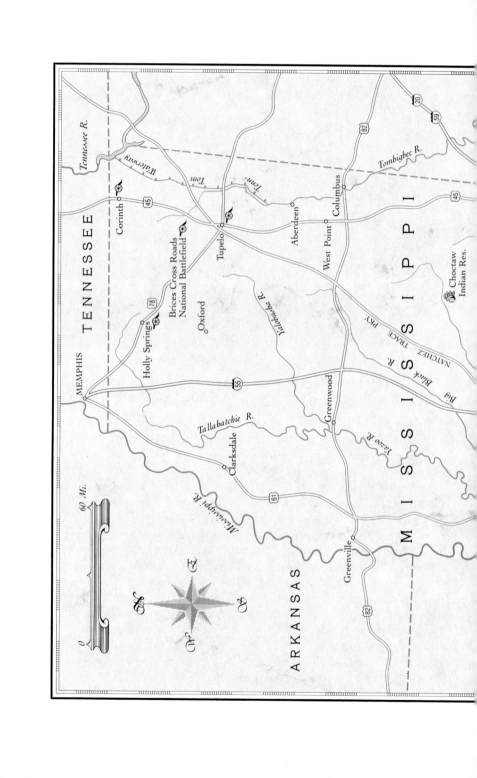

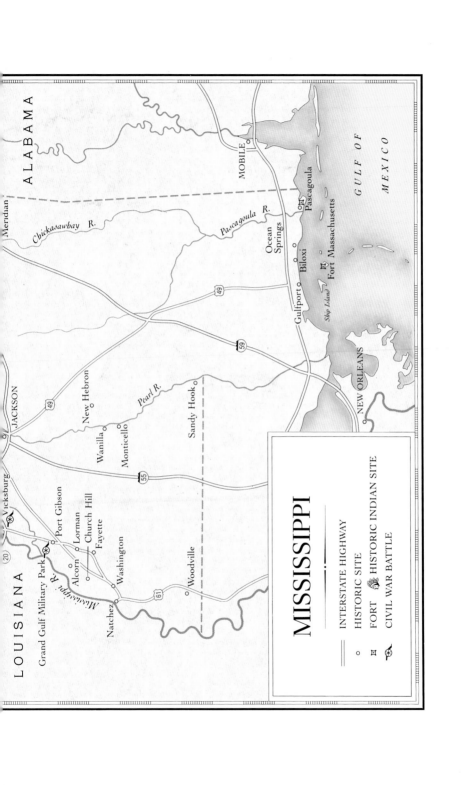

# MISSISSIPPI

—————  INTERSTATE HIGHWAY

∘  HISTORIC SITE

⊞  FORT  🪶 HISTORIC INDIAN SITE

⊗  CIVIL WAR BATTLE

ALABAMA

MOBILE

GULF OF MEXICO

Meridian

Chickasawhay R.

Pascagoula R.

Pascagoula

Fort Massachusetts

Ocean Springs

Biloxi

Gulfport

Ship Island

NEW ORLEANS

JACKSON

New Hebron

Pearl R.

Sandy Hook

Wanilla

Monticello

Vicksburg

Port Gibson

Lorman

Church Hill

Fayette

Alcorn

Washington

Woodville

Natchez

Grand Gulf Military Park

Mississippi R.

LOUISIANA

During the Civil War, Mississippi was a prime strategic target of the Union army, which gained control of the rail lines crossing at Corinth in May 1862 and repulsed a Confederate attempt to retake the town the following October. The river port of Natchez, which, it is said, never flew the Confederate flag, was peacefully restored to the Union early in the war; but General Ulysses S. Grant had to wage one of the war's hardest campaigns to seize Vicksburg, the "Gibraltar of the Confederacy." That campaign included important clashes at Port Gibson, Grand Gulf, and Jackson, which was heavily damaged. Late in the war, two Union pursuits of the Confederate raider Nathan Bedford Forrest led to battles at Brices Cross Roads and Tupelo.

Reconstruction was not successful in Mississippi. After the post-war legislature passed a highly restrictive "Black Code" Congress placed the state under a military governor, Adelbert Ames. A former Union general, Ames was later elected governor with the aid of a large black vote—when blacks were enfranchised after the war they outnumbered white voters. However, in 1875 Democrats prevented blacks from voting through a campaign of murder, beatings, and economic threats, and gained control of the state legislature. The new state constitution of 1890 effectively stripped blacks of the right to vote by imposing an ambiguous literacy test, complicated residence requirements, and a poll tax. Both white and black farm laborers were held in economic bondage by the sharecropper system as Mississippi became even more dependent upon cotton. In 1962, a century after the first battle of the Civil War was fought on Mississippi soil, law student James Meredith broke the state's segregation barrier when he entered the University of Mississippi. Since the Voting Rights Act of 1965, significant gains have been made by Mississippi's blacks and the contributions of slave workers and artisans often figure prominently in tours of the state's historic houses and public buildings.

This chapter begins in the southwestern corner of Mississippi and proceeds north to Natchez and Vicksburg, then east to Jackson and Meridian. Next, after a short section on the Pearl River Valley, it moves to Biloxi and the Gulf Coast. Finally, the chapter covers northern Mississippi, starting with Columbus, then heading north to the Civil War battle sites at Tupelo and Corinth, concluding with a westward swing to Oxford, the heart of William Faulkner's Mississippi.

# SOUTHWESTERN MISSISSIPPI

## WOODVILLE

Settled in the late 1700s, Woodville has been the seat of Wilkinson County since its incorporation in 1811. One of the great live oaks in the courthouse square is known as the **Jefferson Davis Oak** in commemoration of the Confederate president, whose boyhood home, Rosemont, is outside of town. Built in 1903, this courthouse is the third on the site.

Three of the town's churches are among the most significant in the state. With white columns and a cupola rising from its slightly elevated plot of land, **Woodville Baptist** (Natchez Street) is the oldest church in Mississippi, founded in 1798 and built in 1809. The oldest Methodist church in the state is the **Woodville Methodist** (Main Street), built in 1824. Similar in appearance, with white clapboard, cupola, and an enclosed foyer, is **Saint Paul's Episcopal** (South Church Street), completed in 1825. The organ in Saint Paul's, containing 1,000 pipes, was an 1827 gift, manufactured by Henry Erben of New York. An 1885 addition was made by the Pilcher Pipe Company of Louisville, Kentucky. The donor of the organ was Major A. M. Feltus, a Philadelphian who came to Natchez in about 1819 and built the large Neoclassical house at First South and Depot streets (private).

### *Rosemont*

Rosemont was built in 1810 by Samuel Davis of Fairview, Kentucky, who brought his wife, Jane, and their ten children to live here. The youngest child was Jefferson, and Rosemont's historical significance is as the boyhood home of the first and only president of the Confederacy. After attending nearby Jefferson College he was selected, in 1824, as a cadet at West Point. In 1835 he married Sarah Knox Taylor, resigned from the Army, and became a planter near Vicksburg. A few months later, Sarah Davis died of malaria; a decade passed before Davis married his second wife, Varina Howell, who was from Natchez. In 1845 he won a seat in the U.S. House of Representatives. He resigned to lead Mississippi volunteers in battle in the Mexican War, emerged a hero, and was appointed to the U.S. Senate, where he vigorously protected the institution of slavery in the South and promoted its expansion to

*Rosemont, Jefferson Davis's boyhood home, built by his father in 1810.* OPPOSITE: *Rosemont's wide central hall, with large doors on both ends to admit cooling breezes, is dominated by an original 1845 whale oil chandelier.*

the West. Under President Franklin Pierce, he served as Secretary of War (1853 to 1857) and was thereafter elected to the Senate. With Mississippi's secession in 1861, Davis resigned his seat and was elected president of the Confederacy.

Five generations of Davises lived at Rosemont until it was sold in 1895, six years after Jefferson Davis died in New Orleans. Named for Jane Davis's rose garden, Rosemont is a handsome planter's cottage with a symmetrical exterior. A Palladian window in the front gable seems to crown the double front doors, which are framed with a row of small glass panes and sidelights. The one-and-a-half-story cottage is modestly scaled, especially considering the large family that lived here. Four rooms open off the wide central hallway that extends from front to rear galleries. The hallway is lit by an 1845 chandelier, designed to burn whale oil. Many furnishings are either original to the house or belonged to various members of the Davis family: portraits; Jane Davis's spinning wheel, four-poster, and dining room chairs; and an 1880 Eastlake bed. Beyond the main house are gardens, split-rail fences,

outbuildings typical of a nineteenth-century working plantation, and the Davis family cemetery. Jefferson Davis, however, is buried at Hollywood Cemetery in Richmond, Virginia.

LOCATION: Highway 24 East. HOURS: March through December: 10–4 Monday–Saturday. FEE: Yes. TELEPHONE: 601–888–6809.

# NATCHEZ

Natchez is so rich in antebellum architecture and romance that it is easy to overlook its earlier heritage. By the mid-1500s, the Natchez Indians had built a thriving culture on these bluffs of the Mississippi. Observers of the sun, corn growers, and hunters, the Natchez lived in about thirty villages. Their "capital," or Grand Village as the French called it, was located on the banks of Saint Catherine Creek, now within the city limits. In 1716 the French explorer Jean-Baptiste Le Moyne, sieur de Bienville, raised Fort Rosalie on the Natchez bluffs, and at first the Europeans coexisted peacefully with the Indians. In his journal a French carpenter described the

*The last passenger-carrying Mississippi River steamboats, the 1926* Delta Queen *and the 1975* Mississippi Queen, *rafted together at Natchez.*

Natchez as "one of the most polite and affable nations on the Mississippi . . . [the Grand Village] is embellished with magnificent natural scenery, covered with a splendid growth of odoriferous trees and plants, and watered with cool and limpid streams."

But in 1729 the Natchez, determined to reclaim their homeland, attacked Fort Rosalie, killing most of the men stationed there. Although the French later launched a punitive expedition, killing many Indians and driving the rest away, their outpost at Natchez was finished as a viable colony. The **Grand Village of the Natchez Indians** (400 Jefferson Davis Boulevard, 601–446–6502) is now an archaeological site on Saint Catherine Creek. Earth mounds where temples and chieftains' houses once stood are clearly visible, separated from one another by expanses of green, which were once ceremonial plazas. Also on the grounds is a reconstructed Natchez house, corn granary, and a museum containing Indian artifacts and exhibits of the everyday workings of the Grand Village.

During the eighteenth century, when the area passed from French to English to Spanish rule, generous land grants attracted settlers, who came down the Mississippi. In 1798, Natchez was named capital of the U.S. Territory of Mississippi. Further settlement of the area was encouraged when an 1801 treaty with the Choctaw and Chickasaw Indians opened the Natchez Trace, a 500-mile wilderness path between Natchez and Nashville.

The steamboat era (the first steamboat to serve Natchez, the *New Orleans,* docked in 1811) marked the beginning of the city's Golden Age, at least for those who had enormous cotton and indigo plantations and the slaves to run them. With their slave labor, planters and merchants built an opulent world for themselves, the grandeur of which is evident today—Natchez, like New Orleans, was occupied by Federal forces early in the Civil War and was spared destruction.

Many significant churches, commercial buildings, and houses are contained in the center of Natchez, a grid of eight north-to-south and eight east-to-west streets, with its western edge at the river. Other mansions are scattered among parks outside of the grid. The **Historic Natchez Foundation** (109 North Commerce Street, 601–442–2500) provides information about the city's sites. Many of the private houses described here are open to the public on the spring and fall "pilgrimages" sponsored by **Natchez Pilgrimage Garden Club** (800–647–6742). This tour of Natchez starts in the center, then covers the outlying sites.

**Trinity Episcopal Church** (305 South Commerce Street), where services have been held since 1823, was built in a simple, vernacular style with a gilded dome. It has resembled a Greek temple since the late 1830s, when the dome was removed and a great Doric portico added. Smaller changes were made to the exterior and interior in the 1880s (when the impressive Romanesque parish house next door, **Kuehnle Hall,** was built) and again in 1897. **Temple B'nai Israel** (213 South Commerce Street) is a 1904 structure standing on the site of the state's first synagogue.

The 500 and 600 blocks of **Franklin Street** are distinguished by nineteenth-century storefronts and townhouses, some of them built before the Civil War, most of them from the 1870s to the turn of the century. Both blocks comprised the city's lively wholesale district. **Meyer's Marble Store** (410 Main Street) was built in 1855 with marble cast-iron Corinthian columns and a stucco facade. The Agricultural Bank, now **Britton and Koontz First National Bank** (422 Main Street), was the city's first temple-form building when constructed in 1833. Five years later another Greek Revival bank building went up, on Main Street, the **Commercial Bank.** As with similar buildings in the north, it is really a complex, with an attached house for the bank's chief officer. The vault sits beneath one of the bedrooms. Since 1946 the bank has been home to the First Church of Christ Scientist; the house is privately owned.

**Texada Tavern** (222 South Wall Street) was probably the first brick house in Natchez when built in 1792. In the early nineteenth century, it served as Territorial Legislative Hall. Across from it is **Holly Hedges** (214 Washington Street), designed with formal detailing ca. 1823. The **House on Ellicott's Hill** (also known as Connelly's Tavern) is situated on the spot where the American flag was first raised over Natchez in 1797. Built about a year later, the house reflects Creole influence, with double verandahs, connected by an outside staircase.

Flatboatmen and others who plied the Mississippi in the late eighteenth century stayed at **King's Tavern** (Jefferson Street near Rankin), a three-story brick-and-cypress building dating to about 1789. In 1866 the Second Presbyterian Church (built in 1858) became the **Zion Chapel African Methodist Episcopal Church** (Jefferson and Pine streets), and one of the city's first black congregations.

Restoration is planned for the **William Johnson House** (State Street, between Canal and Wall streets), a brick townhouse built in 1841 by William Johnson, who was born a slave in 1809 and freed in 1820. By that time there were nearly 500 free blacks in the state, most of them in Natchez. Like many free blacks, he worked as a barber, first in Port Gibson, then in Natchez, where he owned his own shop. Johnson eventually acquired some land, built this house, and bought slaves himself. He also kept a diary, which is a valuable record of the life of free blacks in the antebellum South. In 1851 Johnson was killed in a land dispute; because all the witnesses to the slaying were black and thus could not testify in court, his killer was never convicted.

Since about 1855 **Weymouth Hall** (1 Cemetery Road, 601–445–2304), a raised plantation house distinguished by fine mill-work, has overlooked the Mississippi from its bluff northwest of town. The house has been restored and is furnished with pieces attributed to John Henry Belter and Prudent Mallard.

From Broadway, Silver Street descends below the Natchez bluff and leads to a row of buildings facing the river and boat landings. Settled in the late 1700s, **Natchez-under-the-Hill** attracted boatmen and outlaws on the run. Stories of bloody fights and outrageous conduct among the denizens of Silver Street are legendary. Its location—literally beneath Natchez proper—is an area long known as the shame of the city, derided with such epithets as "Cesspool of the South" and "Sodom of the Mississippi." An inn, shops, and restaurants now occupy sites where rowdy bordellos and saloons once stood. The balcony of the **Silver Street Inn** (1 Silver Street), an 1840 bordello, overlooks the river.

## Linden

This imposing columned mansion grew from a two-story cottage built in ca. 1792. Thomas B. Reed, Mississippi's first U.S. senator, bought the house in 1818. Reed and subsequent owners expanded the house, making it over into a large residence—the white-columned gallery that stretches nearly a hundred feet across the front of the house was constructed in various stages. The house was sold again in 1849 to Mrs. Jane Conner; she had thirteen children (the west wing of Linden housed their schoolrooms), and the property remains in the family. Open for tours, it is known for such Federal details as the fanlight over the front doorway and for its fine furniture collections: Sheraton, Hepplewhite, Chippendale, and early Empire.

LOCATION: 1 Linden Place. HOURS: 9–5 Daily. FEE: Yes. TELEPHONE: 601–445–5472.

## Auburn

The architect of Auburn introduced the great columns of the Greek Revival to Natchez in 1812. One Yankee, its owner, Judge Lyman Harding, commissioned another Northerner, Levi Weeks, to design the house. Weeks was a New York carpenter-builder who had been successfully defended from a murder charge by a team of lawyers headed by Aaron Burr and Alexander Hamilton. In Natchez he built this grand, formal residence of red brick, fronted by four Ionic columns that soar two stories in height and frame elaborate doorways on upper and lower galleries. Weeks wrote that Auburn was the "first house in the Mississippi Territory on which was attempted any of the orders of Architecture." Judge Harding, the first attorney general of the Mississippi Territory, died eight years after the house was finished, but Auburn passed to an appreciative new owner, Dr. Stephen Duncan, a physician from Carlisle, Pennsylvania. Though he was a slave owner, Duncan grew to support the abolitionist cause and abandoned Auburn during the Civil War. His descendants later willed the property to the public trust. The house, a pavilion next door (formerly Duncan's billiard room), and the oak-shaded grounds are now part of a city park. The house is known for its hand-carved cypress doorways and the freestanding spiral stairway in the foyer. Parlors and bedrooms contain many period furnishings, including Rococo parlor sets, a Regency dining table and chairs, and beds by Mallard.

LOCATION: 400 Duncan Avenue. HOURS: 9:30–5 Daily. FEE: Yes. TELEPHONE: 601–442–5981.

## Stanton Hall

Fronted by tall Corinthian columns, this palatial mansion is named for its builder, Frederick Stanton, who spared little expense on its construction and decoration. Stanton sent overseas for the best and costliest materials and ornaments: silver doorknobs and hinges from England, mantels of white Carrara marble, mirrors from France, and gas-burning chandeliers, among the finest in the country, from Philadelphia. From the front doors, the central hallway extends seventy-two feet. The lavish plasterwork is an opulent example of Greek Revival ornament. In 1858 the house was completed, and Stanton, an Irishman, christened the place "Belfast."

OPPOSITE: *Auburn's striking spiral staircase, rising unsupported to the second floor.*
OVERLEAF: *The columned facade of Stanton Hall.*

*Stanton Hall's unusual triple parlor, its spaciousness enhanced by large mirrors. The house's furnishings include some Stanton pieces.*

He died a few months later. The house, later a girls' school, is now an inn. Stanton's previous residence had been **Cherokee** (217 High Street, private), a modest Neoclassical house built in the 1790s.

LOCATION: 401 High Street. HOURS: 9–5 Daily. FEE: Yes. TELE-
PHONE: 601–442–6282.

## Dunleith

A contemporary of Stanton Hall, this plantation house stands on forty acres of grounds. Surrounded by twenty-six columns, Dunleith is a mammoth raised cottage with Greek Revival details. Planter Charles Dahlgren built the house on property given to him by his father-in-law, Job Routh, who parlayed a large Spanish land grant into a fortune. The Dahlgrens sold the house in 1859 to Alfred V. Davis, who raised thoroughbred horses. Stables and other outbuildings have been restored, along with the main house.

LOCATION: 84 Homochitto Street. HOURS: 9–5 Monday–Saturday,
12:30–5 Sunday. FEE: Yes. TELEPHONE: 601–446–8500.

## Rosalie

This formal mansion, sited on a bluff over the river, was built in 1820 by Peter Little, a lumber trader, as a wedding present for his teenaged bride, the former Eliza Lowe. The house was made for entertaining, with a large double parlor and dining room. But, deeply religious, Eliza shunned the role of hostess. It served as a Union headquarters during the Civil War. Now owned by the Mississippi DAR, the house is grandly furnished, mostly as it was in 1858, with a twenty-piece rosewood parlor suite in the "Rosalie pattern" created for the house by John Henry Belter, a harp and piano, damask curtains and upholstery, Reed and Barton silver, and Sèvres porcelain. When he used the house in 1863, General Grant slept in the four-poster bed in an upstairs bedroom. The gold-leaf mirrors were wrapped in blankets and buried during the Civil War. The white picket fence surrounding the property, dating from 1840, contains no nails or other fasteners—the graceful pickets and rails are slotted together. The back-porch steps are made from individual cypress logs.

LOCATION: 100 Orleans Street. HOURS: 9–5 Daily. FEE: Yes. TELE-PHONE: 601–445–4555.

Farther north on Broadway is the **Parsonage** (305 South Broadway, private), a raised brick structure built in 1852 by Rosalie's Peter Little so that his wife, Eliza, could put up traveling evangelists and others who shared her religious beliefs. The house is a sturdy, modest version of Rosalie.

## Longwood

Longwood is one of the most fascinating houses in America, all the more so because it is an empty, ornate shell—construction wound slowly to a halt during the Civil War. Dr. Haller Nutt, a Renaissance man—scientist, inventor, cotton planter, and staunch Unionist—meant the house to be the showplace of the city, as well as a fashionable dwelling for his wife and eight children. He hired prominent Philadelphia architect Samuel Sloan, who delivered plans calling for an enormous house based on an octagon. The style had been advocated in design books and magazine articles of the day, as it was said to combine novelty with convenience and utility. Construction commenced in 1859 and progressed slowly. By 1861 the exterior was finished, and it was perhaps the most exuberant in the state, the eight sides of the brick house faced with

*Longwood, the largest and most elaborate octagonal house in the United States.* OPPOSITE: *Three floors of rough brick and exposed beams, above, remain as they were when construction stopped in 1861. Longwood's octagonal plan, below, was designed to provide increased space, greater convenience, and better heating.*

white Moorish columns and arches. Soaring in height, the house was topped by a gleaming onion dome. Mirrors, to be installed inside the dome, would have thrown light to other mirrors below, filling the house's great rotunda with sunlight. The plans called for thirty-two rooms, eight on each of the four main floors. Each room would open onto the rotunda as well as its own terrace. Sloan brought workmen from Philadelphia, and once the exterior was completed they began work on the basement level, building offices and storage rooms. Though Sloan's Northern crew kept working in the midst of the war, local hostility drove them out.

During the war, while Confederate and Federal troops burned their cotton fields, the Nutts made do by living in the basement. Nutt died in 1864 of pneumonia, and the house stayed in the family for a century. Family heirlooms fill the basement floor; crates and tools still litter the upper floors, where construction-in-progress is evident. The house is now a property of the Pilgrimage Garden Club.

LOCATION: 140 Lower Woodville Road. HOURS: July through August: 9–6 Daily; September through June: 9–5 Daily. FEE: Yes. TELEPHONE: 800–647–6742.

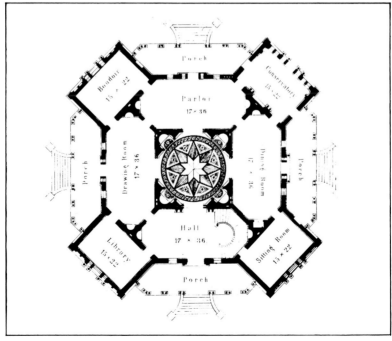

*Fair Oaks, Natchez, with a long gallery that was the center of daily life in warm weather—*
*"Here they wash, lounge, often sleep, and take their meals," wrote one traveler in the 1830s.*

## Melrose

A stately hybrid of Greek Revival and earlier, eighteenth-century
Georgian styles, Melrose has been called the Mount Vernon of
Natchez. It stands on an eighty-four-acre estate meant to recall that
of an English country house, though this one is thick with such
Southern vegetation as azaleas and dogwood, redbud, cypress,
magnolia, and live oak trees. Melrose was built from 1841 to 1845
as a self-sufficient compound; behind the house are slaves' quarters, a working kitchen, a dairy, a gazebo, stables, and a carriage
house. The main house was built by one of Natchez's most prominent lawyers and planters, John T. McMurran; his wife, Mary
Louise, decorated it, and much of the original work and furnishings are present, including faux bois doors, a mahogany punkah,
hand-painted floor cloths, whale-oil chandeliers, Gothic Revival
dining room chairs, an 1845 Philadelphia-made sideboard, and a
rare Knable and Gaeble piano. Among the parlor and drawing

room furnishings are such Victorian oddities as a "courtship" sofa (the twin cushions are primly separated) and a "gout stool." Carved with scroll and floral patterns, the rosewood furniture inspired the Gorham Silver Company's "Melrose" pattern of sterling. After the Civil War George Malin Davis, another attorney and planter, bought Melrose, which remained in his family for over a century.

LOCATION: 1 Melrose-Montebello Parkway. HOURS: 9–5 Daily. FEE: Yes. TELEPHONE: 800–647–6742.

A number of other historic houses also administered by the Pilgrimage Garden Club (800–647–6742) and open to the public include the following. **Green Leaves** (303 South Rankin Street), built in 1838, contains all the original furnishings, including carpets, curtains, and wallpaper, of George W. and Mary Roane Koontz, who bought the house in 1849. **D'Evereux** (D'Evereux Drive), built in 1840, is noted for the furnishings that belonged to its first owner. Among them is a set of Jacob Petit porcelain. Outbuildings—including privies—have been restored.

Original wallpapers hang in the quietly handsome **Lansdowne** (Pine Ridge Road), built in 1853. The classical exterior gives way to a surprisingly grand interior, furnished in high Victorian style. Its silver collections also are noteworthy. The front lawn is lit by gas lamps. Though more than a cottage, **Mistletoe** (Airport Road) was a modest residence when it was built by a prominent and rich family on a Spanish land grant ca. 1807. The exterior features a raised porch and balustrade; the rooms contain a range of early American furniture. **The Elms** (215 South Pine Street), with thick stucco walls and wide verandahs supported by colonettes, is clearly Creole. The interior cast-iron staircase is unique in Mississippi. **Fair Oaks** (Route 61 South) is typical of early-nineteenth-century planters' houses of the lower Mississippi valley. The 1822 dwelling rambles horizontally: When built, it was one room deep with front and rear galleries, but the latter were enclosed in the 1830s to add more rooms. The fanlight doorway and other exterior details are in the Federal style.

Distinct architectural styles are evident in **Richmond** (Government Fleet Road), which was built in three stages. The house went up as a raised plantation house in 1784. In 1832 that structure became ancillary to a Greek Revival addition, complete with a formal Ionic-columned portico. Finally, in about 1860, a strangely archaic, eighteenth-century brick wing was added. In the same

family since 1832, the house contains many furnishings original to the house and a Gilbert Stuart portrait. The grounds of **Montaigne** (200 Liberty Road), an 1855 villa, are planted with more than 350 varieties of camellias. Built by Confederate general William T. Martin, the house was looted by Union soldiers during the Civil War. A "suburban villa," **Elms Court** (John R. Junkin Drive), built in the late 1830s, has lacy cast-iron verandahs of the sort made popular by manufacturers in the period. A ground pit for the original gasworks to fuel chandeliers is behind the house.

## NATCHEZ TRACE

This famed wilderness road was first traveled by Indians, then European traders and missionaries. But the heaviest traffic came from the "Kaintucks," men from Ohio, Kentucky, and other points north, who floated merchandise down the Mississippi on flatboats. In Natchez and New Orleans they sold everything they brought with them—tobacco, iron, meat, even their boats. To return home, they thrashed their way overland, along the Natchez Trace.

Recognizing the importance of the trace to the territory, in 1806 the U.S. government appropriated money to clear and develop it, making it more passable to travelers, supplies, and mail. The trace would also have strategic value: During the War of 1812, Andrew Jackson led Tennessee troops down the road to New Orleans and back again. Inns, called stands, were built along the way, some of them operated by Indians or by whites who had married Indian women.

By the 1820s steamboats had taken away much business from the trace. Steaming up the river, if no faster, was certainly easier than walking the trace or riding it on horseback. But today it is the trace, not the river, that enjoys the traffic: The old wilderness path is now a paved road maintained by the National Park Service (601– 842–1572), traversing the historic route. Among the sites marked along the way are **Mount Locust** (eight miles north of Natchez), an inn restored to its 1820s appearance; a phosphate mine and an ironworks; a tobacco farm; a ferry crossing; and a Confederate grave site. Entrance to the Natchez Trace can be made at various points north of Natchez, from Route 61.

OPPOSITE: *Montaigne, built as an Italianate villa in 1855 and extensively remodeled in the Neoclassical style in 1927.*

# WASHINGTON

This village just east of Natchez was the capital of the Mississippi Territory for fifteen years and is the home of **Jefferson College** (College and North streets, 601–442–2901). The first educational institution in the territory, chartered by the General Assembly in 1802 for "the acquirement and dissemination of useful information," the college was named for Thomas Jefferson. The Jefferson campus was the birthplace of the state of Mississippi: In 1817, the first state Constitutional Convention gathered in a Methodist church that once stood on the college grounds. Restored buildings on the campus include the 1819 East Wing (designed by Levi Weeks), the Greek colonnaded West Wing and West Kitchen (1839), and Raymond Hall (1915). Jefferson Davis was a student at the college; John Jay Audubon may have taught here.

North of Washington, located in the fork of the Natchez Trace and Route 61, is **Brandon Hall** (private), one of the largest houses in Mississippi. Built in 1856 by Gerard Brandon III, grandson of an Irish immigrant who became an important cotton and indigo planter, the house is surrounded by galleries, which are supported by Ionic columns and trimmed with cast-iron railings.

Nearby, between Fayette and Church Hill, is **Springfield** (off Route 553, 601–786–3802), one of the state's large plantation houses. Built as early as 1789 by Virginia planter Thomas Marston Green, Jr., it may have been the first house in the Mississippi Valley with a full colonnade. It is still a working plantation, as it has been for over two hundred years. Inside, door and window frames and mantels reflect Georgian, Adam, and Federal styles. It is often said, although without firm evidence, that Andrew Jackson's 1791 marriage to Rachel Robards took place here. The late-eighteenth- to mid-nineteenth-century furnishings include a grandfather clock, a pencil-post field bed, and a Georgian Sheffield chandelier.

In the rolling hills slightly east of Springfield is the village of **Church Hill,** settled in the late eighteenth century by a group of Maryland pioneers. Among the small churches dotting the settlement is **Christ Episcopal Church** (Route 553), a dark Gothic structure of stuccoed brick surrounded by two-hundred-year-old grave markers. The village's country store was built in 1837; the doctor's office, little more than a cabin, dates from 1860.

OPPOSITE: *A solitary walker on the Natchez Trace, a hunting trail blazed by the Indians that later became the chief route from Nashville, Tennessee, to Natchez, Mississippi.*

# LORMAN

The town of Lorman is the location of **Alcorn State University** (Route 522, 601–877–6130), which was the first land-grant college for blacks in the United States when it was established in 1871. It occupies some of the site and original buildings of Oakland College, founded in 1830 and closed at the beginning of the Civil War. The wrought-iron steps of the Greek Revival **Oakland Chapel** came from the Windsor mansion farther north.

## *Rosswood*

Rosswood was once the 1,250-acre cotton plantation of Dr. Walter Wade. His 1857 Greek Revival mansion was designed by David Shroder. The architect intended it to be an all-brick house, but the locally made bricks turned out to be too soft, and the house was built of cypress. Construction costs totaled $10,850. The generously scaled house—the four main downstairs rooms are each twenty by twenty feet—was Wade's wedding gift to his bride, Mabella Chamberlain. Wade's journal, preserved at the house, offers an account of plantation business, Southern society, and the Civil War. On July 4, 1864, when Federal troops seized cotton from a warehouse in a skirmish that has been called the Battle of the Cotton Bales, the house served as a hospital—it is said that Mrs. Wade went out and brought back the wounded herself. Also among the papers at Rosswood are accounts of an 1845 revolt that ensued when slaves were freed from Ross's grandfather's neighboring plantation, Prospect Hill. A sharecropper tenant house in the 1930s, Rosswood has been restored and furnished to the mid-1800s.

LOCATION: Route 61. HOURS: 10–5 Daily. FEE: Yes. TELEPHONE: 601–437–4215.

Farther north on Route 522 is the 1855 **Canemount Plantation House** (private), an example of the Italianate Revival style that was popular in Claiborne County.

# PORT GIBSON

Chartered in 1803 as Gibson's Landing, this former capital of the Choctaw nation was named for the man who put a dock on Bayou Pierre, Samuel Gibson. It has been the seat of Claiborne County since 1803. Commercial traffic on Bayou Pierre was crucial to its growth, as flatboats brought trade goods, supplies, and people.

After boats were unloaded, they were broken up and the wood used to build simple houses. Port Gibson grew quickly—Mississippi's first library was chartered here in 1818, and the town published a newspaper, the state's second, in 1817. Grander houses and many churches were built here prior to the Civil War. In the May 1, 1863, Battle of Port Gibson, Confederate infantry made a brave but futile stand in a sharp, day-long fight, until they were forced to retreat before General Grant's onrushing column, which had just crossed the Mississippi and was marching quickly north to attack the town of Jackson and engage Pemberton's army defending Vicksburg. The route taken by Grant and his troops, Old Bruinsburg Road, remains a primitive dirt road along which two battle sites are marked: the A. K. Shaifer House, where the first skirmish took place, and the site of the Old Magnolia Church (no longer standing), where the second skirmish took place. Just outside of town, another marker at Main and Carrol streets commemorates the main battle.

Route 61 leads straight into the town, where it becomes Church Street, passing Port Gibson's oldest structure, the 1805 **Samuel Gibson House** (Church and Idlewild streets, 601–437–4351). The small brick cottage now houses the Port Gibson–Claiborne County Chamber of Commerce and is the starting point for walking and driving tours of Port Gibson and the surrounding area, which has a variety of Indian, architectural, and military sites. There are three separate tours, each clearly marked—the Port Gibson tour, Windsor–Battlefield tour, and Grand Gulf tour.

In the town itself, the **Port Gibson Tour,** marked by green signs, passes nineteenth-century churches, houses, and commercial buildings. There are eight houses of worship along Church Street. The 1859 **First Presbyterian Church,** built with a rear gallery for slaves, is known for the unusual decoration atop its steeple: a gold-leafed hand with its index finger pointing heavenward. Chandeliers in the church came from the steamboat *Robert E. Lee.* The Gothic Revival **Saint Joseph's Catholic Church,** built in 1849, is the town's oldest church building. The synagogue **Temple Gemiluth Chassed** was built in 1891. Also on the route are the **Claiborne County Courthouse, Port Gibson Bank,** and other public and commercial buildings. Several private houses are also marked. **Oak Square** (1207 Church Street, 601–437–4350), a thirty-room mansion of the 1850s, is the town's most impressive house, with a large stair hall and furnishings in the Empire and Rococo Revival styles.

On the southeastern outskirts of town is **Wintergreen Cemetery,** where Federal and Confederate soldiers are buried, as are many of the town's early settlers. One marker proclaims forever the political leanings of Henry Devine, who died in 1844: "... the deceased often expressed a wish only to live long enough to vote for Henry Clay for the Presidency. His wish was granted. The last act of his life was to vote the Whig Ticket, having done which, he declared that he died satisfied. . . ."

The **Windsor–Battlefield Tour** (marked by red signs) follows Bayou Pierre west from town, toward the Mississippi River. Along the route are Natchez Indian mounds and, at **Lookout Point,** a log replica of Port Gibson's first Presbyterian church. Sections of the tour follow the route of General Grant's army between Port Gibson and Bruinsburg, where the Union invasion came ashore after its river crossing on April 30, 1863. This area was rich cotton country, and many plantations were built along the bayou.

## Windsor Ruins

Now a ghostly skeleton, Windsor was a great Greek Revival mansion designed by architect David Shroder and built by slave labor between 1859 and 1861. Planter Smith Coffee Daniell II was the owner, though he died at thirty-four, a few weeks after the house was finished. It remained in his family, and during the Civil War, its high roof was used by Confederates as an observation deck. Federals later turned the house into a hospital. Windsor was destroyed by a fire in 1890; all that remains are twenty-three towering Corinthian columns. Only the ruins of Millwood, the Wade Hampton II house in Columbia, South Carolina, can compare as an evocation of the vanished antebellum South.

LOCATION: Route 522, ten miles west of Port Gibson. HOURS: Dawn–Dusk Daily. FEE: None. TELEPHONE: 601–437–4351.

## GRAND GULF

As it leaves Port Gibson the **Grand Gulf Tour** (marked by blue signs) leads northwest past Indian mounds to the once-lively river town of Grand Gulf. This Mississippi port was first settled by the French in 1785. Fifty years later it became an important link between Southern cotton fields and Northern textile mills. By 1840 Grand Gulf had a population of about 1,000 and was catching up with Natchez and Vicksburg as a cultural center—it was a stop for the touring theater companies that arrived by stern-wheeler. Grand Gulf's business district sprawled over fifty-five blocks, and the town had two banks, a newspaper, hospital, school, and several churches. Then a series of disasters struck. In 1843 a yellow fever epidemic killed many citizens. A decade later a tornado destroyed much of the town. But the worst damage came slowly, as the Mississippi River shifted its course over a five-year period from 1855 to 1860 and gradually wiped out the entire business district. The last of the town's buildings were burned by Grant's soldiers.

### Grand Gulf Military Monument Park

General Grant had originally planned to put his Vicksburg invasion force ashore at Grand Gulf, which was defended by two strong Confederate forts. In preparation for a landing, Union gunboats, commanded by Admiral David Dixon Porter, bombarded the forts on April 29, 1863 but were repulsed by the return fire. Grant then put into effect his contingency plan to make the crossing slightly downriver, selecting Bruinsburg as the spot.

The remains of Grand Gulf—both town and battle site—are preserved in the 400-acre Grand Gulf Military Monument Park. In addition to original Civil War mortar and cannon and replicas of stockades and observation towers, the compound includes the town **watermill,** a 1768 **dogtrot house** of hand-hewn yellow pine (moved from Scotia), and the **Sacred Heart Catholic Church,** built in the Carpenter Gothic style in 1868 and moved here from the town of Rodney. A carriage house contains horse-drawn carriages and a restored Confederate ambulance wagon. A **museum** displays Civil War and Indian artifacts, as well as fossils.

LOCATION: Grand Gulf Road, 3.5 miles north of Port Gibson. HOURS: 8–12, 1–5 Monday–Saturday, 10–6 Sunday. FEE: Yes, for museum. TELEPHONE: 601–437–5911.

## VICKSBURG

Before the war, Vicksburg had grown into one of the state's busiest commercial centers. The Spaniards who settled the bluff in 1790 called the place Nogales, meaning "walnut trees," after the black walnut trees that grew here; the English knew the area as Walnut

OVERLEAF: *Towering Corinthian columns are all that remain of Windsor Castle, a stately Greek Revival mansion that survived the Civil War only to burn to the ground in 1890.*

Hills. A Methodist minister, Reverend Newit Vick, arrived in 1811 as steamboats were plying the Mississippi and the cotton industry was burgeoning. Vick bought 1,120 acres on the river from the territorial government and in 1819 laid out a town on the northern 200 acres. Both he and his wife, Elizabeth, died of yellow fever that same year. His executors and thirteen children developed the city, known as Vicksburg by 1819 and incorporated as such in 1825.

From Vicksburg, bales of cotton were shipped north and south, and as the city grew richer, merchandise from the eastern United States and Europe arrived via New Orleans. By 1830 the city boasted a population of Southerners, Northerners, and Easterners, who arrived by river and the Natchez Trace, and Vicksburg remained the largest city in Mississippi until 1910, when Jackson outgrew it.

Situated on a bluff 200 feet above the Mississippi, Vicksburg was known as the "Gibraltar of the Confederacy." By late 1862, General Grant knew that he could succeed in dividing Texas, Arkansas, and Louisiana from the rest of the Confederacy only by commanding the Mississippi, and that required the capture of Vicksburg. Lieutenant General John C. Pemberton, in command of some 50,000 Confederate troops, opposed him. For months Grant's army ardu-

*The remains of the Union ironclad gunboat Cairo, on display at Vicksburg National Military Park. The gunboat was sunk during an attempt to destroy Vicksburg's Confederate batteries on December 12, 1862.*

ously maneuvered toward Vicksburg from the western (Louisiana) side of the Mississippi, chopping through forests and swamps and digging canals—"labors seldom equalled in war" in the estimate of one military historian. These "bayou expeditions" failed. Grant then decided to march his 45,000 troops down the western bank and cross the river below Vicksburg. Trying first to cross at Grand Gulf, Grant was repulsed. Farther south, however, the Federals crossed readily at Bruinsburg and took up their eastward march, capturing Port Gibson and Raymond on their way to Jackson, which fell on May 14. From the capital, Grant and his men were now positioned to approach Vicksburg from the east. Paralleling the east–west line of the Southern Railroad, they knocked back Pemberton's troops at Champion Hill and Big Black River Bridge. Grant's first attacks on Vicksburg, however, were not successful, and he coordinated further land attacks with Admiral Porter's gunboats, which by late May had moved into position to fire against Vicksburg from the Mississippi. The city was surrounded, and the siege lasted forty-seven days, from May 22 to July 4. There were few civilian casualties—during the attack, which cut off all supplies to the city, many moved into caves in the nearby hills. Grant had won his objective: The river was now in Union hands.

*Admiral David Porter's fleet running under the rebel guns at Vicksburg, April 16, 1863, to aid General Grant's operations below the city, as depicted in a Currier & Ives chromolithograph.*

## Vicksburg National Military Park

The vast military park is the site of Grant's siege, its rolling green land studded with monuments and markers at fort and battery sites. At the park's entrance, a visitor center presents several exhibits and a film about the campaign. A paved road loops sixteen miles through the battlefield, among **Ransom's Gun Path,** where Illinois soldiers and infantrymen installed two twelve-pounder cannon; the **Stockade Redan,** where repeated Union attacks failed; **Fort Garrot,** where Confederates—Brigadier General Isham W. Garrot among them—suffered great casualties from Federal sharpshooters; the **Second Texas Lunette,** a fortification, protecting a road to Vicksburg, that was attacked repeatedly by Federals; and **Hovey's Approach,** where zigzagging trenches dug by Union troops under General Alvin P. Hovey are visible.

The interior walls of the **Illinois Memorial** are covered with bronze tablets listing the names of the state's soldiers who fought in the Vicksburg campaigns. A bronze eagle is alighted on the pediment of the rotunda, built in 1906. **Shirley House** is the only structure in the park that survives from the Civil War. It was the headquarters of the Forty-fifth Illinois Infantry.

Nearly 17,000 Union soldiers are buried at the **Vicksburg National Cemetery.** Confederates are buried in **Vicksburg City Cemetery.** Adjacent to the national cemetery are the restored remains of the Union ironclad *Cairo,* sunk north of Vicksburg in the Yazoo River in December 1862. Salvaged a century later, the *Cairo* is now a Civil War naval museum.

LOCATION: 3201 Clay Street, off Route 20. HOURS: 8–5 Daily. FEE: Yes. TELEPHONE: 601–636–0583.

## Balfour House

During the siege, Emma Balfour, wife of a local doctor, kept a diary that is now in the Mississippi Department of Archives and History. From her three-story house, on Crawford and Cherry streets, Balfour could hear and see the conflict. "As I sat at my window," she wrote, "I saw mortars from the west passing entirely over the house and the . . . shells from the east passing by— crossing each other and this terrible fire raging in the center . . . I have almost made up my mind not to think of retiring at all at night. I see we are to have no rest. . . . All night they fired so that our poor soldiers have no rest and as we have few reserves, it is very hard on them." The Balfour house—the scene of great entertainments before the fall of Vicksburg—was built in 1835 and is one of the finest examples of the Greek Revival style in the state. It is famous for its original Balfour furnishings and elliptical spiral staircase.

LOCATION: 1002 Crawford Street. HOURS: 9–5 Monday–Saturday, 1–5 Sunday. FEE: Yes. TELEPHONE: 601–638–3680.

## Martha Vick House

One of Newit Vick's children, Martha, lived in this handsome Greek Revival house built for her in the 1830s, the last remaining of all the Vick family homes. The house is furnished with English and American pieces from the seventeenth to the late nineteenth century, among which are a 1690 chest from England and chairs by New Orleans cabinetmaker François Signouret. On rotating exhibit are paintings by French landscape artist Frederick Ragot.

LOCATION: 1300 Grove Street. HOURS: 9–5 Monday–Saturday, 1–5 Sunday. FEE: Yes. TELEPHONE: 601–638–7036.

The **Duff Green Mansion** (1114 First East Street, 601–636–6968) is named for the merchant who built it in 1856 as a wedding present for his bride. During the siege of Vicksburg, Green's wife fled to a nearby cave where she gave birth to their son, whom she named Siege. For the remainder of the war, the house was converted into a hospital for both Confederate and Union soldiers. The house, now an inn, has elaborate cast-iron grillwork—original in front, reconstructed from the original molds on the back and sides.

Modified in 1836, **McRaven** (1445 Harrison Street, 601–636–1663) is believed to have originated in the 1790s as a simple brick pioneer house. In the 1830s, the Warren County sheriff bought the property, today located inside the city of Vicksburg, and built a new two-story house. In 1849 a new owner made additions and remodeled the house in the Greek Revival style. With its three distinct stages of construction, the house is resonant with Vicksburg history. Gunshells hit it during the Civil War, and Confederates camped out in its three-acre gardens. McRaven has been restored to its prewar condition and is known for its elaborate carvings and plasterwork, furniture attributed to Prudent Mallard and John Henry Belter, and porcelain and needlepoint collections. The kitchen is equipped with eighteenth- and nineteenth-century utensils. **Anchuca** (1010 First East Street, 601–636–4931), built ca.

1830 in the Greek Revival style, and **Cedar Grove** (2200 Oak Street, 601–636–1605), a ca. 1840 mansion with formal gardens, are now inns, but offer house tours to the public.

## The Old Court House Museum

The centerpiece of downtown Vicksburg, this Greek Revival edifice was built in 1858 by slaves on a high hill overlooking the Mississippi River. Architecturally, it is impressive, with porticos supported by thirty-foot Ionic columns. It is topped by a clock tower and cupola, which Confederates used as a lookout and signal station. Crowding display cases throughout the building are artifacts from Vicksburg's Indian era and French settlement; from the city's affluent antebellum days are furniture, porcelain, and silver. From the war years, there are letters and other documents, weapons, uniforms, civilian clothing, and flags.

LOCATION: 1008 Cherry Street. HOURS: 8:30–5 Monday–Saturday, 1:30–5 Sunday, closing at 4:30 during Daylight Saving Time. FEE: Yes. TELEPHONE: 601–636–0741.

*Vicksburg's 1858 Old Court House. From its portico, General Grant and his staff reviewed the victorious Union Army after the surrender of Vicksburg in 1863.*

The nearby **Vicksburg City Cemetery** (Sky Farm Avenue) is the chief burial site of Confederates who died during the 1863 siege. In 1894 a Vicksburg candy merchant, Joseph A. Biedenharn, became the first person to bottle Coca-Cola, until then available only as a fountain drink. He sold it throughout Vicksburg and outlying areas, eventually securing franchises to bottle the drink in parts of Louisiana and Texas. It was the beginning of the soft drink's global bottling and distribution network. The **Biedenharn Candy Company** (1107 Washington Street, 601–636–5010), with reproductions of bottling equipment and many Coca-Cola artifacts dating from 1890 to 1980, has been restored and is operated as a museum by the Vicksburg Foundation for Historic Preservation.

# J      A      C      K      S      O      N

According to legend, a French Canadian trader, Louis Le Fleur, built a cabin on a high bluff on the Pearl River some time prior to 1800. The location of his trading post came to be called Le Fleur's Bluff. In 1821 the state legislature voted to move the capital from Natchez to a more central part of the state. A three-man commission dispatched to find the ideal place for the seat of government came upon Fleur's Bluff, which they described as having "beautiful and healthful surroundings, good water, abundant timber, navigable waters, and nearness to the Natchez Trace." The legislature was convinced. In November of that year it announced that the state capital would be moved and that a town would be established and named after Major General Andrew Jackson, the hero of the War of 1812 and the Battle of New Orleans. The new city fanned out from the west bank of the Pearl, its centerpiece being the two-story brick statehouse. The opening session was convened in December 1822. This building, no longer extant, was located at the corner of President and Capitol streets. Railroads arrived in the late 1850s, linking Jackson, which had dwindled in size, to such prosperous cities as Vicksburg, Natchez, and New Orleans. The second capitol, designed by English architect William Nichols in 1833 and completed in 1840, is much grander than the first was, with a towering portico and rotunda. Henry Clay, Andrew Jackson, and Jefferson Davis are among those who addressed the state legislature in this building, and secession was approved here in 1861. Now known as the **State Historical Museum** (100 South State Street, 601–354–6222), it houses exhibits on such major chapters in Mississippi history as de Soto's sixteenth-century explorations, Indian and

pioneer settlements, the Civil War and Reconstruction, and the civil rights movement. The far more ornate **New Capitol** (400 High Street, 601–359–3114), opened in 1903.

Built in 1842, Mississippi's **Governor's Mansion** (601–359–3175) greets East Capitol Street with a soaring rounded portico of Corinthian columns. The architect—again, William Nichols—wrote that his Neoclassical design was intended to "avoid a profusion of ornament, and to adhere to a plain republican simplicity, as best comporting with the dignity of the State." After Vicksburg's surrender, and the subsequent Federal occupation of Jackson in July 1863, a Union victory dinner was held in the mansion's dining room. A recent governor saw fit to replace Nichol's spare and elegant interiors with a decorator's version of "colonial." The mansion's furnishings include an Empire-style sofa and sideboard attributed to Duncan Phyfe, and pieces in the Rococo Revival, French Restoration and Renaissance Revival styles.

In the heart of downtown Jackson, the Governor's Mansion is part of **Smith Park Historic District,** bounded by Amite, North West, Yazoo, and North Congress streets. A grazing area for many years, Smith Park itself was named for a Scottish resident of the town, James Smith, who donated $100 to build a fence around the 320-square-foot green. Buildings in the district reflect a range of architectural styles from 1840 to 1940. Among them are the former **First Baptist Church** (Yazoo and North West streets), built with an imposing temple facade in 1844 and used as a hospital by Confederate and Federal troops. It is now headquarters of an insurance company. The Gothic Revival **Saint Peter's Cathedral** (North West and Amite streets) was built in 1897. At 304 East Capitol is the 1903 Gothic Revival **Saint Andrews Episcopal Church.** Jackson's first skyscraper, the ten-story **Lamar Life Building,** erected 1924 to 1925, has a crenelated clock tower. A tin mansard roof and steeply gabled pavilions mark the Second Empire styling of **Galloway House** (304 North Congress), built in 1889 for Methodist bishop Charles Betts Galloway. Across the street, the **Galloway Memorial United Church** is the third church on a lot continuously occupied by Jackson Methodists—Bishop Galloway

OPPOSITE: *The 1903 Beaux Arts Mississippi State Capitol, known as the New Capitol, replaced an 1840 building that now contains the State Historical Museum. Mississippi's original statehouse, a modest wooden structure where the legislature first convened in 1822, is no longer standing.*

built the second church on the site in 1883. Also significant are the 1932 Art Deco **Post Office and Federal Building** (245 East Capitol Street) and the 1906 **Old Emporium** (400 East Capitol Street), a dry goods store. Fronted by two pair of massive columns, **City Hall** (219 South President, 601–960–1034) also serves as headquarters for the Masons and was a hospital during the Civil War. Completed in 1847, it is still municipal headquarters.

Jackson suffered badly during the war. In May 1863, during the Vicksburg campaign, General William Tecumseh Sherman occupied and burned the town to prevent its being used as a base by Joseph E. Johnston's Confederate relief force, then marched toward Vicksburg to oppose Grant. After the surrender of Vicksburg, Johnston retreated to Jackson and rebuilt the earthworks defending the city. General Sherman besieged the town for six days in July 1863, until Johnston skillfully evacuated his men and equipment by night. Thereupon Sherman occupied the city and again set fire to it. So many buildings had been burned that Jackson became known as "Chimneyville," for the numerous brick chimneys rising from charred ruins. Among the public buildings Sherman spared were the Old Capitol, Governor's Mansion, and City Hall. During one occupation, General Sherman stayed at **The Oaks** (823 North Jefferson Street, 601–353–9339), the simple one-story cottage of James H. Boyd, mayor of Jackson during the 1850s. Built in 1846 of hand-hewn timber, it may be the oldest house in Jackson. It is surrounded by a white picket fence and contains period furnishings from the early to mid-nineteenth century.

## MANSHIP HOUSE

Also spared was the residence of the mayor who surrendered the city to the Union forces. Charles Henry Manship had arrived in Jackson in 1836 from Maryland, where he was a decorative painter. As a craftsman he worked on Jackson's Old Capitol, and he later opened a paint and wallpaper shop. In 1862 he was elected mayor of the city. Manship House, built in 1857 on what was then the outskirts of town, reflects its owner's many skills—he painted baseboards to resemble slate, pine mantels to look like black-and-gold marble, and wallpapers to resemble oak and mahogany. In a state where Greek architectural details were often used, his Gothic Revival house was unusual, though by no means unique. Complete with bargeboard and pointed arches, it was patterned on a design in Andrew Jackson Downing's popular 1850 manual *The Architecture of Country Houses*. Manship and his wife, Adaline Daley, had fifteen children; they celebrated their fiftieth wedding anniversary in the house in 1888. Standing on one-and-a-half acres of its original four-acre grounds, the house has been restored to the 1888 period, with furnishings and appointments, original paint colors, and reproductions of the original wallpaper. The house stayed in the family until 1975, when the Mississippi Department of Archives and History acquired it and began restoration. Manship House and the exhibits at the visitor center next door give a complete sense of the daily life of an accomplished nineteenth-century family in Mississippi.

> LOCATION: 420 East Fortification Street. HOURS: 9–4 Tuesday–Friday, 1–4 Saturday–Sunday. FEE: None. TELEPHONE: 601–961–4724.

A highly conjectural replica of the trading post of Jackson's original settler, Louis Le Fleur, stands at the entrance of the **Mississippi Agriculture and Forestry Museum** (1150 Lakeland Drive, 601–354–6113). Exhibits in this museum convey the history of the state, from the handicrafts of early Indian tribes to the development of such important industries as pine logging and cotton cultivation through the railroad era, the expansion of the road network, and the use of aircraft for crop dusting.

Also of historic interest in downtown Jackson, **Spengler's Corner** (East Capitol and North State streets) contains the oldest commercial structure in the city. Standing opposite the Old Capitol, the building was erected by Alsatian immigrant Joseph Spengler, the eldest of three brothers who arrived in Mississippi in 1836.

## MERIDIAN

East of Jackson, through Bienville National Forest, is Meridian, an industrial center taken after a siege by General Sherman in 1864, four years after its founding. "For five days," Sherman wrote in his report on the destruction of its war-making capacity, "10,000 men worked hard and with a will . . . of destruction, with axes, crowbars, sledges, clawbars, and with fire, and I have no hesitation in pronouncing the work as well done. Meridian, with its depots, storehouses, arsenal, hospitals, offices, hotels . . . no longer exists."

**Merrehope** (905 Martin Luther King, Jr., Drive, 601–483–8439), an exuberant architectural potpourri, was built around an 1859 cottage that belonged to the daughter of one of the town's founders. Another turn-of-the-century treasure in Meridian is the **Dentzel Carousel** (in Highland Park, 19th Street and Forty-first Avenue), with twenty-eight hand-carved horses and other animals.

Northwest of Meridian and west of the town of Philadelphia is the 21,000-acre **reservation of the Mississippi Band of Choctaw Indians,** whose major community is Pearl River (Route 16, 601–656–1521). The reservation's **Choctaw Museum** (601–656–5251) stresses the cultural continuity of the tribe with displays of contemporary work in basketry, costumes, drums, and other items. There is also a video presentation about the Choctaw culture. About 6,000 Choctaw live in the area in seven communities. The **Nanih Waiya State Historical Site** northeast of Philadelphia (Route 397, 601–773–7988) preserves a Choctaw sacred mound.

# PEARL    RIVER    VALLEY

Beginning in the early 1800s, farmers settled the fertile plains of the lower Pearl River. Generally the houses here are in the simple vernacular, providing an important contrast to Mississippi's antebellum mansions. Lawrence County has twenty-one notable examples of vernacular domestic architecture, from one-room log cabins to four-room cottages, dogtrot houses, and simple expressions of the Greek Revival. These dwellings are typical forerunners of the more pretentious mansions of a later period. Information about these houses can be obtained from the Lawrence County Historical Society (601–587–7731).

Moving south along the Pearl River, near **New Hebron,** is the 1834 **Buckley Cabin** (601–694–2287), beautifully wrought of heart pine. The small residence, expanded with galleries on three sides, was home to Benjamin Buckley, his wife, Rebecca, and their twelve grandchildren, who shared the sleeping loft.

    **The Fox House** (seven miles north of Monticello, in Wanilla, 601–587–7175) faces one of the oldest cemeteries in the state, called **Fox-Arrington.** Buried there is General Arthur Fox, a Virginian who served in the War of 1812 and was elected to the Mississippi House of Representatives and Senate. The Greek Revival house he built in 1850 is actually two separate buildings, one containing the kitchen and dining room.

    **Longino House** (Caswell Street, 601–587–7731) is the oldest surviving house in the town of **Monticello.** Two years before the house was built in 1884, a tornado wiped out much of the town. The builder of the five-room cottage was Andrew Houston Longino, Mississippi governor from 1900 to 1904.

South down the Pearl River in the community of **Sandy Hook** is the **John Ford House** (Route 35, 601–736–5378), also known as Ford's Fort. Once a stockaded fort and post office serving New Orleans–Nashville travelers, the frontier-style house was the site of an 1816 meeting—known as the Pearl River Convention—to determine Mississippi's boundary lines prior to filing petition for statehood. Ford, a Methodist minister, believed to have built the frontier house in the late 1790s, put up General Andrew Jackson on his way to the Battle of New Orleans.

# THE     GULF     COAST

At the close of the seventeenth century, the expedition of Pierre Le Moyne, sieur d'Iberville, commissioned by Louis XIV to settle France's Louisiana Territory, arrived on the Mississippi seacoast. Landing on the east side of the bay (at present-day Ocean Springs), he called the place Biloxi, after the Indians whose land it was. D'Iberville's Biloxi Bay Colony was the first permanent European settlement in the region. The coastal lands were not particularly good for farming, but the colonists fished, traded for furs, and

*Horn Island, on Mississippi's Gulf Coast, part of the Gulf Islands National Seashore.*

raised cattle. From its base in Biloxi Bay, the colony expanded its reach along the Mississippi coast for the next century, even under English rule, from 1763 to 1779, and the Spanish, from 1779 to 1798.

## GRASS LAWN

In 1836 Hiram Alexander Roberts, a Port Gibson surgeon and plantation owner, built this summer home on the Gulf. Now surrounded by the twentieth-century town of Gulfport, the estate originally had 235 acres. Upper and lower galleries, ten feet deep and surrounded by a triangular-patterned balustrade, face the sea. Pine and cypress timbers harvested from nearby forests were used to build the house, and an exposed section on the second floor shows details of wooden-peg construction. The house contains furniture from the period 1800 to 1840.

LOCATION: Route 90, between Gulf and Roberts streets, Gulfport. HOURS: 10–4 Monday, Wednesday, Friday. FEE: Yes. TELEPHONE: 601–864–5019.

*The Gulf of Mexico as seen from the lower gallery of Grass Lawn, built in 1836.*

# BILOXI

Biloxi grew rapidly in the nineteenth century as it became a popular seacoast resort. Not even the Civil War caused much upset. In 1862 Union gunboats anchored south of town, at Fort Massachusetts on Ship Island, peacefully capturing Biloxi. When the railroad arrived after the war, the resort life of the town resumed, and seafood industries began to attract an international population of workers. In the modern city are a few landmarks dating from the French and Spanish period and more from the nineteenth century. Though spared the ravages of the Civil War, Biloxi and other coastal towns have suffered severe weather damage—most notably by Hurricane Camille in 1969—and many historic buildings have been destroyed. The history of Biloxi and its coastal neighbors is presented in the **Seafood Industry Museum** (off Route 90 at the Biloxi–Ocean Springs Bridge, 601–435–6320), with exhibits on geology, the Biloxi Indians, and the growth of the town as a French colony, as part of Spanish West Florida, as a nineteenth-century resort, and as a center of the seafood industry. Among the objects in the museum are equipment used in fishing, crabbing, shrimping, and oystering, as well as anchors, nets, a lighthouse lens, trawls, and Biloxi-made skiffs and other boats.

Walking tours of the town's historic buildings begin at the 1895 **Brielmaier House.** Conspicuous for its ornamental woodwork in the Eastlake style, it is now the city's **visitor center** (710 Beach Boulevard, 601–435–6248). The oldest documented building in Biloxi is the ca. 1835 **Old French House,** now a restaurant on the Magnolia Street Mall; the **Old Spanish House** (Water Street, private) was built about 1840. Other sites on the tour include the 1896 Romanesque Revival **Old People's Bank** at Howard Avenue and Lameuse Street; the 1908 Neoclassical **City Hall** (Lameuse Street); and the 1908 Colonial Revival **Redding House** (Jackson Street). Dating to the 1840s, Biloxi's earliest days as a resort, is the **Magnolia Hotel** (Magnolia Street Mall, 601–432–8806), one of the oldest hotels on the Gulf Coast. It now houses the Biloxi Mardi Gras Museum. The **Old Brick House** (Bay View Drive, 601–432–5836), now occupied by the Biloxi Garden Center, may have been built as early as 1830.

Its tall front gallery open to the Gulf, the ca. 1840 **DuBuys House** (Beach Boulevard, private) is typical of Creole cottages of Louisiana and Mississippi, with a wooden second floor above an elevated brick basement. The **Tullis-Toledano Manor** (360 Beach

Boulevard, 601–435–6293) was built by New Orleans cotton broker Christoval Toledano as a summer house in 1856. The brick house, now used as a community center, has been restored after being severely damaged by Hurricane Camille.

Jefferson Davis was a vestryman at Biloxi's ca. 1875 Gothic Revival **Episcopal Church of the Redeemer** (Bellman Street and East Beach Boulevard). The church was deconsecrated and moved to its present location when a new church was built in 1891; the older building served as a parish house until 1969, when a hurricane destroyed the newer church. At that time, the original church was repaired and reconsecrated; it now serves once again as a place of worship. Davis spent the last twelve years of his life as a Biloxi resident, at Beauvoir, and the Davis family pew is located in the nave of the church.

## Beauvoir

Former Confederate president Jefferson Davis spent many of his postwar years at this house. Captured in Georgia on May 10, 1865, he was charged with treason and with being part of the conspiracy to assassinate Abraham Lincoln, in which he actually had no part. He was held for two years at Virginia's Fortress Monroe, but he was never brought to trial. After his release he accepted an invitation from Mrs. Sarah Dorsey, a family friend, to stay at her house, Beauvoir, named for the beautiful view it has of the Gulf of Mexico. Davis stayed in a cottage on the grounds; two years later he purchased the property. He was joined here by his wife, Varina, and daughter Winnie. It was here that he wrote his two-volume *Rise and Fall of the Confederate Government* and *A Short History of the Confederate States of America.*

Beauvoir was an ideal retreat, with an atmosphere conducive to reflection and work. Built in the early 1850s by a Mississippi planter, the house suits the climate. Raised on brick piers, it is cooled by breezes blowing beneath the main floor and through the ceiling-height windows. It is modest in design, although a front staircase leading up to the gallery creates some formality. After Davis's death in 1889 in New Orleans, his widow wrote a memoir here. She kept the house until 1903, finally selling the property to the United Sons of Confederate Veterans, an organization that

OPPOSITE: *Biloxi's 1895 Brielmaier House, a Victorian cottage with Eastlake-style ornamental woodwork, serves as the city's visitor center.*

agreed to maintain the property as a shrine to Davis and as a rest home for Confederate veterans of the Civil War (many of whom are buried in Beauvoir Cemetery).

Beauvoir preserves many Davis family possessions, from furniture and writing utensils to needlepoint. The basement level houses a museum displaying artifacts of Jefferson Davis's public life and of the Confederacy, along with the 1978 joint resolution of Congress, signed by President Jimmy Carter, that restored Davis's United States citizenship. An additional museum, located in the old veterans' hospital, contains artifacts from the war years and exhibits about the postwar life of Confederate soldiers.

LOCATION: 2244 Beach Boulevard. HOURS: 9–5 Daily. FEE: Yes. TELEPHONE: 601–388–1313.

The **Biloxi Lighthouse** (Route 90 at Porter Avenue, 601–432–2563), built in 1848, remained in Confederate hands during the Civil War. Its keepers did not light the oil-burning lamp, lest it aid the navigation of Yankee vessels. It was electrified and automated in 1926. The forty-eight-foot cast-iron tower and an exhibit on its construction and history are open to the public.

*Jefferson Davis's study in the Library Cottage at Beauvoir, where he wrote* The Rise and Fall of the Confederate Government *and* A Short History of the Confederate States of America.

*Davis holds a granddaughter in this family photograph taken at Beauvoir ca. 1885.*

In 1969, Hurricane Camille split **Ship Island,** south of Biloxi, into two islands. The area now known as East Ship Island served as a base of British coastal operations during the War of 1812. In 1855 Jefferson Davis, then the U.S. Secretary of War, recommended the construction of **Fort Massachusetts** (601–875–9057) on what is now West Ship Island. Congress did not authorize the necessary funds until 1857, and construction was finally completed after the Civil War. During the war the unfinished fort was used by the U.S. Navy as a base of operations for the coastal blockade. Even before it was completed, the fort had been rendered obsolete by technical advances in artillery. The fortification—forming a giant D—is in excellent condition, and visitors may tour it and see one of the few fifteen-inch Rodman guns left in the United States, along with a guardroom containing implements for firing the cannons.

## OCEAN SPRINGS

A replica of the early-eighteenth-century **Fort Maurepas** is under construction on Front Beach. Younger Ocean Springs landmarks are associated with Louis Sullivan, one of the great American

*Fort Massachusetts on West Ship Island, a federal naval base during the Civil War.*

architects of the late nineteenth and early twentieth centuries. A Chicago resident, Sullivan summered on the Gulf Coast. While in Ocean Springs, Sullivan stayed at a compound he designed with some assistance from a young man in his office, Frank Lloyd Wright. The octagonal cottage and two bungalows (Shearwater and East Beach drives) are private residences.

Also of architectural interest is the High Victorian Gothic **Saint John's Episcopal Church** (705 Rayburn at Porter), designed entirely of wood construction by Manly H. Cutter of New York. It was built in 1891 with a complex, many-faceted facade and unusual stained-glass windows.

Farther east, in **Pascagoula,** is the oldest structure in the Mississippi Valley, surviving from the early years of French colonization. Known inaccurately as the **Old Spanish Fort** (4602 Fort Drive, 601–769–1505) since the years of Spain's rule in the territory, it was built from 1718 to 1721 and is actually a carpenter's or blacksmith's shack. The structure has a cypress-and-pine frame, a shingled roof, and walls of tabby (a mixture of clay, burned oyster shells, and Spanish moss). Also on the grounds are several cannon captured by Andrew Jackson in the 1815 Battle of New Orleans and the **Krebs Cemetery,** where some of the region's early European settlers are buried. A modern building on the site houses a **museum** operated by the Jackson County Historical Society.

# NORTHERN MISSISSIPPI

The hilly, forested lands of northern Mississippi, fed by abundant streams, were a stronghold of the Chickasaws. Eastern settlers began to arrive in the early 1830s. After the Indians were deprived of their lands in the 1828 Treaty of Pontotoc, speculators and surveyors descended to divide the area into counties, towns, and farms and build saw and grist mills on streams. Abundant timber for building came from the region's forests, and the local clay made strong bricks.

## COLUMBUS

Formerly a trading post in Chickasaw territory, the land that would become Columbus was ceded by the Indians to the U.S. government in 1816. Five years later the town was incorporated, and many settlers arrived from the East and from other Southern states, drawn by the government's offer of land for about a dollar an acre. Columbus was well situated for settlement and trade, both of which developed briskly. The town had direct water access to Mobile via the Tombigbee River. Many of the settlers were farmers who had elsewhere exhausted thin soil by planting the same crop every season; in eastern Mississippi they found a richer land on which they rotated cotton, corn, potatoes, and tobacco. In 1821 the town established the state's first free public school, **Franklin Academy** (501 Third Avenue North). The 1847 Columbus Female Institute was the antecedent for the **Mississippi University for Women** (College Street, 601–329–7119), the first state-supported educational institution for women in the United States. Its campus is a complex of handsome Gothic buildings dating from 1860 to the turn of the century.

A Tiffany window decorates **Saint Paul's Episcopal Church** (318 College Street), a pointy Gothic edifice built in 1860 that contrasts with its simpler **rectory** next door. The rectory was the boyhood home of playwright Tennessee Williams, born in Columbus in 1911. The **Columbus Historic Foundation** (618 College Street, 601–329–3533) conducts tours of Saint Paul's and two other antebellum churches, the Catholic **Church of the Annunciation** (808 College Street) and **First United Methodist** (602 Main Street). These and other churches served as hospitals during the Civil War. Although no battles were fought in Columbus, thousands of wounded soldiers, Confederate and Federal, were cared for here.

In 1866 a group of Columbus women declared a "Decoration Day" and marched to **Friendship Cemetery** (Fourth Street South) to lay flowers on the graves of Confederate soldiers. According to local stories, one of the women, a war widow, impulsively placed flowers on the Union graves as well, saying "After all, they are somebody's sons." The event resulted from a tea at **Twelve Gables** (601–327–5087), an 1838 cottage at 220 South Third Street. The decoration of graves at Columbus was one of many such acts around the country that evolved into the national observance of Memorial Day; additionally, every April 25, Columbus celebrates Decoration Day in Friendship Cemetery.

Generally, the houses in Columbus are situated differently from those in Natchez. Prosperous antebellum towns were often built as compounds for plantation owners whose overseers lived more simply on the plantations themselves. In Natchez, however, a rural feeling is maintained by many lacy, parklike settings, unusual in the South. Columbus is more typical; its houses—though large, with attendant kitchens, stables, smokehouses, and other detached structures out back—are relatively close together, but, taken together, they are an extraordinary assemblage. A dozen, all but one privately owned, are on an annual spring tour conducted by the Columbus Historic Foundation.

When it was completed in 1850, the four-story **Riverview** (514 Second Avenue South, private) and its grounds occupied a full city block; it still is among the most stately of Mississippi's antebellum houses. Its perfectly proportioned facades—identical front and rear arrangements of square Tuscan columns, brick pilasters, and shuttered windows—face the Tombigbee River and Second Avenue. The cupola is very large—typical of Columbus and neighboring Alabama—and served the practical purpose of venting warm air. The builder, Charles McLaren, had extravagant tastes: The rooms are rich in plaster moldings, colored glass, and gilt cornices. Chandeliers, marble mantels, pier mirrors, and other appointments are original to the house.

**White Arches** (122 Seventh Avenue South, 601–328–4568) has the distinction of a central octagonal tower and observatory. Without the trimmings, White Arches might seem like a fortress, but the builder, a transplanted Georgian, ordered an abundance of cast-iron railings and brass finials and etched glass and cloverleaf-pattern tracery for the front porch. Among the period furnishings is an 1857 grand piano.

Unique to Columbus are amalgams of Gothic and Greek elements at **Errolton** (216 Third Avenue South, private); **Shadowlawn** (1024 Second Avenue South, private), built by a town merchant in 1860; and **Snowdoun** (906 Third Avenue North, private), built in 1854 around an octagonal center. **The Colonnade** (620 Second Street South, private) also displays elements of different styles, with Italianate roof brackets above its Grecian doorway. A Georgian planter, Dr. William T. Baldwin, built it as a townhouse in 1860 across the Tombigbee River from his plantation. He used the river for transportation of his cotton to Mobile, and to receive building materials and furnishings for his house. Formal gardens extending behind the house to the river contain boxwood mazes, orchards, and cutting, kitchen, and herb gardens, elements typical of Southern gardens of that era. **Amzi Love** (305 Seventh Street South, private) was named for its first owner, a Columbus lawyer who built it as a present for his bride. The 1848 cottage is a hybrid of Greek Revival and Gothic Revival, with bracketed cornices adding some gaiety to the exacting facade. The house and many of its original furnishings have remained in the Love family.

A former North Carolina general built **Temple Heights** (515 Ninth Street North, 601–328–0599) on a sharp rise of land in about 1837, as a copy of his wife's Federal-style family home in North Carolina, complete with a Classical columned facade across the rear. A decade later a Georgia statesman put up new eastern and northern facades for a total of fourteen Doric columns with a carved frieze overhead.

## WAVERLEY PLANTATION

One man's empire on the Tombigbee River, Waverley was one of the largest plantations in the pre–Civil War South, anchored by a remarkable house. Designed with identical inset, Classical facades in front and back, it is built around an enormous octagonal rotunda. As great an impression as it makes on the exterior, the eight-sided rotunda is even more spectacular inside.

Waverley was the home of George Hampton Young, a New York–educated lawyer who came to Columbus from Georgia in 1835, when the U.S. government put land up for sale at bargain prices. He bought an enormous parcel, which already had a house large enough for his wife, Lucy, and their ten children. But Young wanted something grander, and he set about building a self-contained community for himself.

The identity of the architect of the house is uncertain, but he was undoubtedly a good student of style books that advocated the octagonal form, as seen at Longwood in Natchez, and of the "tribune," or central space of the Regency style. Though the floor plan is almost a square, the octagonal core rises from the first floor, so that most interior spaces are made to seem eight sided. Two gently curving staircases lead to cantilevered balconies on the second, third, and fourth levels—past parlor, library, and dining room, to bedrooms, to storage rooms. The second-story bedrooms open onto their outside galleries as well as the interior balconies. The cupola above fills the rotunda with light and also acts as a giant chimney, venting warm air through its windows.

The rotunda below could not have made a better ballroom had it been designed as one, and it perhaps gives a clue to the expansiveness of the man of the house: People who lived in places such as Waverley were great entertainers and fancied themselves not just hosts but social and intellectual arbiters. One of Young's contemporaries, a fellow planter, wrote that "Young was a man of wealth and high social standing and his elegant home . . . was a centre of refined and extended hospitality." Young's modern showplace boasted a built-in china cabinet and secretary, and interior details

*Built during the mid-nineteenth-century vogue for octagonal houses, Waverley combines an octagonal cupola with a more traditional square base.*

complemented the spectacular scale of the house. Waverley's rooms displayed all that was fashionable in decoration—sculptural cornices and medallions, marble mantels, woodwork painted with trompe l'oeil effects.

Surrounding the house were not only gardens and orchards but the outbuildings that were the scene of plantation work and Young's enterprises: a brick kiln and lumber mill (for ongoing construction), a cotton gin, and livestock pens. Though Mrs. Young died before the house was completed, she left it a green legacy in the English boxwoods that now nearly touch the second-story windows. After the last Young descendant died in 1913, the house fell into a half-century of disrepair. In 1962 new owners from Philadelphia began to restore it, and the house now appears much as it did when Young entertained here. Among the original appointments are gold pier mirrors, marble mantels, chandeliers (including the one made of brass that hangs from a sixty-five-foot chain from the top of the rotunda), Venetian door glass, an English carpet, and some original curtains.

LOCATION: Route 50, between Columbus and West Point. HOURS: Dawn–Dusk Daily. FEE: Yes. TELEPHONE: 601–494–1399.

*Waverley's spectacular open hall, which provides excellent ventilation, keeps the house five to ten degrees cooler than the outdoors.*

# ABERDEEN

North of Columbus, Aberdeen was founded in 1835 by a Scotsman, Robert Gordon, who saw the potential of the gently rolling, fertile lands fanning out west of the Tombigbee River. Two years after his arrival, the town was incorporated and on its way to being one of the richest in Mississippi's cotton kingdom. By 1850 Aberdeen was not only the largest port on the Tombigbee but also the second-largest city in the state and the seat of Monroe County. Late in the century Aberdeen experienced a second boom. Ornate Victorian residences and shopfronts along Commerce and Franklin streets create a rich architectural scene. There are a large number of outstanding antebellum, Victorian, and Queen Anne-style homes, as well as cottage types, open for tour on spring "pilgrimages" (information can be obtained from the Aberdeen-South Monroe Chamber of Commerce, 601–369–6488).

Two of the most interesting houses face each other across West Commerce Street: **Sunset Hill** (number 803, 601–369–2610) was built in 1847 by a cotton broker who used stout Doric columns to support an overhanging roof. Three years later **The Magnolias** went up at number 732. Built by Virginians, the house contains furnishings from 1850. The town's antebellum cottages include the 1848 **Parson-Gunn** (519 West Monroe) and the 1856 **Showboat** (109 West Madison). A few miles west on Route 25 is **Lenoir Plantation,** built as a story-and-a-half residence in 1847 and enlarged after the turn of the century.

The **Monroe County Courthouse** (Chestnut Street) was built in 1857. **Saint John's Episcopal Church** (402 West Commerce Street) went up between 1851 and 1853; its first pastor, Joseph Holt Ingraham, a popular novelist of the day, claimed to have designed the structure himself. Stained glass and chandeliers in the **First Methodist Church** (300 College Place), which replaced an earlier structure when it was built in 1912, are attributed to Louis Comfort Tiffany.

The **Amory Regional Museum** (Third Street and Eighth Avenue South, 601–256–2761), located in a former hospital, exhibits Indian and military artifacts, medical instruments, and furniture. A railroad coach attached to the building displays railroad memorabilia.

# TUPELO

Part of the fertile northeastern woods ceded by the Chickasaws in 1832, the Tupelo area quickly attracted Easterners and others who saw an opportunity to start over on new farmland. The new village thrived, even before the Mobile & Ohio Railroad arrived in 1859. Three houses from that period survived a 1936 tornado and are being restored (North Broadway). The site of a **Chickasaw Village** is marked on the Natchez Trace three miles north of the town.

## *Brices Cross Roads National Battlefield Site*

On June 10, 1864, Confederate General Nathan Bedford Forrest, the raider known for fast strikes and tough fighting, won a victory here over General Samuel D. Sturgis. General William Tecumseh Sherman, fearing that Forrest would destroy the Nashville-to-Chattanooga rail line that was supplying the Union Army in Georgia, dispatched Sturgis with a powerful 8,300-man force to track down Forrest. The Confederate general was indeed advancing toward Tennessee to cut the railroad when he was urgently summoned back to face Sturgis. Forrest, with about 3,500 men, attacked the Federal column near Brices Cross Roads. Confused by Forrest's maneuvers and feints, the Federal commanders believed themselves outnumbered, but Sturgis was simply outgeneraled: In hard fighting, Forrest's men outflanked the Northerners and burst into the rear, sowing panic. Fleeing pell-mell back to Tennessee, the Federals abandoned their supply wagons of food, ammunition, and weapons. The Confederates could not call the battle a total success—the Tennessee rail line remained open, bringing supplies to Sherman's campaigners advancing on Atlanta, Georgia—but Forrest remained at large, forcing Sherman to order yet another hunt for him. Information about the battlefield is available at the Tupelo Visitor Center on Natchez Trace Parkway.

LOCATION: Route 370, west of Baldwyn. TELEPHONE: 601–842–1572.

## *Tupelo National Battlefield*

Admitting that Forrest "had whipped Sturgis fair and square," Sherman gave orders to "follow Forrest to the death, if it costs

10,000 lives and breaks the Treasury." With 14,000 men, General
A. J. Smith marched to Tupelo and surrounded his force with
strong defensive works. Forrest, at the command of General Stephen Lee, reluctantly attacked Smith's position on July 14, 1864
and suffered heavy losses. Forrest himself received a painful
wound in the foot. Despite holding the advantage, Smith ordered a
retreat because his food and ammunition supplies were running
low. Sherman's order to pursue Forrest to the death had not been
carried out, but the Confederate raiders were again kept from
harassing Sherman's supply line. The battlefield, within the present city limits of Tupelo, is not preserved, but the one-acre Tupelo
National Battlefield commemorates the engagement; information
is available at the Tupelo Visitor Center on Natchez Trace
Parkway.

LOCATION: Route 6, west of Route 45. TELEPHONE: 601–842–1572.

The **Tupelo Museum** (Route 6, 601–841–6438) offers a broad view
of local history, exhibiting archaeological finds, Indian artifacts, a
primitive log cabin and other examples of indigenous architecture,
Civil War weapons and other relics, a one-room schoolhouse, and a
country store.

# CORINTH

Located at the junction of two important Southern railroads—the
Memphis & Charleston and Mobile & Ohio, this town in the northeastern corner of Mississippi was an important transit point for
Confederate troops and supplies. In May 1862, more than 128,000
Federal troops under General Henry W. Halleck surrounded the
town. Realizing how badly his Confederates were outnumbered,
General Pierre G. T. Beauregard ordered a nighttime evacuation
via rail south toward Tupelo. To deceive the Federals as the empty
trains rolled into Corinth for the evacuation, the Southerners
cheered and bugles sounded as if reinforcements had arrived. The
next morning, Halleck found an empty town. The Confederates
attempted to recapture the rail junction the following October.
The Southerners, led by General Earl Van Dorn and Major General Sterling Price, were repulsed, suffering heavy casualties—1,400
killed and 5,700 wounded, compared with the Federals' 300 killed
and 1,800 wounded. **Battery Robinette** (West Linden Street) is the
site of the heaviest fighting in the two-day Battle of Corinth.

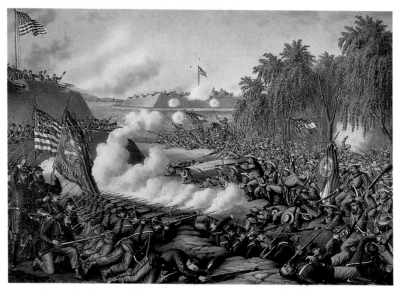

*Union forces under General William S. Rosecrans repulse a Confederate attempt to recapture Corinth on October 3 and 4, 1862.*

The famous intersection of train tracks lies at Fillmore and Cruise streets. Men who died in the Battle of Corinth are buried in the **National Cemetery** (Horton and Cemetery streets). At Washington and Fourth streets, the **Corinth Museum** contains local-history exhibits, including many documents and relics relating to the occupation and fighting at Corinth. A self-guided tour of the town begins at the museum and leads to battle sites and significant buildings. The 1854 Federal style **Jacinto Courthouse,** just outside Corinth in the town of Jacinto, has been furnished to give the atmosphere of a typical courtroom of that day. Nearby a ca. 1850s doctor's office has also been restored.

For his headquarters in Corinth, General Halleck took over **Curlee House** (715 Jackson Street, 601–287–2231). It is now a museum containing antebellum furniture, decorative objects, and Civil War memorabilia. Before the occupation, General Beauregard stayed at the 1856 **Fish Pond House** (708 Kilpatrick Street, private).

## HOLLY SPRINGS

Northwest of the Holly Springs National Forest is the cotton-growing and -brokering town of Holly Springs, incorporated in

1837. Raw cotton fiber was carted west to the Mississippi and
floated down to New Orleans to be sold to mills in New England
and in Great Britain. Area plantations also grew tobacco, hay,
wheat, and corn, and fortunes were made in livestock. Van Dorn
Avenue, on the south side of **Court Square,** was planned as the
town's original commercial row.

In 1860 the Mississippi Central Railroad linked Holly Springs
to New Orleans. In 1862 General Grant made the town his major
supply base in his first campaign against Vicksburg—enormous
amounts of food, clothing, medicine, and ammunition were stored
in boxcars and in buildings throughout the town. On December 20,
Confederate raiders under General Earl Van Dorn stormed the
town and destroyed the stockpiles, forcing Grant to retreat, tempo-
rarily, to Tennessee. This and some sixty other Confederate raids
on the Union-occupied town seriously set back the Union's chief
aim in Mississippi, the seizure of Vicksburg.

At the **Marshall County Historical Society Museum** (College
Avenue, 601–252–2943) the collections include Chickasaw Indian
artifacts, relics of the Civil War and the War of 1812, paintings by
local artists, farm tools, and a collection of antique clothing.

Among those buried in the 1837 **Hillcrest Cemetery** were
Confederate soldiers and victims of an 1878 yellow fever epidemic.
The elaborate cast- and wrought-iron fences that surround some of
the graves were created at the Jones-McIlwain Iron Works, also
known as the Holly Springs Iron Works. The workmanship was
superior—local artisans also produced many of the iron railings,
galleries, and fences for private residences.

Four of Holly Springs's churches were built before the Civil
War: the 1849 **First United Methodist** (Van Dorn and Spring
streets); **Christ Episcopal** (Van Dorn and Randolph streets), designed along Gothic Revival lines and dedicated in 1858; the Romanesque Revival **First Presbyterian** (Memphis Street and Gholson Avenue), which was occupied by Federal troops in the middle
of its construction; and **Saint Joseph's Catholic Church** (College
Avenue), a quaint, bell-towered frame building dating from 1837.

Most of the historic houses of Holly Springs are private (with
the exception of Montrose, which is open by appointment), but
may be seen on an annual spring tour (601–252–2943). Among the
antebellum houses are two examples of the Gothic Revival, **Airliewood** and **Cedarhurst,** both located on Salem Avenue. General

OPPOSITE: *The author William Faulkner at Rowan Oak, 1962.*

Grant used Airliewood, painted salmon pink and sporting a crenelated roof, as his military headquarters in 1862. Cedarhurst is a twin, though not quite an identical one, of Airliewood. It too has a double chimney and three gables rich with decoration, but its exterior is brick rather than stucco, and a balustrade of white cast iron, rather than crenelations, trims the roof.

When she visited her husband in 1862, Julia Grant stayed at **Walter Place** (Chulahoma Avenue), conspicuous for its towering Corinthian portico and, on each side, octagonal, battlemented towers. Elaborately carved marble mantels were installed in each room. The extraordinarily large house was built in 1859 by a local lawyer and businessman for his wife and their ten children.

**Montrose** (Salem Avenue and Walthal Street, 601–252–2672) was a wedding present from planter Alfred Brooks to his daughter Margaret. Completed in 1858, it could stand beside the grandest houses of Natchez or the River Road, with its bold four-columned portico. Its bricks were made locally by slaves, who also laid the fine parquet floors. The house is now headquarters of the Holly Springs Garden Club and open by appointment. Across Salem Avenue is a virtual mirror image of Montrose, **Oakleigh,** the 1858 home of Judge J. W. Clapp. **Crump Place** (127 Gholson Avenue), a handsome Greek Revival cottage from about 1840, was built around a much simpler log structure. During the Civil War it served as officers' quarters.

Stark and huge, **Fort Daniel** (184 South Memphis Street) is mysteriously named: It was built as a residence, not as a fort, in 1850, and no one called Daniel has ever been associated with the house. During the Civil War it was occupied by Union officers. The first brick building in Holly Springs, the 1836 **Yellow Fever House** (104 Gholson Avenue) got its name in 1878 when the epidemic of that year claimed the owner of the house.

The oldest historically black college in Mississippi, Methodist-affiliated **Rust College** (Memphis Street and Rust Avenue, 601–252–4661) traces its origins to 1866, when Reverend A. C. McDonald of the Freedman's Aid Society and Reverend Moses Adams, a local preacher, began teaching classes in a Methodist church in Holly Springs. In 1870 the school was chartered as Shaw University; it was renamed in 1890 to honor Richland S. Rust, Secretary of the Freedman's Aid Society.

# OXFORD

Nestled into the green hills south of the Holly Springs National Forest, Oxford looks like what it is, a college town. The **University of Mississippi** was chartered here in 1844 and four years later opened its doors to eighty students. The first building on the 640-acre campus was the 1848 **Lyceum,** possibly designed by William Nichols, architect of the second capitol and Governor's Mansion in Jackson. The university's other antebellum structures are the ca. 1857 **Barnard Observatory** and the 1853 **Old Chapel.**

## Rowan Oak

The university owns Rowan Oak, the home of Oxford's most famous resident, the author William Faulkner. Built in 1840 and acquired nearly a century later by Faulkner, this typical "planter's house" is set back among oak and cedar trees but is still visible from the street. Faulkner did prodigious amounts of work here, basing his fictional Yoknapatawpha County and its denizens on the world just beyond Oxford, where he grew up. The Snopes trilogy—*Sanctuary, Light in August,* and *A Green Bough*—and *Absalom, Absalom!* were among the works written at Rowan Oak. Eventually Faulkner made some changes to the house and added an office. On the walls of that room he outlined *A Fable,* his 1954 Pulitzer Prize–winning novel. The outline has not faded from the walls of the office, which remains as it was when Faulkner died in 1962—his portable typewriter still sits on the small desk that he made himself. On view are the simply furnished rooms and Faulkner's gardens, smokehouse, and stable. Many of Faulkner's papers, including his Nobel Prize citation, are in the University of Mississippi library.

LOCATION: Old Taylor Road. HOURS: 10–12, 2–4 Monday–Friday, 10–12 Saturday, 2–4 Sunday. FEE: None. TELEPHONE: 601–232–7237.

In **Clarksdale** the 1914 Tudor-style Carnegie Public Library houses the **Delta Blues Museum** (114 Delta Avenue, 601–624–4461), honoring one of America's unique musical forms, pioneered by such artists as McKinley Morganfield, known as Muddy Waters; John Lee Hooker; Charlie Patton; and W.C. Handy, all of whom were born in Clarksdale.

# ALABAMA

OPPOSITE: *The 1848 Teague House served as headquarters for the staff of Union General James H. Wilson when his raiders swept into Montgomery in April 1865.*

Alabama—the name means "brush gatherers" in Choctaw and referred to the Alibamu tribe, members of the powerful Creek Confederacy—consists of a surprising mix of influences. The French, Spanish, and British vied for dominance during the seventeenth and eighteenth centuries; a highly civilized native population, much reduced in numbers by European diseases, was "removed" to Oklahoma during the eighteenth and early nineteenth centuries. Cotton planters controlled the state prior to the Civil War; but during the last quarter of the nineteenth century an important coal and iron center developed around Birmingham. The great hydroelectric projects of the Tennessee Valley Authority helped transform northern Alabama during the first half of the twentieth century, and the creation of the Marshall Space Flight Center at Huntsville has turned that once-sleepy town into a metropolis during the last half of this century.

It is only fitting that Alabama's seal shows the state's rivers, since it is on these that its wealth and evolution are based. The landscape varies dramatically from the Appalachian hill country of the northeast to the bayou lands around Mobile, and the people vary likewise from the northeastern mountaineers to the cosmopolitan residents of Huntsville, Montgomery, and Mobile, to the pinewoods Cajuns (no relation to Louisiana's Cajuns), whose ancestry mixes Indian, French, English, and Spanish blood.

Alabama's rivers have been important since the earliest Indian settlements nearly 10,000 years ago. Along the Black Warrior River, in the western part of the state, for example, is Moundville, one of the great concentrations of mounds created by a highly advanced native culture, about which little is known. The mound culture spread up and down all the state's river systems, and its tribes engaged in trade that brought them obsidian from the west, copper from the north, and shell from the Gulf of Mexico.

When the first Europeans appeared in the middle of the sixteenth century, they poked up river valleys inhabited by assemblages of tribes later called Creek, Choctaw, Chickasaw, and Cherokee. (It was later traders from South Carolina who gave the Creek their name, abbreviating a designation that originally indicated which creek they lived on.) Hernando de Soto—who had first landed near Tampa Bay in 1539, seeking gold but discovering the Mississippi River instead—penetrated the site of present-day Alabama with a band of 500 Spaniards in 1540, descending the Tennessee River and Coosa River valleys. At an Indian town called

*A 1735 watercolor by the French traveler Alexandre de Batz shows painted Choctaw warriors displaying scalps on poles.*

Mauvila on October 18, 1540, his force attacked a large party of Indians under Chief Tuscaloosa with firearms and horses, killing at least several thousands of them in one of the bloodiest Indian-European fights in American history.

Two decades later, in 1559, another Spaniard, Tristan de Luna, made the first efforts at settlement, establishing short-lived forts at present Mobile Bay and on the Alabama and Coosa rivers. De Luna's towns lasted less than two years. Thereafter, the Spanish sporadically asserted their claim to the area, while the English— who had included the region in their Carolina Charters of the mid-seventeenth century—began to send traders and trappers into the Alabama River valley.

But it was the French who first succeeded in creating permanent settlements. Fur was the booty they sought. To handle the trade, they created first Fort Louis (1702) near the present site of Mobile, then Port Dauphin on Dauphin Island. The main port town was reestablished at Mobile in 1711. To control the river basins, meanwhile, the French implanted Fort Toulouse (1714) between the arms of the Coosa and Tallapoosa rivers, and Fort Tombigbee (1736) on the river of the same name. They also started growing indigo and rice on their coastal holdings, laying the foundation of the export-crop pattern that would later characterize much of the South; to work the land, they began to import black slaves in 1719.

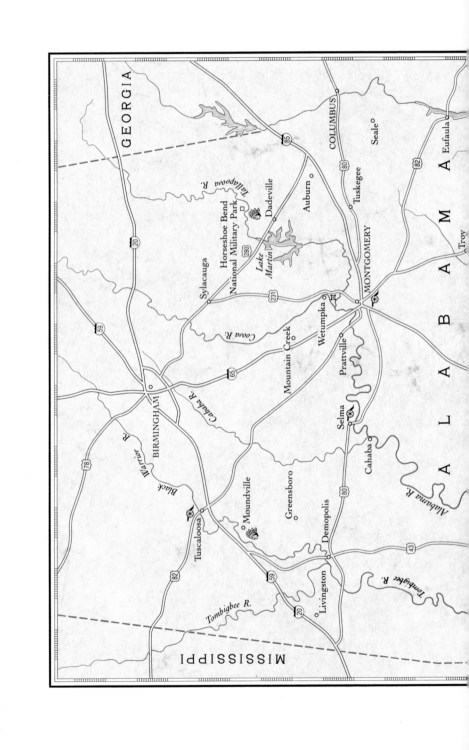

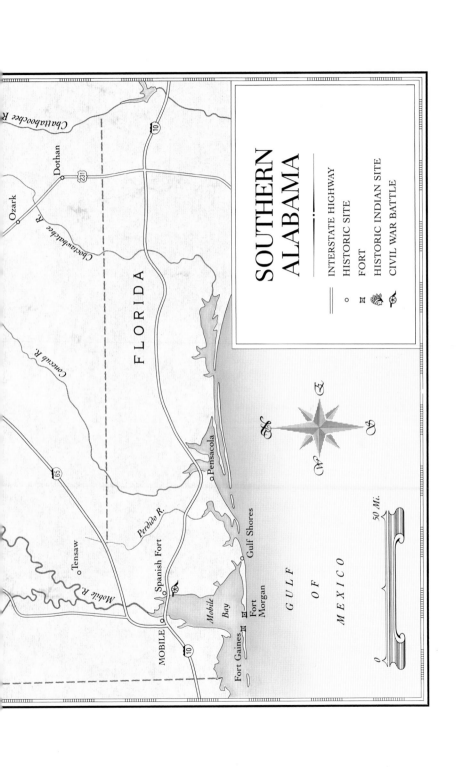

# SOUTHERN ALABAMA

— INTERSTATE HIGHWAY
o HISTORIC SITE
⊨ FORT
HISTORIC INDIAN SITE
CIVIL WAR BATTLE

Chattahoochee R.

Ozark

Dothan

231

10

Choctawhatchee R.

FLORIDA

Conecuh R.

65

Perdido R.

Pensacola

Tensaw

Mobile R.

Spanish Fort

Gulf Shores

MOBILE

10

Mobile Bay

Fort Morgan

Fort Gaines

GULF

OF

MEXICO

0    50 Mi.

*Vice Admiral David Farragut observes the gunners of his flagship* Hartford *firing a broadside into the Confederate ironclad* Tennessee *during the Battle of Mobile Bay, shown here in an 1883 painting by William Heysham Overend.*

For most of the eighteenth century, shifting alliances and intrigues among the white and Indian populations characterized the region. The Creek and the Chickasaw favored the British; the Choctaw fought for the French. Finally, the English were the winners; Alabama became British property under the terms of the Treaty of Paris, in 1763. Well treated by their allies, the tribes of the Creek Confederacy gained in power, and some British traders, such as Lachlan McGillivray married into the tribes.

The Creek were thus favorably disposed to the Loyalists during the American War of Independence, while the Cherokee sided with the rebels. The American victory brought most of Alabama into the United States (as part of the Georgia Territory), though it would take another string of treaties and purchases to bring Mobile and the Gulf coast under American control in 1813.

Neither Cherokee nor Creek nor Choctaw nor Chickasaw fared well under American rule. Settlers pressed the Indians on all sides, demanding their removal. In 1813, sensing the opportunity afforded by the War of 1812, the Creek went to war. They won the Battle of Burnt Corn, and in August 1814 swept over Fort Mims—strategically placed where the Alabama and Tombigbee rivers met—killing perhaps as many as 250 white settlers.

The triumph was short-lived. Andrew Jackson, leading the Tennessee militia, fought the Creek all the way down the Coosa River, until their final defeat at the Battles of Talladega and Horseshoe Bend on March 27, 1814. In the treaty dictated by the victor, the Creek lost much of their land. The pattern of Indian removal continued, though with less bloodshed, through the next two decades until at last even the peace-loving Cherokee farmers had been routed out of the region, leaving it open to white settlement.

Alabama became a state in 1819. During the ensuing three decades, the state capital moved from one river town to another: from Cahaba, to Tuscaloosa, and finally to Montgomery in 1847. The city of Montgomery had had its first boost, however, in 1821, when steamboat service connected it with Mobile. (Some would say the boost came earlier, in 1802, when a Jewish immigrant named Abraham Mordecai built the region's first cotton gin nearby.) Situated in the heart of the Black Belt, a very fertile plain of black loam soil girdling the middle of the state, Montgomery was the natural shipping and commercial center for the area that would in the following decades become one of the leading cotton producers in the world. The developing textile industries, particularly in Great Britain, created an apparently limitless demand for cotton, and during each decade between 1800 and the Civil War, the South doubled its production.

The planters, whose voices were heard loudest in state politics, advocated the extension of slavery to the territories gained during the Mexican War of 1846–1848. This engendered a controversy about expansion of slavery that, together with federal enforcement of fugitive slave laws and (ironically) "states' rights," led Alabama to the brink of seceding from the Union. The announcement of Abraham Lincoln's election to the Presidency was enough to push Alabamans over the edge: The state seceded on January 11, 1861. (Interestingly, more than 3,000 young men from the northeastern section of the state went north to fight for the Union.)

Less than a month later Jefferson Davis was inaugurated as president of the Confederate States of America in Montgomery, which remained the capital of the Confederacy until May 21. The state was of great value to the Confederacy, not only because of its prominence in cotton production—the rebellion's chief source of cash—and its strategic location, but because it was the young nation's main source of iron. No fighting reached Alabama until 1862, when Union raiders took Huntsville and pressed south.

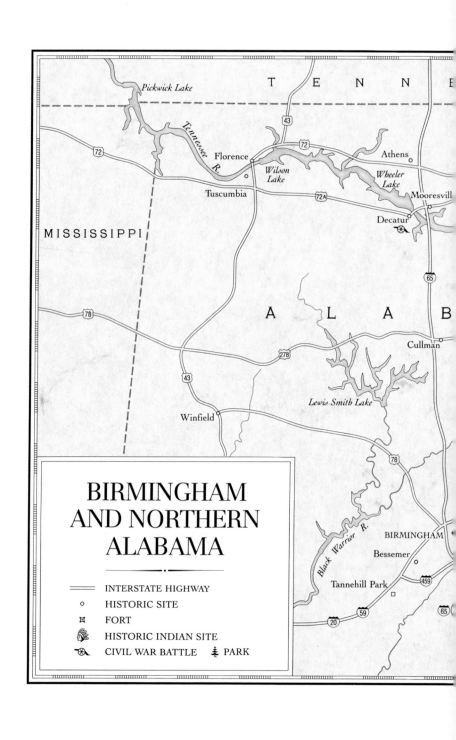

Pickwick Lake

T E N N E

Tennessee R.

72

Florence

Wilson Lake

Tuscumbia

43

72

72A

Athens

Wheeler Lake

Mooresvill

Decatur

65

MISSISSIPPI

A L A B

78

Cullman

278

43

Lewis Smith Lake

Winfield

78

BIRMINGHAM
AND NORTHERN
ALABAMA

Black Warrior R.

BIRMINGHAM

Bessemer

Tannehill Park

459

20

59

65

INTERSTATE HIGHWAY

○ HISTORIC SITE

⊟ FORT

HISTORIC INDIAN SITE

CIVIL WAR BATTLE    ♣ PARK

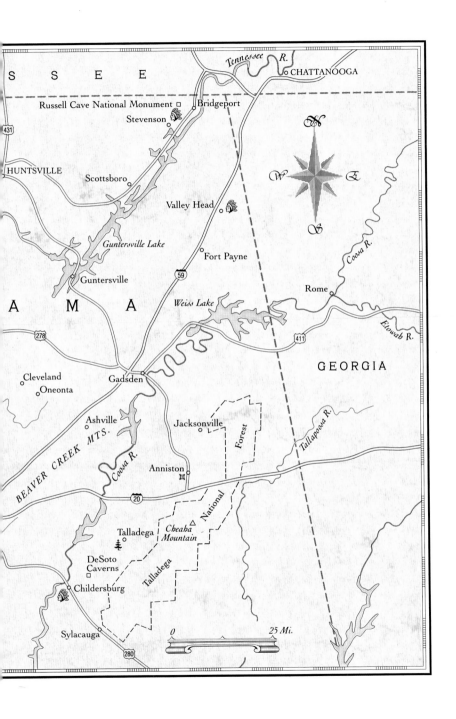

Tennessee R.

CHATTANOOGA

S S E E

Russell Cave National Monument □ Bridgeport
Stevenson

431

HUNTSVILLE

Scottsboro

Valley Head

Guntersville Lake

Fort Payne

Coosa R.

Guntersville

59

Rome

A M A

Weiss Lake

278

Etowah R.

Gadsden

411

GEORGIA

Cleveland
Oneonta

Ashville

Jacksonville

National Forest

Tallapoosa R.

BEAVER CREEK MTS.

Coosa R.

Anniston

20

Talladega

Cheaha Mountain

National

DeSoto Caverns □

Talladega

Childersburg

0            25 Mi.

Sylacauga

280

Mobile was one of the Confederacy's critical ports. This lifeline remained open until August 1864, when Vice Admiral David G. Farragut, uttering his famous "Damn the torpedoes! Full speed ahead!" won the Battle of Mobile Bay. In March and April 1865, 13,000 Federal raiders under General James H. Wilson descended from Tennessee, struck Birmingham, Tuscaloosa, and Montgomery, and destroyed their main objective—the shipyard and arsenal at Selma.

On May 4, 1865, at Citronelle, north of Mobile, General Richard Taylor surrendered the last active Confederate units east of the Mississippi River. The war and the Reconstruction period (1865 to 1874) brought down the slave-based institutions of Alabama, but the Reconstruction administrations, run first by the military and then by carpetbaggers, were unable to establish any lasting reforms. Alabama's large black population was free in name, but the freedom consisted largely of the liberty to become a tenant farmer instead of a slave. After 1874, white supremacy was reestablished with increasing segregation, the prevention of voting by blacks, and a virtual one-party system of Southern Democrats, challenged only briefly by Populists in the early 1890s.

Cotton continued to be the major crop until 1915, when the boll weevil destroyed the crop and at last ended its dominance. Meanwhile, northern Alabama was beginning to come to the fore as an industrial center. The city of Birmingham, now the largest in Alabama, was not founded until 1871, when it was laid out at the junction of two railroad lines. The railroads themselves had been attracted by the Jones Valley, an area rich in iron, coal, and limestone—the ingredients of steel.

The state's rivers again came to prominence during the Great Depression. Floods in the southern regions compounded the damage caused by the market crash of 1929. The creation of the Tennessee Valley Authority in 1933 marked the beginning of the great hydroelectric projects in northern Alabama. The importance of the north increased during the 1950s, when the Redstone Arsenal in Huntsville served as the center for the development of the first U.S. satellite, *Explorer 1*.

Despite industrialization, Alabama was very slow to urbanize. It wasn't until 1960 that the urban population of the state outnum-

OPPOSITE: *The Little River Canyon in De Soto State Park, the deepest canyon east of the Mississippi, was an important base for military expeditions during the Creek Wars.*

bered the rural, in part because of the considerable black emigration from the farms to the cities of Alabama. In recent years, Montgomery and Selma were cradles of the modern civil rights movement. Building on the legacy of other great black Alabamans like Booker T. Washington and George Washington Carver, the Reverend Martin Luther King, Jr., galvanized the urban black population to oppose segregation. The Montgomery Bus Boycott of 1955, the Freedom Rides of 1961, and the constant voter registration and school desegregation fights were the leading efforts in the nation on behalf of black citizens.

The entries for Alabama begin with Mobile and the Gulf Coast, then move to the southeastern Wiregrass country; the central Black Belt; the Birmingham region; and finally, the north.

# MOBILE AND THE GULF

The southern third of Alabama is a mixed region. Once regarded as wasteland, these plains dotted with islands of pine are now an important agricultural area. West and south, the coastal plain slopes gently down to the Gulf of Mexico and to broad, shallow Mobile Bay and the barrier islands beyond.

## MOBILE

Mobile's wealth and the antiquity of its European settlement arose from its fortunate location as the state's only port and the outlet of its major river systems. The French settled here first in 1711. Jean-Baptiste Le Moyne, sieur de Bienville, transferred his main base of operations to what he called Fort Condé, after a disastrous flood at the original settlement, Fort Louis de la Mobile, at Twenty-Seven Mile Bluff on the Mobile River. The British took Mobile in 1763, changing the name of Fort Condé to Fort Charlotte. Seventeen years later, the Spanish sailed into the bay and occupied the town, holding it for more than three decades until in 1813, when it finally came into the possession of the United States.

Mobile is unique in Alabama for its cosmopolitan tradition. Once capital of France's whole Louisiana Territory, it later shipped cotton to ports around the world, and later still, timber products.

After the Civil War, Mobile fared better than its inland neighbors, because whatever had to be shipped had to come to Mobile. Streets and houses show influences from around the world, and a profusion of exotic flowers—azaleas, crape myrtles, and camellias among them—cloak walls and fill gardens. The city's Mardi Gras has been held, with a break during the Civil War years, since it was instituted by Bienville in 1704.

The reconstructed **Fort Condé** (150 South Royal at Church Street, 205–434–7304) re-creates the period when the fort housed the capital of the Louisiana Territory. It displays a small collection of china, tools, and other artifacts discovered in the excavations preceding the reconstruction. The fort serves as a visitor center for the city. Next door is the ca. 1845 **Condé-Charlotte Museum House** (104 Theatre Street, 205–342–4722). There are authentically furnished rooms from each period of Mobile's history: an 1813 Federal dining room, a 1780 Spanish courtyard, two 1860 Confederate parlors, a 1763 English Council Chamber, and a French sitting room (1815) and bedroom (1825).

Mobile's **Cathedral of the Immaculate Conception** (Dauphin and Claiborne streets) was built between 1835 and 1850 in the

*German stained glass lights the interior of Mobile's Cathedral of the Immaculate Conception.* OVERLEAF: *Mobile's reconstructed Fort Condé, originally built by the French to protect Alabama's only port between 1724 and 1735.*

Romanesque style. Its portico and towers were added in the 1890s. The windows, made in Munich, Germany, are particularly noteworthy.

Mobile boasts two remarkable Greek Revival churches from the 1830s: **Christ Episcopal Church** (St. Emanuel and Church streets) and **Government Street Presbyterian Church** (Government and Jackson streets). Both were probably built from designs by James and Charles Dakin, who were assisted by Cary Butt in the work for the Episcopal church, and by James Gallier, Sr., in the work for the Presbyterian church, which is one of the nation's most distinguished church buildings. These two structures, plus the domed **Barton Academy** (504 Government Street), memorialize Mobile's boom years in the 1830s, when its leading citizen, Henry Hitchcock, commissioned a series of splendid buildings from these architects.

The **Richards–D.A.R. House** (256 North Joachim Street, 205–434–7320) sits in the middle of a district full of fine old homes. This Italianate residence, built for a riverboat captain in 1860, has exterior ironwork showing allegorical figures representing the four seasons. It is maintained as a museum, with 1860s period pieces, marble mantles, a cantilevered staircase, and door lights of red Bohemian glass.

Nearby is the **Museum of the City of Mobile** (355 Government Street, 205–434–7569), housed in a graceful 1872 Italianate townhouse. The history of Mobile from prehistory to the present day is traced in the museum's collections, which include Mardi Gras queens' costumes from years past, an assortment of horse-drawn carriages, an extensive Civil War collection, maritime antiques, porcelains, and paintings. Around the corner, the **Phoenix Fire Museum** (205 South Claiborne Street, 205–434–7554) is housed in an 1859 brick fire station, featuring horse-drawn, motorized, and steam-driven fire engines and a collection of firefighting memorabilia dating back to 1819.

## Oakleigh

This outstanding antebellum mansion, situated in the middle of the Oakleigh Garden District—rich in fine homes—was built between 1833 and 1838 by cotton broker James W. Roper. An elabo-

OPPOSITE: *The 1860 Richards-DAR House, encrusted with ornamental ironwork.*

*The parlor of Oakleigh, which was named for the stand of giant oaks that surrounds it.*

rate, T-shaped Greek Revival mansion, it is furnished with fine eighteenth- and nineteenth-century silver, china, and antiques of the Empire, Regency, and Victorian periods. Also on the grounds is the 1850 **Cox-Deasy House,** a Creole cottage characteristic of Gulf Coast plantations of the nineteenth century.

LOCATION: 350 Oakleigh Place. HOURS: 10–4 Monday–Saturday, 2–4 Sunday. FEE: Yes. TELEPHONE: 205–432–1281.

The **Carlen House Museum** (54 Carlen Street, 205–470–7768) is a simple Creole cottage built in 1842, typical of local farmhouses of the period. Furnishings are appropriate to the house and period.

The University of South Alabama campus, with many nineteenth-century structures, contains the **Heustis Medical Museum** (2451 West Fillingim Street, 205–476–3752), a miscellaneous collection of anatomical models, drug items, and surgical instruments.

Mobile's **Fine Arts Museum of the South** (Museum Drive, Langan Park, 205–343–2667) contains a collection of fine art from the seventeenth century forward. The Southern Heritage Collection focuses on furniture and decorative arts of the Southeast. Most pieces date from the nineteenth century, including an 1806 hunt board (a high sideboard) from the Piedmont region. The museum's collection of American paintings of the 1930s and 1940s is national in scope, as is its contemporary crafts collection, containing fine examples of modern glass and handmade furniture.

### USS Alabama Battleship Memorial Park

Here is the World War II battleship *Alabama*, refurbished and open for inspection. The ship carried a crew of 2,500. The submarine USS *Drum* is also on display, along with a collection of planes and weaponry that includes a B-52 bomber.

LOCATION: Battleship Parkway, Mobile Bay. HOURS: 8–Dusk Daily. FEE: Yes. TELEPHONE: 205–433–2703.

## BELLINGRATH GARDENS AND HOME

Walter Bellingrath bought the first of 800 acres of riverside and woodland near Theodore as a fishing camp in 1918, but he and his

*Bellingrath Gardens, south of Mobile.*

wife more and more came to see their property as an opportunity to garden. Today, along with much wild acreage, there are 65 acres of gardens, mostly of subtropical plantings, with a quarter of a million azaleas. Something is blooming every month of the year. In 1937 the Bellingraths built a fifteen-room home in the middle of their garden, furnishing it with antiques collected during their travels. The collection of china and porcelain is particularly fine.

LOCATION: Twenty miles south of Mobile, in Theodore. HOURS: 7–Dusk Daily. FEE: Yes. TELEPHONE: 205–973–2217.

## FORT GAINES AND FORT MORGAN

Guarding the entrance to Mobile Bay, these two forts failed to hold off Vice Admiral Farragut during the Battle of Mobile Bay in 1864. **Fort Gaines** (Dauphin Island, 205–861–6992) is a brick fort completed in 1857. It is furnished with eight cannon, a barracks and kitchen, and a museum that includes documents, shells, maps, the anchor from Farragut's flagship, and other artifacts. **Fort Morgan** (Route 180, 20 miles west of Gulf Shores, 205–540–7125), the best preserved fort in the Mobile area, is a star-shaped brick fort constructed between 1819 and 1834. It endured a fourteen-day siege during the Civil War. The museum's numerous military artifacts and documents detail the role of fortifications on this site.

At 5:30 AM on August 5, 1864, the fourteen-ship fleet of Vice Admiral David G. Farragut began its desperate race under the guns of Fort Morgan. Of equal concern to the Federal commander were the mines, then called torpedoes, protecting the bay. In order to see over the smoke of his own ship's guns, Farragut had himself lashed to the rigging high above the deck. The lead vessel in Farragut's column, the ironclad *Tecumseh*, struck a mine and sank within minutes, taking over ninety men to their deaths. The next ship in the line stopped and began to reverse course, stalling the entire fleet under the Confederate gunfire until Farragut shouted his famous order, "Damn the torpedoes! Full speed ahead!" The fleet surged ahead, bumping into mines that failed to go off. Ahead of them waited the formidable, but slow, Confederate ironclad *Tennessee*, which held out against the Federals for an hour of furious fighting. The Federal victory closed the port (leaving Wilmington, North Carolina, as the Confederacy's only open harbor), but Mobile itself was not taken until the following spring.

OPPOSITE: *Fort Morgan, whose gunners were unable to prevent Farragut's fleet from entering Mobile Bay in August 1864.*

**Historic Blakely Park** (Route 225), just across Mobile Bay near the town of Spanish Fort, preserves breastworks, rifle pits, and redoubts left from the March 1865 defense of the fort against a Union attack. The 3,800-acre site features an annual reenactment of the fight for the fortifications whose batteries guarded the Tensaw River. The park also contains middens (refuse heaps) and mounds that indicate Indian habitation over a period of 4,000 years.

Northeast of Mobile, just off Route 37 about four miles from Tensaw is a simple monument marking the site of **Fort Mims.** It was here on August 30, 1813, that forces of the Creek Confederacy, goaded by white invasions of their lands, overwhelmed a fortified settlement, killing between 250 and 500 people. This was the attack that galvanized Andrew Jackson to lead his Tennessee militia against the Creek.

# T H E   W I R E G R A S S

The far southeast corner of the state is called The Wiregrass, after the stiff native grasses that grow there. The region's chief trade center is **Dothan,** a town that did not really boom until the railroad reached it in 1889. The origin of the town's name is obscure, though there is some suggestion that it refers to a passage in Genesis, "Let us go to Dothan." There is an attractive 1915 **opera house** (115 North St. Andrews Street, 205–793–0127) in town.

Nearby, **Landmark Park** (Route 431 North, about 2.5 miles from Ross Clark Circle, 205–794–3452) contains an 1890s farmstead, blacksmith shops, a barn with old tools, a pioneer log cabin, a planetarium, and a variety of nature trails.

The town of **Ozark** is supposed to have received its name in 1855 from a postmaster who happened to be reading about the Ozark Indians at the time. Once a center of the cotton monoculture, the town's economy has since diversified into peanuts, hogs, and other produce. It is also home to Fort Rucker and the **U.S. Army Aviation Museum** (Novosel and Andrews avenues, Fort Rucker, 205–255–4516), where army aircraft are displayed along with the world's largest collection of helicopters. On East Andrews Avenue is the **Claybank Church,** a split-log Methodist church built in 1852. Its roughness and simplicity reflect the character of life in the region.

Near the town of **Troy,** seat of Pike County, is the **Pike Pioneer Museum** (Route 231 North, 205–566–3597), an excellent

*Eufaula's Shorter Mansion.*

introduction to the culture of The Wiregrass. The complex is comprised of ten structures, including a fully furnished tenant house, a split-log house, and a general store. There are buggies, carriages, harnesses, furniture, and clothing. Demonstrations of old-time crafts are given on a regular basis.

## EUFAULA

Though actually on the edge of The Wiregrass region, Eufaula's location on a bluff above the Chattahoochee River made it an important trade center and cotton embarkation point. (The dammed river now forms Lake Eufaula.) As a result, the town contains many structures of great interest, including the **Shorter Mansion** (340 North Eufaula Avenue, 205–687–3793). Built in 1884 and remodeled in 1906, it contains an excellent museum of Confederate items, Alabama memorabilia, and decorative arts from a wide range of periods. The **Sheppard Cottage** (504 East Barbour Street, 205–687–6664), one of Eufaula's oldest pioneer cottages, is a simple, 1837 home with a back-sloping roofline and a double door with window lights. The **Hart-Milton House** (211 North Eufaula Avenue, 205–687–9755) is a Greek Revival home, hardly altered since the time it was built about 1843.

# T  H  E        B  L  A  C  K        B  E  L  T

The swath of fertile prairie that girds Alabama's midsection, covering a 4,300-square-mile area, takes its common name not from the
slaves who once worked its cotton plantations but from the rich,
black, limestone-and-marl soil. The red hills and the pine and
hardwood cover of the north here give way to broad plains inter-
spersed with woodlands and crisscrossed by rivers. This was the
heart of Alabama's agriculture, and as such, contained for many
years almost all the towns of importance. In the succession of state
capitals—Cahaba, Tuscaloosa, Selma, and Montgomery—all were
located in the Black Belt along a major river artery. (Cahaba in fact
was too near the river; repeated floods were responsible for the loss
of its position as capital.)

The first cotton gin came to the Black Belt around 1800. From
that time until the Civil War, production of cotton was constantly
on the upswing, helped by the continuing importation of slave
labor to work the large and economically efficient one-crop plantations. Most Black Belt residents lived on the land, not in cities, and
at the height of King Cotton's reign, fully 70 percent of them were
black slaves.

Though the Civil War broke the slave system, for the most part
it simply led the planters or their successors to resort to the scarcely
less onerous tenant-farmer system. Cotton was still king, even if a
puppet king, until 1915, when the boll weevil infestation ended the
crop's long dominance. The weevil forced the Black Belt to diversify its agricultural base; the increased availability of farm machinery
also reduced the need for tenant farmers, who flowed out of the
countryside into the local cities and northward to the industrial
centers of the Midwest and East.

## TUSCALOOSA

Tuscaloosa—which means Black Warrior, in Choctaw—copies the
name of a nearby 1809 Creek settlement that was wiped out in the
Creek War of 1813. The current city was established in 1816. The
citizens' bitter disappointment at losing the original state capital,
which went to rival Cahaba in 1819, turned to joy when floods
forced the removal of the seat of state government to Tuscaloosa in
1825. Though the city was destined to keep this honor for scarcely
two decades, it benefited substantially. Citizens planted water oaks
along their streets, adding the nickname "Druid City" to the town.

*The heavily laden* Mary S. Blees *calls at a plantation landing along the Tombigbee River.*

(The Druid City District on the east side of Tuscaloosa is still a good place to see the fine homes that are the town's pride.) The city also captured the state's cultural and intellectual prize, the University of Alabama, in 1831.

Through the time of the Civil War, Tuscaloosa was a sort of ideal of the agrarian, plantation-dominated South, although having lost the state capital in 1846, it was already a conservative and quiet place compared with burgeoning Montgomery. In April 1865, a column of Wilson's raiders led by Colonel Croxton burned most of the university along with stores of military supplies and cotton. Postwar Reconstruction ruined what was left of the local economy. Today Tuscaloosa is a pleasant, small city preserving a strong Old South atmosphere.

## University of Alabama

Among the more stately monuments in Tuscaloosa are the historic buildings of the main campus of the University of Alabama. The **Gorgas House,** a porticoed brick building, was built in 1829 as a dining hall and stewards' residence. It is the only surviving building of the university's original campus designed by the architect William Nichols (he also designed many buildings in Mississippi, most of them destroyed). On display are some items that belonged to Dr. William Crawford Gorgas, a pioneer in the prevention of yellow fever who eradicated disease-carrying mosquitoes from Panama during the construction of the canal. He was the son of one of the university's early presidents. The home is open as a museum, with an extensive collection of silver decorative arts, and many furnishings from a variety of nineteenth-century periods.

Another antebellum structure on campus is the 1841 Greek Revival **President's Mansion** (University Boulevard), a stuccoed brick home with a colonnade of six Ionic columns and a double winding staircase leading to the second-story entrance. When Federal troops came to burn the place down after they captured Tuscaloosa in 1865, the president's wife talked them out of it. Also surviving is the Sentry Box, or **Little Round House** (it is actually octagonal). When Union troops under General Croxton moved into town, they destroyed most of the older public buildings of the campus, but left intact one old classroom, the **Old Observatory,** which dates from 1844. A Tiffany window dedicated to the Alabama Corps is located on the third floor of the Amelia Gayle Gorgas Library (for information, call 205–348–6010).

The **Battle-Friedman House** (1010 Greensboro Avenue, 205–758–2238) was built around 1835 by plantation owner Alfred Battle. He meant it to last: The walls are brick and eighteen inches thick. Battle himself was ruined by the war, and he sold the house for taxes in 1869. For almost a century the home remained in the Friedman family, who remodeled it extensively. Furnished with antiques, it also displays the portraits and silver of the Battles. The **Strickland House** (2828 6th Street) was begun in 1820 by Moses McGuire, a Revolutionary War veteran and the county's first probate judge. Although converted to offices, it remains a striking example of the four-by-four raised-cottage style.

Four private antebellum houses of note are the Greek Revival **Dearing-Swain House** (2111 14th Street, private), a restored building with sixteen columns on three sides, built about 1838. Built in 1835, the **Collier-Booth House** is a two-story mansion at 905 21st Avenue. The **Christian Harper House** (512 Main Avenue, Northport, private) is a solid brick (inside and out) raised cottage dating from 1840, with four chimneys and eight fireplaces. The oldest brick home in the city, the **Gild-Verner House** (1804 University Boulevard, private) dates from 1820.

Tuscaloosa's short era as the state capital is chronicled at the **Old Tavern Museum** (28th Avenue and University Boulevard, 205–758–8163). The building itself is an example of the French balconied style, with French doors leading onto the balcony. Its collection of beds, china, and domestic furnishings includes some from the old state house.

The **Mildred Warner House** (1925 8th Street, 205–553–6200), originally a two-room house built in 1820 that was greatly expanded and remodeled, contains an excellent collection of furniture and art including a Federal dining table with seventeen chairs made in Williamsburg, Virginia; landscapes by two Hudson River school painters, Thomas Cole and Asher B. Durand; Southern landscapes by William Aiken Walker; Western views by Henry Farny; and works by George Catlin, Thomas Moran, Albert Bierstadt, John Henry Twachtman, and Childe Hassam. There is also a collection of antique dolls.

## MOUND STATE MONUMENT

There are twenty mounds on this 320-acre site of an ancient city nestled in wild woodlands. Probably 3,000 people—they may have

*Mound State Monument, the site of a prehistoric Indian city.*

been ancestors of the Choctaw—lived here during the twelfth and thirteenth centuries, when this city was at its height. Another 7,000 people living in smaller towns along the Black Warrior River probably paid tribute to the chiefs of this town.

A fine small museum shows some of the remarkable materials excavated from the mounds, including ceremonial vessels, incised jewelry, trade items, and other artifacts. The people conducted burials in the "floors" of their houses, and excavations have revealed items that had been buried with the dead along with some skeletons, several on exhibit. A reconstructed village on the site illustrates the life of the people who lived here.

LOCATION: Sixteen miles south of Tuscaloosa on Route 69. HOURS: 9–5 Daily. FEE: Yes. TELEPHONE: 205–371–2572.

Another quiet county seat is the town of **Livingston,** named for Edward Livingston, Andrew Jackson's secretary of state. The **Alamuchee-Bellamy Covered Bridge** (on the campus of Livingston University) was built some time before the Civil War with heart of pine, its members joined with wooden pegs.

# DEMOPOLIS

French refugees, exiles from the defeat of Napoleon, founded a colony here in 1817 as part of a two-pronged Bonapartist plan. (The other, militant part was an invasion of Texas and the foundation of a military outpost there.) The peaceful colonists settled here on a bluff above the Tombigbee River, and then at Aigleville, named for the Napoleonic eagle, and tried to raise grapes and olives. Neither imported grapes nor olives would grow, and the neighbors were rude and threatening. By the middle of the next decade, the disappointed French dispersed, but their settlement grew into a burgeoning Black Belt town.

## Gaineswood

Originally a plain log house, Gaineswood was transformed, between 1842 and 1860, by General Nathan Bryan Whitfield into a Regency villa of great elegance. The columned ballroom is breathtaking, and much of the home, with interior details taken from the pattern books of Minard Lafever, is still furnished with the general's antebellum possessions. Though its once extensive grounds (which included a lake) have been reduced, it remains one of the

*Gaineswood, the elegant Demopolis house of General Nathan Bryan Whitfield, was the result of twenty years of planning and building.* OVERLEAF: *Gaineswood's drawing room.*

three or four most interesting houses in America—remarkable for its lavish Greek Revival interior and for the imposing arrangement of its porticos and other architectural elements.

LOCATION: 805 South Cedar Street. HOURS: 9–5 Monday–Saturday, 1–5 Sunday. FEE: Yes. TELEPHONE: 205–289–4846.

**Bluff Hall** (407 North Commission Avenue, 205–289–1666) is named for its commanding position on the limestone bluffs above the Tombigbee. Built as a Federal brick home—the wedding gift of a doting father—in 1832, it received Greek Revival additions in 1840. Furnishings are Empire and mid-Victorian, and there is a room of memorabilia of the Vine and Olive Colony.

## GREENSBORO

This Black Belt town preserves more than 150 nineteenth-century structures in its downtown historic district, including mid-century cottages, Greek Revival houses, and late-nineteenth-century

commercial buildings such as the Queen Anne style **Greensboro Hotel** and the **opera house**. The **Noel-Ramsey House** (Market and South streets) was built about 1820 by the French settlers Thomas and Anne Hurtel Noel. It served as the Catholic church for settlers of the Vine and Olive Colony. At the western end of the historic district is **Magnolia Grove** (Main and Hobson streets, 205–624–8618), an austere, eight-room Greek Revival house built ca. 1840 as a townhouse by a cotton planter, Isaac Croom. It was the childhood home of Croom's nephew, Richmond Pearson Hobson, a naval hero in the Spanish-American War and, as U.S. congressman, the author of the Prohibition Amendment to the Constitution. The house displays furnishings from the 1830s to the early 1900s.

## CAHABA

Southwest of Selma is Cahaba, a town that once was among the principal cities in the state. In 1819, it became the state capital, only to lose that eminence six years later, largely owing to frequent floods that once compelled the legislature to evacuate by boat. Still, it remained the county seat until after the Civil War, when even that honor was shifted slightly north to Selma. For many years, Cahaba was a virtual ghost town, but is being rehabilitated as the **Cahaba Historical Park** (Route 22, eight miles southwest of Selma, 205–875–2529). The complex includes a visitor center, reconstructed streets with interpretive signs on various ruins, a single wood-frame house dating from the 1840s, and archaeological exhibits at the sites where research is underway. During the Civil War, Union prisoners were held here at "Camp Morgan."

## SELMA

The town of Selma is in the heart of the Black Belt. It was named by one of its founders, Senator (and later Vice President) William Rufus King, for a place in a poem by the legendary Gaelic poet Ossian. Like so many important Alabama towns, Selma is located on the bluffs above a river, the Alabama River in this case, and its situation has made it both an important trade stop and agricultural area since it was first platted in 1819.

During the years before the Civil War, Selma had a plantation aristocracy second to none. Cotton planters vied in the creation of fine homes and raised prize thoroughbreds on the side. Selma's central location and excellent river and rail communications made

*The Reverend Martin Luther King, Jr., leading a civil rights march in Selma in March 1965.*

the town an important munitions depot and foundry for the Confederacy—three battleships were built here as well as rifles, cannonballs, and other war materiel—making it a prime target for
General James H. Wilson's raiders when they swept into Alabama
in 1865. The fall of Selma on April 2, 1865, was notable not only
for its effect on Confederate industrial strength and for the capture of most of General Nathan Bedford Forrest's defenders, but
for the behavior of Wilson's guerrillas, who looted the town.

Today, Selma is the industrial and commercial center of a
diversified agricultural area. Many still remember it for the violent
confrontation at the Edmund Pettus Bridge on March 7, 1965,
when Sheriff Jim Clark's deputies and Alabama state troopers
attacked the Selma-to-Montgomery voting rights march. The
bridge and Brown Chapel A.M.E. church, a headquarters for the
civil rights movement where marches were organized, are monuments to the movement that helped achieve the passage of the
Voting Rights Act only six months later.

## Sturdivant Hall

The best surviving example of antebellum Selma homes, the mar-
velously ornate Neoclassical Sturdivant Hall was built over a period
of almost three years beginning in 1853. The builder, Thomas
Helm Lee, brought in craftsmen to execute the marble mantles, the
plaster ceilings, and the ornate vine-and-grape-leaf molding, much
of which can still be seen today. Frescoes were added in the 1870s.
Furnishings include a few pieces from the original owners, but
most are appropriate to the 1850s period. Among these is a rare
George Washington commemorative clock, made in France in
1807.

Next door to the mansion, several buildings of the 1820s,
brought here from other parts of the state, are being restored.

LOCATION: 713 Mabry Street. HOURS: 9–4 Tuesday–Saturday, 2–4
Sunday. FEE: Yes. TELEPHONE: 205–872–5626.

The **Joseph T. Smitherman Historic Building** (109 Union Street,
205–874–2174) was built by the local Masonic lodge to be a college-

*Selma's Old Depot Museum contains exhibits ranging from the Civil War to civil rights.*

level academy. The brick structure in the Greek Revival style has been used for many purposes and now houses civic organizations and a small museum featuring displays of old maps, Confederate money, and munitions from the navy foundry.

The **Old Depot Museum** (Water Avenue and Martin Luther King, Jr., Street, 205–875–9918) is housed in an 1891 Louisville & Nashville railroad station. The history of railroads in Selma is a growing specialty here: A Western Railway boxcar and a Southern Railway caboose are on exhibit, reminders that the town once saw twenty-seven daily runs on three different rail lines. There is also an interpretive history museum, with Civil War artifacts and paper and photographic memorabilia on local heroes like William Rufus King, generals E. W. Pettus and J. T. Morgan, and Benjamin Turner, the first black man from Selma elected to the U.S. House of Representatives. Voted in during the Reconstruction 1870s, Turner was said to have been so incensed at the behavior of Wilson's raiders during the war that he sponsored the introduction of a bill in Congress to return to Confederate veterans their right to vote and hold office.

## PRATTVILLE

Just northwest of Montgomery is the town of Prattville, named for Daniel Pratt, the state's leading industrialist, who founded a much-improved cotton ginning factory here in 1833. Nearby is **Buena Vista** (County Road 4, between Highways 31N and 14, 205–361–0961), a mansion built between 1835 and 1840, reputedly for a riverboat captain named Major William Montgomery. A portico was added, and changes made in the interior, during a 1916 renovation. It is furnished with antiques.

## MOUNTAIN CREEK

Toward the top of the Black Belt are several towns with interesting local history museums, including the **Confederate Memorial Park** (Route 63, off Route 23, 205–755–1990), on what was once the site of the twenty-two-building Confederate Soldiers Home. Two cemeteries remain, as does a small museum displaying uniforms, weapons, and historical photographs of the home. Two simple country buildings from the 1890s, a gabled church and a post office, have been moved here.

# MONTGOMERY

Montgomery city and Montgomery County were named for different Montgomerys, both military men. The city is named for General Richard Montgomery, a Revolutionary War hero—a compromise arrived at by the two groups of land speculators trying to start towns here on the banks of the Alabama River in the 1810s.

The city officially came to exist on December 3, 1819, and within a few years it was in steamboat communication with Mobile and stagecoach communication with points east. Located in the heart of the rich Black Belt, it quickly became the center of plantation Alabama, a status recognized when Montgomery was made the state capital in 1846, supplanting Tuscaloosa. Five years later, railroad communications had been established both to the northeast and the southwest.

Alabama was among the first states to secede from the Union at the outset of the Civil War, and the Alabama Secession Convention met in Montgomery on January 6, 1861. A little over a month later, Jefferson Davis was elected president of the Confederacy and took the oath of office standing before the state capitol. The Confederate States of America had its capital here briefly, until it was moved to Richmond, Virginia, the Confederacy's major industrial center, in May 1861.

Nevertheless, Montgomery itself was not spared invasion by Federal troops. On April 12, 1865, Wilson's raiders entered the city and retreating rebels burned the city's cotton stores. The raiders finished the job, demolishing whatever communications and industrial facilities might have served the Southern cause. Montgomery was a shambles when Reconstruction came, but it gradually rebuilt its influence by serving as the seat of state government, as well as by diversifying agriculture, raising livestock, and attracting light industry. In the twentieth century, with the decline of the tenant farm system and an increase in the number of industrial and service jobs in the cities, the urban blacks who concentrated in Montgomery gradually organized and gained political strength, becoming a politically active force in the city. The first major victory of the civil rights movement came with the Montgomery Bus Boycott of 1955, during which local blacks—the overwhelming

OPPOSITE: *Alabama's State Capitol, where Jefferson Davis was sworn in as president of the Confederacy.*

majority of the bus system's riders—refused to ride the buses until seating was desegregated. At that time Martin Luther King, Jr., had his church and his base of support in Montgomery.

The domed **State Capitol** (Bainbridge Avenue, between Washington and Monroe avenues) was completed in 1847, burned down in 1849, and was rebuilt in 1851, with Neoclassical additions constructed between 1885 and 1912. The additions and remodelings have not destroyed its harmonious proportions. On January 11, 1861, the Alabama Secession Convention passed the Ordinance of Secession in the current House of Representatives chamber; a little over a month later, Jefferson Davis was inaugurated on the front portico—today a bronze star marks the approximate spot.

Across the street is the **First White House of the Confederacy** (644 Washington Avenue, 205–261–4624), a simple frame house built in the 1830s and remodeled in the Italianate style in the 1850s. Jefferson Davis lived with his family here for the three months that Montgomery was the Confederate capital. Restored and furnished with some of the Davis family's belongings, the building also houses other Confederate artifacts.

A more capacious view of Alabama's past is available next door at the **Alabama Department of Archives and History** (624 Washington Avenue, 205–261–4361). The museum there contains a fine collection of Indian artifacts from the Montgomery area, including some rare effigy vessels and a large number of Spanish, French, and English trade goods. Military artifacts from the 1830s to the present are also on display, as well as many examples of decorative arts and material culture items used by Alabamans during the nineteenth century. A room is devoted to Alabama native son William Rufus King, who was elected vice president of the United States, sharing the ticket with Franklin Pierce. King was inaugurated in March 1853 and served until his death a month later.

The **Rice-Semple-Haardt House** (725 Monroe Street, 205–261–3184), up the street from the capitol, was built in 1855 by a local judge as a one-story Greek Revival cottage with a box-columned portico. Later a second story was added with Italianate and Gothic Revival influences. There are some period furnishings in the house, but it is chiefly known for the **Lurleen B. Wallace Museum,** two rooms dedicated to the memory of George Wallace's wife, who succeeded him as governor.

OPPOSITE: *Confederate Navy memorabilia in the collection of the Alabama Department of Archives and History.*

A rich and interesting tour that traces much of Montgomery's history in a brief area is the **Old North Hull Street Historic District** (205–263–4355), north of the capitol. There are twenty-seven restored buildings in the area, many refurnished according to their period, beginning with an 1818 tavern and ending with an 1898 one-room schoolhouse. There are barns, carriage houses, pioneer cabins, a shotgun house, and more.

Several well-restored homes line South Perry Street. The **Teague House** (468 South Perry Street, 205–834–6000) is an ornate Greek Revival mansion, built by a livery stable magnate in 1848. The refurbished interior has original full-length mirrors, free-standing columns in the hall, and a collection of period furnishings. **Knox Hall,** a private office down the street at 419 South Perry, is even more opulent; it is not open to visitors, but its exterior Corinthian columns are impressive in themselves. Another fine Greek Revival mansion is the **Lomax House** (235 South Court Street). Built in 1847, the Doric-columned building shows some Virginian influences in its portico and parapet chimneys. It now houses an insurance company. A sort of capstone to the neighborhood is the **St. John's Episcopal Church** (113 Madison Avenue, at North Perry Street). Built in the popular Gothic Revival style in

OPPOSITE: *Part of Montgomery's Old North Hull Street Historic District, which comprises twenty-seven restored buildings.* ABOVE: *A one-room schoolhouse in the district.*

1855, this was the church where the family of Jefferson Davis worshiped; their pew is marked. The elaborate painted ceiling has been restored.

The **Dexter Avenue King Memorial Baptist Church** (454 Dexter Avenue, 205–263–3970) was the church of Rev. Martin Luther King, Jr. As pastor during the early 1950s, the Reverend Vernon Johns tried unsuccessfully to get Montgomery blacks to boycott the segregated city bus lines. In 1954 he resigned, to be replaced by Dr. King. A year later, the Montgomery Bus Boycott was underway. The restored brick church—Victorian with Italianate influence—has a mural in the basement which depicts King's participation in the struggles from Montgomery to Memphis.

Running west, Dexter Avenue terminates at **Court Square,** a focal point of the old downtown and home of the county courthouse, first erected here in 1822. The restored square still contains the 1885 **Court Square Fountain,** topped by a statue of Hebe, goddess of youth. The **Old Central Bank** (1 Dexter Avenue) is a solid Renaissance Revival building built by Philadelphia architect Stephen Decatur Button in 1856. Across the square is the **Winter Building,** an early 1840s Italianate structure, from which the telegram was sent instigating the attack on Fort Sumter, the first clash of the Civil War.

West of Court, a block of old streets runs down to the riverfront. At the corner of Coosa and Bibb streets is the 1850s **Murphy House** (205–240–1600), a fine Greek Revival mansion erected for the cotton broker John H. Murphy, who was also a founder of the city waterworks. Appropriately, the town's water company has its offices here today, and an elegantly furnished double parlor with its original chandeliers is open to the public.

Commerce Street, toward the river, preserves brick commercial buildings built in the last quarter of the nineteenth century to serve the nearby railroad and river depots. The **Union Station** (300 Water Street), built by the Louisville & Nashville line in 1898, is noted for its 600-foot-long gabled train shed with beautiful trusses and stained glass.

## FORT TOULOUSE AND JACKSON PARK

About twelve miles northeast of Montgomery is a park that recreates two forts that once stood at this spot. The first, Fort Toulouse, was created by French settler Bienville in 1717 to control trade with the Creek Indians; the second, Fort Jackson, was built by Andrew Jackson during his war against the Creeks. Both palisades have been reconstructed from the ground up, and a small museum displays items found in archaeological digs, including cannonballs, gun parts, and old bottles. Indian arrowheads, vessels, and other artifacts come from an Indian mound located on the site.

LOCATION: Route 231, one mile south of Wetumpka. HOURS: April through October: 6–9 Daily; November through March: 8–5 Daily. FEE: None. TELEPHONE: 205–567–3002.

## HORSESHOE BEND NATIONAL MILITARY PARK

In the "horseshoe bend" of the Tallapoosa River near present-day Dadeville, the remnants of the Creek Confederacy met Andrew Jackson's forces in the decisive battle of the Creek War of 1813–1814. On March 27, 1814, Jackson's 3,000 Tennessee militiamen defeated a force of 1,000 Creek, killing about 800 of them. This victory brought the first fame to the man who would later become president of the United States. The Creek's defeat led to their signing a treaty which ceded their ancestral lands to white settlers.

*Antagonists at the 1814 Battle of Horseshoe Bend: Andrew Jackson and the Creek Chief Menawa. Jackson's portrait was painted by John Wesley Jarvis, Menawa's by Henry Inman.*

The park maintains exhibits on the Creek War and on Creek culture, as well as a marked tour of the battle site.

LOCATION: Route 49, 12 miles north of Dadeville. HOURS: 8–6 Daily. FEE: None. TELEPHONE: 205–234–7111.

## TUSKEGEE INSTITUTE NATIONAL HISTORIC SITE

East from Montgomery in the heart of the Black Belt is Tuskegee, its name a corruption of a local Indian word designating a village that once stood nearby. The Creek, French, and British have all occupied the area, but the town's enduring fame is owed to Booker T. Washington, the man who founded the Tuskegee Institute here in 1881. The great campus that began a year later was raised with student-made bricks and student labor.

Washington's pioneering effort to create a trade school for black people was lauded around the nation and attracted contributions from the likes of John D. Rockefeller, Collis P. Huntington, and Andrew Carnegie. Though there was controversy between Washington and other black leaders such as W. E. B. Du Bois as to

*The Tuskegee Institute, founded in 1881 as a trade school for black students by Booker T. Washington, became a degree-granting college in 1927.*

*The den of Booker T. Washington's house, The Oaks, with original furnishings.*

whether black students should be steered to trade schools instead of colleges, there is no question that the institute served as a source of skills and, perhaps more importantly, of a cadre of teachers for Southern blacks. The issue became moot in 1927, when under Washington's successor the school became a degree-granting college. The campus comprises some 160 buildings.

Washington's campus home, **The Oaks,** was built in 1899 also by students with their own manufactured bricks. The Queen Anne Revival house designed by R. R. Taylor, the first black graduate of M.I.T. and a Tuskegee professor, is furnished with original family furniture and is open for tours.

Also on campus is the **George Washington Carver Museum,** containing everything from Dr. Carver's plant collections to his art and needlework. A genius of applied horticulture and chemistry, Carver came to work as head of the agriculture department at Tuskegee in 1896, spurning higher paying work. His advances with peanuts and other southern crop plants were important, and in 1917 he was made a fellow of the Royal Society.

LOCATION: 1212 Old Montgomery Road. HOURS: 9–5 Daily. FEE: None. TELEPHONE: 205-727-6390.

# NORTHERN ALABAMA

Roughly the northern third of Alabama consists of the trailing
edge of the Appalachian Mountains, together with the great Tennessee River Valley, which crosses the state from east to west.
Cheaha Mountain, the highest point in the state, is here, measuring
2,407 feet above sea level. Some of the oldest Indian settlements
and caves are to be found in this area as well, together with the
state's most modern industrial and high-tech urban centers.

White settlement in the region came very early, with settlers
moving in from the Piedmont of Virginia, the Carolinas, and
Georgia. Culturally and politically, the highland settlers had more
in common with the Appalachian mountaineers of Tennessee,
Kentucky, and Virginia than with the planters of Alabama's Black
Belt. This is where a group of fiercely independent small farmers
proposed seceding from the Confederacy during the Civil War to
set up their own state of Nickajack. Union general William T.
Sherman's personal bodyguard was made up of north Alabama
cavalrymen. Most development in the highlands has come since
World War I with the creation of the Tennessee Valley Authority
during the depression and, later, the Redstone Arsenal and then
the Marshall Space Flight Center in Huntsville.

## BIRMINGHAM

Birmingham sits in the Jones Valley, ringed by hills so red with iron
hematite that one was simply called Red Mountain. The valley was
first settled around 1813 by a man who gave the place his name;
previously the local Indians—known as "Red Sticks" for the red
paint they daubed on themselves—came into the valley to hunt and
trade. A few small villages grew up during the nineteenth century,
the most important being a hamlet called Elyton, named for the
government land surveyor who had managed the sale of its lots.
The Confederates found some use for the local iron ore during the
Civil War, though most of it was forged at Selma.

In 1870, the South & North and the Alabama & Chattanooga
railroads (later to become the Louisville & Nashville and the Alabama Great Southern) crisscrossed in the middle of the Jones
Valley, and there, with the help of a team of shrewd land speculators, Birmingham was born. Those who named the town knew its
potential: Coal, iron, and limestone—the ingredients of steel—
were plentiful in the surrounding hills; they named it after the

great British industrial center. Despite a cholera epidemic and a national financial panic within two years of the town's 1871 founding, Birmingham was bound for boom times. The attitude of its capitalists was perhaps typified by one of their ranks, Henry F. DeBardeleben: "Life is just a big game of poker."

The boom continued until the Great Depression, creating a major city so quickly that it often seemed but half finished. Foundries lit the sky with their shining molten metal, smog filled the air, but yesterday's mansions were today's ruins. Birmingham's iron and steel industry never really recovered after the depression. Birmingham's largest employer is no longer the steel mills but the University of Alabama.

The reverberations of the civil rights movement were felt deeply here; Martin Luther King, Jr.'s famous "Letter from a Birmingham Jail" was written in 1963, at the height of desegregation demonstrations, mass arrests, the pelting of black children with high-pressure fire hoses, and the eventual murder of four black girls in the firebombing of a church.

*A massive statue of Vulcan, cast of Alabama iron for the 1904 Saint Louis Exposition, stands as a monument to Birmingham's iron industry.*

A bird's-eye view of Birmingham can be had from its most prominent monument. On top of Red Mountain is a fifty-five-foot-high **statue of Vulcan** (Valley View Drive, 205–254–2699), standing on a 124-foot pedestal. The ancient god of metallurgy was made out of native Alabama iron for the 1904 Louisiana Purchase Exhibition in St. Louis by sculptor Giuseppe Moretti. At the fair Vulcan held a giant jar of pickles in his hand; today he holds a lamp (it burns green when everyone in town drives safely and red when there has been a recent fatality).

The geology on which Birmingham's steel industry is based can be seen at the nearby **Red Mountain Museum** (1421 Twenty-second Street South, 205–933–4104). A walkway leads along a cutaway face of the mountain, where markers show the history of the area as revealed by rocks deposited over 150 million years. There is also a specimen of the marine dinosaur called a mosasaur on display. Alabama is unusually rich in fossils of prehistoric whales, sloths, sabertooth tigers, and other large mammals because in prehistoric times the region was twice covered by the sea and twice emerged lush and fertile.

In Birmingham itself is the **Sloss Furnaces National Historic Landmark** (First Avenue North and Thirty-second Street, 205–324–1911), whose proximity to Red Mountain gives a very clear idea of how natural it was to make iron here. Constructed between 1902 and 1931, the furnaces operated until 1971. A tour takes visitors through boilers, ovens, and casting areas.

An unusual and interesting museum in the northeastern part of town is the **Southern Museum of Flight** (4343 Seventy-third Street North, 205–833–8226), with displays ranging from a 1966 F-4 Phantom fighter to a 1910 Curtiss Pusher and the 1935 Fairchild, as well as other antique planes and equipment. It is not widely known that the Wright Brothers opened America's first flying school near Montgomery, Alabama, in 1910. A display case commemorates the school. The museum also has a 1925 plane that was among the first ever flown by Delta Air—a crop duster.

The **Birmingham Museum of Art** (2000 Eighth Avenue North, 205–254–2565) has a notable collection of Renaissance art, bronzes by Frederic Remington, a varied collection of decorative arts, and the largest Wedgwood collection outside of England.

OPPOSITE: *John Singer Sargent's 1904 portrait of Lady Helen Vincent, Viscountess of d'Abernon, is part of the Birmingham Museum of Art's varied collections (detail).*

There are also archaeological exhibits about Alabama's Indians, smaller collections of American and Oriental art, and a growing collection of Alabama textiles and furnishings.

On the campus of the University of Alabama at Birmingham is the **Alabama Museum of the Health Sciences and Reynolds Historical Library** (1700 University Boulevard, 205–934–4475). Dr. Lawrence Reynolds, a prominent radiologist, left the university his collection of antique medical instruments and books, some of which date to the thirteenth century.

## Arlington Antebellum Home and Gardens

This stately colonnaded home was once part of Elyton, the small town that stood here from the early nineteenth century until absorbed by Birmingham. It is now the only antebellum house left in Birmingham. It was built by Judge William Mudd in the mid-nineteenth century, possibly after design examples printed in a popular pattern book, Asher Benjamin's *The Practical House Carpenter.*

Mudd served in both pre– and post–Civil War legislatures, and was one of the ten founders of Birmingham. Robert Munger, a subsequent owner, renovated the house at the turn of the century, adding Colonial Revival features: a rear portico, porte cochere, and a second-floor balcony in front. The interior of his house, redecorated in the Colonial Revival mode by later owners, displays an extensive collection of decorative arts and Southern furniture, including a bedroom suite attributed to the noted New Orleans cabinetmaker, Prudent Mallard, as well as fine English furniture. A portrait of a young girl, attributed to Nicola Marschall, who designed the first Confederate flag, hangs in the house. Also of interest is the portrait of the Seminole chief Osceola, painted by William Laning in 1838, while the chief was a prisoner at Fort Moultrie, South Carolina, during the Seminole War.

LOCATION: 331 Cotton Avenue SW. HOURS: 10–4 Tuesday–Saturday, 1–4 Sunday. FEE: Yes. TELEPHONE: 205–780–5656.

# BESSEMER

Industrialist Henry F. DeBardeleben founded Bessemer in 1886. From the name of the town—homage to the man who invented the steel-making process—his intent was clear. The town was an important steel-making center in its day. The **Hall of History Museum** (1905 Alabama Avenue, 205–426–1633) contains a varied collection of local-history material, including Indian artifacts excavated from local Indian mounds, pioneer tools, the printing press used by Bessemer's first newspaper, old photos, jewelry, tools, Indian pottery, and a typewriter "liberated" from Hitler's Eagle Nest by a local GI. The museum is housed in a 1916 Southern Railroad depot with an oriental-looking three-tiered roof.

The **Bessemer Historic Pioneer Homes,** now owned and maintained by the West Jefferson County Historical Society, predate the town's founding. The **Sadler House** was begun as a log house in 1815, then substantially refurbished and expanded in 1840. It ended up being a substantial "dogtrot" home, with its upstairs areas segregated for boys and girls of the family (the only way to get from one upstairs area to another was by going downstairs and across the dogtrot). Also here is an example of a "parson's chamber," a downstairs room with a separate entrance, left open so that the circuit parson, or another traveler, might occupy it during the night without disturbing the sleeping family. Some interesting early furniture is inside, along with a set of china buried by the family during the Civil War. In the yard is an ancient pecan tree, planted by the family during the 1840s to honor a newborn daughter. According to the custom, it ought to have been cut down on her wedding day, and its wood used to make a hope chest. Two other antebellum homes are nearby: the **McAdory House,** home of Bessemer's first mayor, and the **Owen House.** Tours of all three can be arranged through the Bessemer Chamber of Commerce (205–425–3253).

## TANNEHILL PARK

This state park centers around the historic 1855 blast furnaces that were among the first iron-processing facilities in Alabama. There are also over forty restored log homes and early stores or functional buildings on the 1,500-acre property, most of them refurnished. Crafts, from quilting to vintage photography, are demonstrated periodically. A museum houses displays on blast-furnace processes, the Civil War, and other topics of local interest.

LOCATION: Exit 100 off Route 59, thirty miles west of Birmingham. HOURS: 7–Dusk Daily. FEE: Yes. TELEPHONE: 205–477–5711.

# CULLMAN

This prosperous farm town and light manufacturing center north of Birmingham was founded in 1873 by Colonel John Cullman, who envisioned a cooperative agricultural community peopled with industrious immigrants from his native Germany. Exiled from his homeland because of his alleged participation in a plot to assassinate the czar—Russia then controlled his native Landau—Cullman first intended to bring over only his family to the new land. Within a year, however, he had imported five families and created a town with spacious, 100-foot-wide streets. When he had finished, he had been responsible for the immigration of 20,000 Germans to the town.

The **Cullman County Museum** (211 Second Avenue NE, 205–739–1258) offers an excellent introduction to the area. Along with a collection of Indian arrowheads and pottery, it features a re-created nineteenth-century Cullman street scene, with many period shop rooms. Also of interest are displays of furniture and documents relating to the town's founder.

Nine miles west is the **Clarkson Covered Bridge** (Route 278W, 205–739–3530), at 296 feet the longest of many such wooden bridges in the state. Nearby are reproductions of a pioneer log cabin and a gristmill.

The backcountry east of Cullman in Blount County contains a number of covered bridges. (Information and a map are available from the Blount County–Oneonta Chamber of Commerce, 500 New Street, Oneonta, 205–274–2153.) It is a hilly landscape thickly covered with a deciduous forest that creates spectacular autumn scenery. Once the territory of the Creek Indians, it remains relatively untouched by the industrial transformation nearby.

All four surviving bridges were constructed during the 1920s and 1930s to provide safe crossing over the county's many creeks and the two tributaries of the Black Warrior River, the Locust and Mulberry forks. At 96 feet, the **Old-Easley Road Covered Bridge** (near Route 160 at Oneonta) is short when compared with the nearby **Horton Mill Covered Bridge** (off Route 75 at Oneonta), which is more than twice as long. Perched 70 feet above the river, it seems to be a highway between treetops. Westward near the town of Cleveland is the even longer **Swann-Joy Covered Bridge** (off

OPPOSITE: *Tannehill Park, near Bessemer, which contains more than forty restored pioneer buildings.*

Route 79), but the longest of all is the **Nectar Covered Bridge** (off Route 160), a 385-foot four-span bridge across the Locust Fork near the town of Nectar.

## FLORENCE

The town perches on a bluff high above the Tennessee River, with hills rising behind it. The Creek, Cherokee, Chickasaw, and earlier tribes inhabited the area at various times, and the first white settlers leased land from Chief Doublehand as early as 1807. But Florence owes its name to the nostalgia of the surveyor who laid it out, an Italian named Ferdinand Sannoner. Because it was on Andrew Jackson's military road and near the Natchez Trace, and possessed excellent water transportation, the town was popular with settlers heading west.

Hydroelectric power has helped Florence become a modern city. The **Wilson Dam** (Route 133, off Route 72, 205–386–2442) was the grandfather of all Tennessee Valley Authority dams, having originally been constructed as part of a wartime project starting in 1917 and ending in 1925. Now under the control of the T.V.A., it has the biggest generating capacity of any dam on the river. Tours visit the turbine rooms and tunnels deep beneath the dam.

Florence is also home to four monuments that commemorate the range of Alabama culture. The most ancient is the **Indian Mound and Museum** (South Court Street, 205–760–6427), a preserved ceremonial mound whose museum displays fluted points, stone pipes, and pottery dating from the Paleolithic to the Mississippian period. Something of the character of the nineteenth-century American town is preserved at **Pope's Tavern** (203 Hermitage Drive, 205–760–6439), a slave-built tavern dating from ca. 1820. The simple one-and-a-half-story building with its long veranda served as a tavern and as a hospital for both Confederate and Union troops. Recently refurbished, it houses a local-history collection including local and imported furniture of the period and items such as a surgical saw used during the tavern's hospital days. The **W. C. Handy Home, Museum, and Library** (620 West College Street, 205–760–6434) is a simple log cabin where the great bluesman was born in 1873. He lived here until early manhood, when he headed off, first to the steel mills of Birmingham, then to Chicago, St. Louis, and Memphis. The house is furnished with turn-of-the-century antiques, and the adjacent museum displays Handy's trumpet and the piano on which he composed "St. Louis Blues," among other artifacts. The **Kennedy-Douglass Center for the Arts** (217 East Tuscaloosa Street, 205–760–6380) is housed in a 1918 Georgian style mansion. In addition to the performing arts, the center houses rotating art exhibits and one room is set aside as a memorial to Hiram Kennedy-Douglass, son of the man who built the house and an important figure in local history.

Just south of Florence, in the town of **Tuscumbia,** is the birthplace of another famous Alabaman, Helen Keller. **Ivy Green** (300 West North Commons, 205–383–4066) is a one-and-a-half-story frame cottage built by David Keller, Helen's grandfather, ca. 1820. The house is furnished with nineteenth-century pieces and contains mementoes of Keller's early life. A small office building on the grounds was converted to a bedroom; Keller was born there in 1880. Also on the grounds is the pump at which her teacher, Anne Sullivan, taught Keller her first word: water. During the Civil War, Confederate and Union soldiers were nursed in the home.

*Helen Keller lived in this small cottage with her teacher, Anne Sullivan.*

# DECATUR

A busy railroad, market, and industrial center on the banks of the Tennessee River, Decatur is named for the naval hero Commodore Stephen Decatur. By 1832, it had become important as the eastern terminus of the Tuscumbia Railroad, the first railroad west of the Alleghenies, constructed to allow cargo to circumvent the dangerous Muscle Shoals on the Tennessee River.

All but a few buildings of old Decatur were destroyed in seesaw struggles during the Civil War. One survivor is the state bank building built in 1833 and now restored as the **Old State Bank Museum** (925 Bank Street NW, 205–350–5060). The Greek Revival bank features five huge limestone pillars quarried at the nearby plantation of the bank director and president. Its opening was attended by then Vice President Martin Van Buren. Portions of the interior are maintained as the bank was then, including a restored cashier's apartment, with 1830s furnishings. Also of interest are rotating exhibits and, on the grounds, an antebellum log cabin, moved to the site from the banks of the Tennessee. Walking-tour maps identifying the town's antebellum and Victorian buildings are available from the bank. The 1829 **Dancy-Polk House** (901 Railroad Street NW, private) was built in the Palladian style by the town's founding citizen and is now a bed-and-breakfast inn. The **Rhea-McEntire House** (1105 Sycamore Street NW, private), a remarkable 1836 Palladian-Jeffersonian mansion, was built by merchant John S. Rhea. At various times during the Civil War the house was headquarters for officers of both sides.

West of Decatur on Route 20 is the frame plantation dwelling of Alabama's most famous general, Fighting Joe Wheeler, the commander of Confederate cavalry and later an important general in the United States Army and a congressman. Set in an impressive grove of oak trees, the **Wheeler Home** (thirteen miles west of Decatur, 205–637–8513) is preserved with period furnishings.

# MOORESVILLE

Mooresville is one of the best places in northern Alabama to recapture a sense of nineteenth-century town life. Founded in 1818, it is the oldest town in the region, and preserves an unusual number of early buildings, including antebellum houses and a fine brick church from 1820.

# ATHENS

Founded in 1818, with the name Athenson, the town is the site of a number of interesting Greek Revival homes. Information on a walking tour along the town's tree-lined streets is available from the chamber of commerce (205–232–2600). The **Pryor House** (North Jefferson Street, private), now an apartment building, was built ca. 1836. Senator Luke Pryor, who lived in the house from 1854 to 1900, had it remodeled in the Italianate style in 1868. The **Beaty-Mason House** (Beaty Street, private) was built in 1826 by planter Robert Beaty; in 1845 the facade was remodeled in the Greek Revival style. The house is now the residence of the president of Athens College. A slave cabin still stands in back of the house. The 1835 **Houston House** (101 North Houston Street, 205–233–8770), also Greek Revival, was the home of George S. Houston, the first Democratic governor after Reconstruction. It now houses the local library and a museum of local history, including Indian artifacts and Civil War relics.

# HUNTSVILLE

In 1805 a Virginian named John Hunt was looking for a place to settle, and decided to stay in this beautiful, mountain-backed valley. The first substantial settler, Leroy Pope, arrived four years later, promptly naming the nascent town for his namesake Alexander Pope's residence, Twickenham. The less pretentious Huntsville became the name of the town, though its great trove of historic antebellum houses, located south and east of the courthouse in the area bounded by Echols and McClung avenues, Adams Street, Lowe Avenue, and Williams Avenue, is known as the Twickenham District (a walking tour is available from the Convention and Visitors Bureau, 205–535–4230). Here are many distinguished private homes dating as early as the second decade of the nineteenth century. Particularly interesting is the **Leroy Pope Walker Home** (McClung and Echols avenues, private). It was built by Leroy Pope in 1814; its portico was added a generation later, and a wing in 1920. It is possibly the oldest brick house in Alabama. The house is named for Pope's grandson, who, as the Confederate Secretary of War, passed the order to General Beauregard to fire on Fort Sumter, initiating Civil War hostilities. Also in the district is the elegant Palladian residence now known as the **Weeden House Museum** (300 Gates Avenue, 205–536–7718), built ca. 1819. Its beautifully proportioned entrance portico (added later by William Weeden) and its graceful interior staircase are noteworthy. A subsequent occupant, Maria Howard Weeden, was a poet and artist at the turn of the century. The house is furnished as it was during her tenure and displays her work.

Adjacent to the Twickenham District is the reconstructed **Museum Village at Constitution Hall Park** (Franklin Street at Gates Avenue, 205–532–7551). The village consists of four buildings and numerous outbuildings of the period 1805 to 1819, rebuilt on their original sites to commemorate the 1819 Constitutional Convention, at which the document was written that prepared the way for Alabama's statehood. Demonstrations portray life during that era, and the buildings and artifacts focus on social history.

On top of Monte Sano is the **Burritt Museum and Park** (3101 Burritt Drive, 205–536–2882), built by a local physician. His house now features a good local-history museum with collections of Indian artifacts, period furnishings, geology, and art. Among the artworks are important pieces by Maria Howard Weeden. On the grounds are several buildings moved from other sites in the area, including a blacksmith shop, a church, and two cabins. One of these is a typical two-part "dogtrot" cabin, a traditional form linking two cabins with a passage open at both ends—a dog might trot back and forth across the central passage.

## The Space and Rocket Center

This 450-acre complex is the largest space museum in the world, and features a guided tour of the adjacent **NASA–Marshall Space Flight Center,** where space station research and rocket testing are conducted. The museum has an unparalleled collection of memorabilia, models, artifacts, and working simulators relating to America's space and missile programs, as well as the actual *Mercury 7* and *Apollo 16* spacecraft. The U.S. Space Camp's training center and space station–shaped dormitory flank **Pathfinder,** the nation's only full-scale Space Shuttle exhibit. The vast park in back of the museum features examples from the entire history of rocketry, highlighted by the fully assembled, 363-foot *Saturn V.*

LOCATION: Route 565 (Governor's Drive), six miles west of Huntsville. HOURS: 9–6 Daily. FEE: Yes. TELEPHONE: 1–800–63SPACE or 205–837–3400.

*The Saturn V booster rocket at the Space and Rocket Center, near Huntsville, the world's largest space museum.*

Highway 72 continues east out of Huntsville, through the high, forested Tennessee River Valley. The farm town of **Scottsboro** is a quiet county seat, but it was here in 1931 that nine young black men were brought and charged with the rape of two white women. The Scottsboro Boys, as they were known, carried their appeal for a fair trial to the U.S. Supreme Court, becoming important forerunners of the civil rights movement.

The little town of **Stevenson** is notable for the **Stevenson Depot Museum** (Main Street, 205–437–2334). The sturdy brick building dates only from around the turn of the century, but it stands on the site of a depot that was a hotly contested Civil War prize. At the junction of two rail lines, Stevenson was a crucial supply depot for the Confederacy. The museum contains Civil War artifacts of that period and archaeological displays.

# RUSSELL CAVE NATIONAL MONUMENT

Beginning roughly 9,000 years ago, native Americans inhabited this huge cave set into limestone bluffs for about 8,000 years, leaving tools, pottery, and other artifacts. The cave ceiling is twenty-six feet high and the main room is more than half as long as a football field. In earliest times, a small group of perhaps twenty to thirty people made the cave their winter home, moving the seven miles down to the Tennessee River in spring to fish and gather mussels. A self-guided tour passes an exposed archaeological dig in the cave shelter, showing the different strata that represent each period of occupancy. The nearby visitors center has exhibits of artifacts from the excavation.

LOCATION: Eight miles west of Bridgeport, following Route 72, then Route 91 west, then Route 75 northwest. HOURS: 8–5 Daily. FEE: None. TELEPHONE: 205–495–2672.

**Valley Head** was an important Cherokee center before the arrival of white settlers, owing to the important springs that still rise here. The Cherokee leader Sequoya lived during the first quarter of the nineteenth century in a nearby village, where he invented an alphabet for his people and made possible the first Native American newspaper. Today the town is a quiet place, and Sequoya is remembered by several markers.

In the DeKalb County seat of **Fort Payne** is the 1889 **Fort Payne Opera House** (510 Gault Avenue North, 205–845–3761), the oldest theater still in use in Alabama. It contains interesting murals depicting local history.

# GADSDEN

The important industrial city of Gadsden is bisected by the Coosa River. The area was settled as early as the 1830s, following a long occupation by the Creek Indians, who used the nearby springs. Agriculture, river travel, and railroads were sources of wealth to the growing town, but its real prosperity came from the abundant iron and coal in the neighboring hills.

The **Gadsden Museum of Fine Arts** (2829 West Meighan Boulevard, 205–546–7365) contains works by local artists, including some interesting landscapes, as well as historical exhibits.

OPPOSITE: *The ninety-foot Noccalula Falls, near Gadsden, named for a legendary Indian princess who leapt to her death here.*

Among these are a re-created turn-of-the-century home and doctor's office, and collections of radios and locally made textiles.

A reconstructed **pioneer village** at **Noccalula Falls Park** (Noccalula Road, 205–549–4663) is comprised of some late-eighteenth-century structures—a dogtrot cabin, smokehouse, and smithy—plus a general store and a combination church-schoolhouse. Also rebuilt here is the fine ca. 1900 Gilliland-Reese Covered Bridge.

## ASHVILLE VICINITY

Southwest from Gadsden just off the main roads to Birmingham are two sites predating the region's railroad and industrial booms. **Horse Pens 40** (off Route 59 at the Ashville exit), a fortresslike semicircular rock formation, once served as a racetrack and is now a crafts-show venue. According to tradition, the Creek used it to corral horses. A settler, noticing that it was about forty acres in area, named the place Horse Pens 40.

The town of Ashville was founded in 1820 and for many years served as half a county seat (the rugged Beaver Creek Mountains were so impassable that it was necessary to split the county). A relic of Ashville's earliest days is the **Looney House** (on County Road 24, five miles southeast of Ashville, 205–594–7686), an 1820 two-story dogtrot house, possibly the oldest such structure in the state. Inside is a collection of period furnishings and other items from the era of the home's construction.

## JACKSONVILLE

East of the main road to Birmingham, but along important railroad routes, are a series of towns that lie on the curved edge of the Talladega National Forest, one of the wildest and most mountainous areas in the state.

At the northern end of this arc, nestled among rolling Appalachian hills, is Jacksonville, a town founded in 1822 and later given its name to commemorate Andrew Jackson's stay in the vicinity during the war with the Creek Indians. Its main historical monument is the **Dr. J. C. Francis Medical Museum and Apothecary** (100 Gayle Street, 205–435–7611), a general practitioner's office dating from 1850. Dr. Francis practiced in the lovely single-story Greek Revival building for fifty years after he built it, and the office continued to be used by physicians until the 1960s. It now displays some of the medical appliances and apothecary's supplies used by Dr. Francis.

# ANNISTON

With mountains to the east and factories to the west, Anniston (a contraction of "Annie's Town," referring to a local industrialist's wife) is a microcosm of post–Civil War Alabama. Up to the time of the Civil War, the town's site in the Choccolocco Valley was filled with cotton; during the war, a few Confederates began to mine iron here. But it wasn't until 1872 that an iron smelter from Georgia and a Connecticut capitalist founded an important iron company, and with it, the city of Anniston.

The founders brought in architects to plan and create Anniston, and there are still a number of large homes and buildings from the late nineteenth century. Outstanding among them is the **Church of St. Michael and All Angels** (Eighteenth Street and Cobb Avenue), a Richardson Romanesque church built in 1888–1890 of native stone and decorated inside with the detailed stone carving typical of the style.

A boost to the city's fortunes was the building of **Fort McClellan** nearby in 1912, used as a training station during World War I. At building 1077 on the fort's grounds is the **Women's Army Corps Museum** (Route 21, three miles north of Anniston, 205–848–3512), the nation's main memorial to the WACs. The Women's Army Corps was founded to help the war effort in 1942 and finally decommissioned in 1978. Full of vintage uniforms, artifacts, and photographs detailing women's role in the U.S. Army, the museum has also made an effort to document the careers of earlier women in active service, including Belle Boyd, the Confederate spy, and Harriet Tubman, who ran the Underground Railroad for fugitive slaves and spied for the North.

# TALLADEGA

Heading south toward Talladega, the rugged country to the east is clad with southern pine and hardwood forest. Nearby **Cheaha Mountain** (2,407 feet) is the tallest peak in Alabama. The name for Talladega, one of the oldest white settlements in eastern Alabama, is a rough spelling of two Indian words, *Italua* and *Atiti,* meaning "Border Town," which is what the old town was called. Andrew Jackson defeated a band of Creek here in 1813, rescuing a group of whites and friendly Indians who had been surrounded in Fort Leslie, a fort that had grown up around a trading post.

Talladega is a well-preserved place. Its 1836 brick Greek Revival courthouse is the oldest courthouse still operating in the state.

It is set on a classic, southern courthouse square, near the Silk-Stocking District, which encompasses a large number of antebellum houses (walking tour available from chamber of commerce, 205–362–9075). On the campus of the Alabama Institute for the Deaf and Blind is the imposing 1851 brick **Manning Hall**, flanked with Ionic columns and ornamental ironwork.

## SYLACAUGA

Located at the southwest corner of the Talladega National Forest, Sylacauga is famous for the quality of the marble quarried nearby, some of which graces the U.S. Supreme Court building in Washington, DC, as well as other seats of power.

The **Isabel Anderson Comer Museum and Arts Center** (711 North Broadway Avenue, 205–245–4016) is a local-history museum with a good collection of Indian projectile points and pottery, some ironwork dating from the time of de Soto, and a variety of nineteenth-century items. The museum also has a replica of the Hodges Meteorite, the only meteorite ever known to have struck a human being. It came through Mrs. Hodges's roof in 1954, ricocheted off the floor, and hit her as she sat on her sofa. It "bruised her considerably," but otherwise left her unharmed.

## DE SOTO CAVERNS

These vast caverns, found by Hernando de Soto during his month-long stay in the area in July 1540, had been discovered by the Indians long before. The place was sacred to the Creek Indians—Creek creation myths sometimes give this cave as the place from which the spirits rose to create the Creek people. A 2,000-year-old Coopena Indian burial site, excavated in 1964, is displayed in the cave. A trader, I. W. Wright, carved his name here in 1779; the Confederates used part of the cave to store gunpowder, and some of their equipment may be seen. The cave was also home to the Bloody Bucket, a Prohibition speakeasy whose stills and other equipment can now be seen.

LOCATION: Route 76, five miles east of Childersburg. HOURS: April through September: 9–5:30 Monday–Saturday, 12:30–5:30 Sunday; October through March: 10–2 Monday–Friday, 9–5 Saturday, 12:30–5 Sunday. FEE: Yes. TELEPHONE: 205–378–7252.

OPPOSITE: *The view from McDill Point looking south toward Talladega Mountain in Cheaha State Park, a rugged forest region explored by Hernando de Soto in 1540.*

# SAVANNAH
## AND THE
# COASTAL PLAIN

OPPOSITE: *Ruins of Dungeness, built in 1884 by Thomas Carnegie on the site of James Oglethorpe's hunting lodge on Cumberland Island, the largest island on the Georgia coast.*

Last of the original thirteen Colonies, Georgia was the brain-child of an English professional soldier and philanthropist, James Edward Oglethorpe, who convinced King George II (for whom the state is named) to grant his group a charter to a vast tract of land between the Carolinas and Florida, stretching west-ward to the Mississippi. His intent was to bring debtors, dissenters, and the British working poor to a new land of opportunity, where they would harvest the semitropical silks and wines and spices that the home country craved. They were to do so without slaves and without using alcohol to debauch the Indians with whom they traded. The Crown favored the project not only—perhaps not principally—for its mercantile promise, but also because it prom-ised a secure wedge between the already important Carolinas and the Spanish enclave of Florida.

Although high-minded, Oglethorpe was not impractical. Landing with his first group of settlers at Yamacraw Bluff on February 12, 1733, he was welcomed by the Yamacraw Indians and set about building the city of Savannah. That Savannah today, 250 years later, is still an unusually comfortable and beautiful city of shaded streets and many plazas, is a testimony to his skill as a planner. Over the course of the 1730s and 1740s, the philanthro-pist also proved himself an able general: Though he failed in his efforts to capture St. Augustine from the Spanish, he successfully repulsed Spanish assaults on St. Simons Island in 1742, thus estab-lishing the colony securely.

Oglethorpe's colonists were not the first Europeans to appear among the aboriginal peoples of what is now Georgia. Evidence of Indian habitation itself dates back more than 12,000 years, culmi-nating in the so-called Master Farmer culture that built mound cities, such as those at Ocmulgee and Etowah, roughly three-quar-ters of a millennium before the first Europeans arrived. When Hernando de Soto marched through Georgia seeking gold in 1540, the area was inhabited for the most part by the riverside dwellers the English later called "Creeks" and, in the north, by the mountain dwellers they called "Cherokee." French Huguenots tried to occu-py parts of the coast during succeeding decades but were driven out by the Spaniards, who established a string of missions along the coastal islands. The oldest of these, Santa Catalina de Gaule on St. Catherines Island, dates from 1586 and is the site of the oldest European ruins in Georgia. The English, jealous of their position

*James Oglethorpe presents Yamacraw Indian Chief Tomo-Chi-Chi to the lord trustees of the colony of Georgia in London in 1734, in a detail from William Verelst's painting.* PAGES 250–251: *Savannah's Victory Drive, lined with palm trees planted to commemorate the American victory in World War I.*

in Carolina, ejected the Spanish missionaries during the first years of the eighteenth century, leaving the way open for Oglethorpe.

It is hard today to imagine the idealism with which Savannah was founded. The trustees of the settlement banned rum, forbade the importation of slaves, and sought to control the amount of land sold to large speculators. These constraints, together with the difficulty of establishing the crops they wanted to grow, slowed the growth of the colony. By 1749 slaves had been deployed in an effort to found an imitation of Carolina's rice-indigo-cotton economy. When the trustees' charter ran out in 1753, Georgia became a royal colony, and the floodgates were opened both for a rapidly growing population and for every vice that Oglethorpe had sought to prohibit. By the time of the American Civil War, almost half the population of the state were slaves; the Georgia legislature had been involved in one of the nation's great land swindles; and the Creeks and Cherokees had been forcibly removed from their ancestral lands.

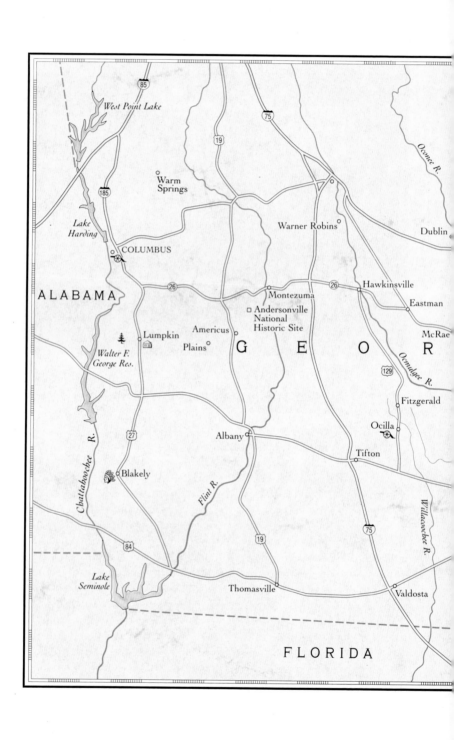

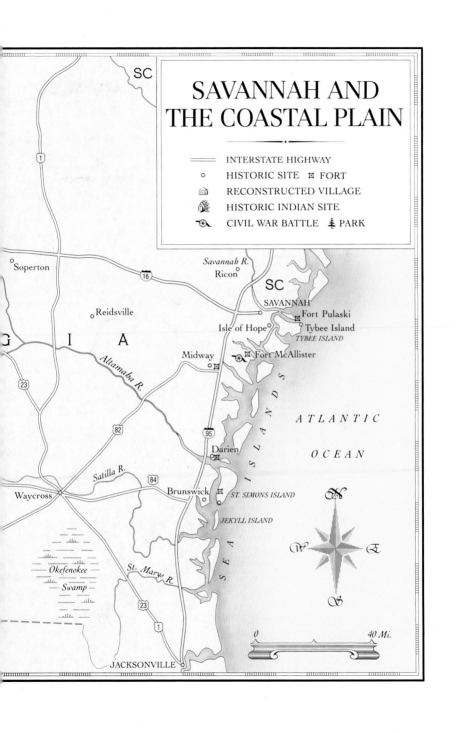

# SAVANNAH AND
# THE COASTAL PLAIN

─────── INTERSTATE HIGHWAY
  ○    HISTORIC SITE   ⊞ FORT
  🏠   RECONSTRUCTED VILLAGE
  🧑   HISTORIC INDIAN SITE
  ⚔    CIVIL WAR BATTLE   🌲 PARK

SC

SC

Soperton

Savannah R.
Ricon

SAVANNAH
Fort Pulaski
Tybee Island
TYBEE ISLAND

Reidsville

Isle of Hope

G  I  A

Altamaba R.

Midway      Fort McAllister

Darien

Brunswick
ST. SIMONS ISLAND

S
E
A

ATLANTIC

OCEAN

Waycross

Satilla R.

I
S
L
A
N
D
S

JEKYLL ISLAND

Okefenokee

Swamp

St. Marys R.

N

W        E

S

0                    40 Mi.

JACKSONVILLE

During the Revolutionary War, many, probably most, Georgians were staunch loyalists. Less than half of Georgia's parishes sent representatives to the Colonies' first congress on January 18, 1775, and both Savannah and Augusta remained in British hands for much of the Revolutionary War. As though to make up for any perceived lagging, however, the postwar Georgia legislature moved rapidly to accept the new Constitution when it was promulgated, becoming the fourth state to ratify the document.

Augusta became the state capital, reflecting a shift of power from the sandy or swampy coast into the great interior Piedmont region, where rich loam soils could grow upland cotton, the sort that Eli Whitney's cotton gin would soon make economically important. The West Indies plantation system, firmly established along the coast, with its attendant slaves, spread westward.

Having been caught by the U.S. government in the fraudulent sale of 50 million acres of land in what is now Mississippi and Alabama to a small group of legislator/land speculators—a scandal known as the Yazoo Frauds—the Georgia legislature agreed to cede the territories to the federal government in 1802, in exchange for cash and a promise that federal troops would be used to drive the Indians off the land within Georgia's boundaries. The federal government proceeded slowly in this invasion of Indian lands; President John Quincy Adams would not press confiscation of the Creek land and Chief Justice John Marshall sought to give some protection to the Cherokee. But the Creek were evicted in 1827, and over the ensuing decade the civilized Cherokee were forced to follow the "Trail of Tears" to Oklahoma.

Many Georgia planters were Unionists in the nullification and states' rights controversies of the 1830s, '40s and '50s, but became increasingly secessionist in the late '50s, and after the election of Abraham Lincoln in 1860, opted for the Confederacy. Union troops occupied the Sea Islands in 1862; the Confederates won a bloody victory at the Battle of Chickamauga in 1863; General William Tecumseh Sherman took Atlanta—the city where three rail lines met, making it the key link between the Confederate states of the Gulf and the Atlantic coasts—on September 2, 1864. Two months later, Sherman set off with his 60,000 troops on the march to the sea. Sherman's self-proclaimed purpose was to "make Georgia howl" in order to destroy popular support for the rebellion. As he wrote to a superior in Washington: "I attach much . . . importance to these deep incisions into the enemy's country, because this war differs from European wars in this particular: We are not fighting armies, but a hostile people, and must make old and young, rich and poor, feel the hard hand of war. . . ." In its wake Sherman's army left a swath of destroyed houses, farms, livestock, and food supplies. Sherman reached Savannah in time to offer the city to Lincoln as a Christmas present.

In an act of hope as much as of defiance, Georgians made Atlanta the capital of the state in 1868, choosing the phoenix as the city's symbol. As elsewhere in the South, Reconstruction in Georgia failed to create a two-party system or a new way of life for former slaves or masters that could bring the region out of the worldwide agrarian depression of the 1870s. By 1870, the state legislature was again firmly in the hands of the Democrats, where it would remain for almost a century. Cotton lost its prominence with the arrival of the boll weevil in 1914 to 1915, and today agriculture is centered around soy, wheat, corn, and, more recently, peanuts. Georgia has also become a leading poultry and egg supplier and an important source of lumber and newsprint.

The first enduring foothold on the Georgia coast is still its most important city. Throughout its history, Savannah has been the depot for all the products of the interior, shipped down rivers, roads, canals, and railways. Darien and Brunswick, farther down the coast, gained status as seaports, but none rivaled Savannah, with its connection directly to the interior via the Savannah River.

The Sea Islands preserve the vestiges of a virtually independent black culture, initiated by Creole slaves who escaped mainland plantations during the early years of settlement. Some black residents still use the patois developed on the islands, a version of English called Gullah, and some have names that derive not from Europe but from West Africa. A more slender strand of Sea Island culture is centered on Jekyll Island, where wealthy vacationers such as John D. Rockefeller established their winter "cottages"—usually palatial homes—beginning in the mid-1880s.

The following entries begin with Savannah on the northern tip of Georgia's coast and proceed southward to Brunswick, near the southern end. A subsequent section describes the coastal plain.

# S    A    V    A    N    N    A    H

Savannah was cosmopolitan from the start. The original settlers attracted by Oglethorpe in 1733 and thereafter included Englishmen, Scotsmen, German Salzburgers, Moravians, Sephardic Jews, Irish Catholics, and French Huguenots. Throughout its history, the city's position as an important port has brought to it factors and agents from the northern cities and from Europe. Unlike many Georgia cities, Savannah is not an insular community. The city is set upon the firm base of Oglethorpe's plan, filled with an ordered series of plazas and parks. It has remained a city full of green, with over 5,000 oaks shading the principal streets and squares.

During the Revolution Savannah was the site of one of the war's bloodiest battles. The British had landed troops in December 1778 and captured the city. Nine months later a combined force of American militia and French troops attempted to oust the British. They launched a poorly coordinated attack on October 9, 1779, against the Spring Hill Redoubt, which stood near the junction of Railroad Street and West Broad. The attack was repulsed at a cost of some 1,000 dead and wounded, among them the Polish cavalry commander Count Casimir Pulaski, who was struck down leading a charge against the enemy rear and died on an American ship two days later. His burial place is unknown—he may have been buried at sea. Savannah is the final resting place of another Revolutionary hero, General Nathaniel Greene, who died peacefully after the war, of sunstroke, and lies buried under a monument at Johnson Square.

At the end of the eighteenth century, tobacco and rice were the important crops; the latter ceased to be cultivated during the 1820s and 1830s when the rice fields were breeding grounds for mosquitoes that brought outbreaks of yellow fever. By that time, rice was becoming less profitable than cotton, largely because of Eli Whitney's invention of the cotton gin in 1793.

Savannah's growth accelerated in the early 1800s, and boomed after 1817 with the introduction of steam navigation up the river to Augusta, which made Savannah the ocean port for all of the upland cotton, much of which used to go overland to Charleston. The Cotton Exchange at water's edge was the world's center for trading in the commodity and effectively fixed the prices that the market would pay.

*Savannah, laid out with ample parks and squares by its founder, James Oglethorpe, is today the fastest-growing port on the South Atlantic coast.*

Savannah's boom was marred by two disasters—an 1820 fire that destroyed much of the residential area and a yellow fever epidemic that killed a quarter of the population—and proved to be short-lived. Maneuvers by British financiers to stem the flow of English gold and silver into the coffers of the cotton planters caused a credit crisis in the 1820s. Savannah's merchants struggled to stave off bankruptcy but most were brought down as the boom imploded. In 1834 an Irish visitor found that some of the city's "ambitious-looking dwellings . . . are mostly deserted, and have that decayed look which is so melancholy. . . ."

Compared to other cities of the Confederacy Savannah did not suffer greatly during the war, although it was blockaded by the Union navy, working from its base at captured Fort Pulaski. As Sherman's army tightened a siege ring around the city in December 1864, its defenders slipped away by night over an improvised bridge across the Savannah River. The city capitulated without a fight on December 22—Sherman was so pleased that he telegraphed Lincoln, "I beg to present you as a Christmas gift, The City of Savannah with 150 heavy guns and plenty of ammunition and about 25,000 bales of cotton." Its occupation was peaceful, indeed almost friendly, as Sherman distributed rations to the people with a generous hand. Since the city's only military installation was its port, now firmly in Union hands, there was no need for destruction of the sort that had been visited upon Atlanta.

Savannah is today the fastest-growing port on the South Atlantic coast, serving as a shipping center for food products, lumber, paper, chemicals, steel, tractor trailers, and jets. They are not only shipped from here but manufactured as well, using some of the same materials that have been arriving from the interior since the earliest days. This tour of Savannah begins downtown at the city's visitor center, then covers the waterfront area, and gradually moves inland through the city's nineteenth-century districts.

The **Savannah Visitor's Center** (301 West Broad Street, 912–944–0456) is housed in a restored 1860 Georgia Railroad depot and features a slide presentation on the city's history. Next door, in the old train shed, the **Great Savannah Exposition** shows a collection of artifacts and reproductions tracing a quarter-millennium of Savannah history, in addition to multimedia presentations on city history. Information on detailed walking tours of Savannah's several restored historic neighborhoods, the remarkable downtown National Historic Landmark District—a two-and-a-half-square-mile tract encompassing all of Oglethorpe's original city plan—and the Victorian District, located just south of the old downtown, is available here. The latter has some of the most elaborate gingerbread homes in America; President Franklin D. Roosevelt once stopped a parade in order to look more closely at one of them.

On the waterfront, along Factor's Walk and Bay Street, monuments recall Savannah's earliest days. The 1905 **City Hall** (Bay and Bull streets) provides a good orientation point with its gilded dome. It stands on the site of the old City Exchange, where the price of cotton was fixed. Next door are the **Washington Guns,** two bronze cannons captured at the battle of Yorktown and given by George Washington to the city in May 1791. The **U.S. Customs House** (3 East Bay Street) is an 1850 Greek Revival colonnaded structure, whose columns are capped with tobacco leaves, instead of the usual acanthus. Oglethorpe himself lived on this site, and John Wesley, the founder of Methodism, preached his first sermon here in 1736.

OPPOSITE: *The elegant house of William Scarbrough, designed by the English architect William Jay. President Monroe visited the house in 1819 when he came to inspect the first transatlantic steamship, the* Savannah.

The 1887 **Old Cotton Exchange** (100 East Bay Street), long the center of the postwar cotton trade, is now used as a Masonic lodge.

The eastern edge of the downtown waterfront is full of memorials to Savannah's history as a port. Not least is the **Old Harbor Light** (East Broad and Bay streets), a cast-iron beacon light built in 1852. The **Ships of the Sea Museum** (503 East River Street, 912–232–1511) is a general maritime museum, among the finest of its kind, with a collection of memorabilia and a particularly fine group of more than one hundred ships' models. The museum also displays seventy-five ships-in-a-bottle, scrimshaw, and paintings by Leslie Wilcox.

To the west of the waterfront is the **William Scarbrough House** (41 West Broad Street, 912–233–7787), an 1819 Regency villa built for a prominent steamboat promoter by the architect William Jay, a young Englishman who came to Savannah in 1817 and in only three years gave it the finest collection of Regency houses in America. Now home to the Historic Savannah Foundation, it is restored and furnished and is one of the best examples of its style in America. Among the highlights is a conjecturally restored atrium entrance hall. Not far east, at 23 Montgomery Street, is the **First African Baptist Church,** built in 1858 for a congregation that was founded in 1788.

Just off Johnson Square is **Christ Episcopal Church** (28 Bull Street), an 1838 Greek Revival church belonging to a congregation that was founded with the colony in 1733. This is the third church to stand on the spot. In 1736, the church was served by John Wesley, who was sent by an English missionary society; he was too rigorous for colonial tastes, however, and returned to England a year later. The church's interior balcony is delicately beautiful.

The **Trustees Garden** (East Broad near Bay Street) is the site of part of the original experimental garden implanted by Oglethorpe in 1734, using seeds from the Chelsea Physic Garden in London. The peach trees planted here are said to have been the foundation of the Georgia peach industry, though the original colonists were more interested in the possibility of growing oranges, coffee, mulberries (for silk), figs, and other exotics. It was intended to help relieve England of her dependency on other nations for such items. There is a ca. 1734 herb house on the site that may be the oldest building in Georgia. Between Liberty and Greene squares there are several important early houses, as well as the Telfair Museum.

# TELFAIR ACADEMY OF ARTS AND SCIENCES

The oldest public art museum in the South, founded in 1875, the Telfair is housed in a fine and harmonious Regency mansion designed by William Jay. The 1818 palazzolike structure has several restored and furnished rooms, including an octagonal reception room, a dining room, a drawing room, and a plantation kitchen. Much of the original Telfair family furniture is still in place here. The museum's painting collection includes an excellent selection of portraiture, with works by Charles Willson Peale, Rembrandt Peale, Henry Benbridge, and Jeremiah Theus. The early-twentieth-century collection includes works by Childe Hassam, George Bellows, Robert Henri, and Arthur B. Davies. The highlights of the strong, early-nineteenth-century furniture collection are a curly maple suite attributed to Joseph Barry and a secretary by Duncan Phyfe. The museum's silver collection features pieces made in Savannah in the early 1800s.

LOCATION: 121 Barnard Street. HOURS: 10–5 Tuesday–Saturday, 2–5 Sunday. FEE: Yes. TELEPHONE: 912–232–1177.

*The Telfair Academy of Arts and Sciences, housed in an 1818 William Jay building, overlooks Telfair Square.*

The **Juliette Gordon Low Birthplace** (142 Bull Street, 912–233–4501) is another Regency home dating from the 1810s. The founder of the Girl Scouts, Low was born here in 1860, and the house museum is furnished with Gordon family possessions. The carriage house features a small collection of Girl Scout memorabilia.

The **Owens-Thomas House** (124 Abercorn Street, 912–233–9743) is another excellent William Jay–designed Regency dwelling, this one completed in 1819. Many superlatives are lavished on Jay's work in Savannah, but this home is regarded by many as his masterpiece, with its portico supported by Ionic columns and its careful detailing throughout. The house is furnished with an outstanding collection of period antiques and decorative arts.

The **Davenport House** (324 East State Street, 912–236–8097) is a brick Federal-style dwelling raised on a high basement to catch whatever breeze might blow. It was built by Rhode Islander Isaiah Davenport between 1815 and 1820. More conservative in style than Jay's Regency buildings, it has at once an air of simplicity and of luxury. Davenport was the son of a shipbuilder, and the house contains an excellent collection of Davenport china, along with period furnishings.

The regular plan of Oglethorpe's squares is interrupted in the next layer of his grid by the **Colonial Park Cemetery,** bounded by Abercorn, Habersham, Oglethorpe, and Liberty streets. This was the second cemetery in the new town and received the remains of citizens between 1752 and 1853. Button Gwinnett, a signer of the Declaration of Independence who died in a duel, is buried here.

In the next layer back from the riverfront, bordered roughly by Pulaski and Troup squares, are two more important houses, both attributed to architect John S. Norris, the man who did for the planters and cotton factors of the mid-nineteenth century what William Jay had done for the previous generation. Both houses are elaborate and daring, especially when compared with what was then coming to be regarded as the outmoded Neoclassicism of Jay. The first is the 1853 **Green-Meldrim House** (14 West Macon Street, 912–233–3845), a Gothic Revival structure with sinuous ironwork verandas on the outside and rooms festooned with plaster detail inside. The double parlor is of particular interest; the house is furnished with antiques. General Sherman was headquartered in this house in 1864. Not far away is the 1848 **Andrew Low**

OPPOSITE: *The asymmetrical entrance hall of the Davenport House, with original decorative ironwork visible on the porch.*

*Juliette Gordon Low, founder of the Girl Scouts of America, was born in this grand house built in 1818 by her great-uncle James M. Wayne, the mayor of Savannah. The portrait of Mrs. Low is a copy; the original is in the National Portrait Gallery.*

**House** (329 Abercorn Street, 912–233–6854), built for the prominent British cotton merchant Andrew Low. Low helped set up his friend Charles Green of the Green-Meldrim House, another Englishman, in the cotton business. The home is an early example of the Italianate style and is furnished with what amounts to a museum of early American and English furniture and decorative arts. Outside is a parterre garden patterned on the original that stood here. Norris provided Savannah with several later, more elaborate Italianate houses; especially noteworthy is that for General Hugh Mercer (429 Bull Street, private) of 1859–1866.

In the heart of Savannah's old downtown is the temple belonging to the third-oldest Jewish congregation in America, established in July 1733. The interesting Gothic **Mickve Israel Temple** (20 East Gordon Street, 912–233–1547) was not built until the 1870s, but it contains the oldest Torah in America, along with a wonderful collection of books and letters, including a letter from George Washington. Savannah's Jewish community was crucial to its cultural life from the eighteenth century onward.

Just beyond the reach of the grid of squares is the **King-Tisdell Cottage** (514 East Huntington Street, 912–234–8000), a Victorian home containing a museum with artifacts of the black culture of Savannah and the Sea Islands, and 1890s furniture.

On the outskirts of Savannah are the sites of several old forts that protected the city from seaborne attack. Three miles east from the center of town on President Street is **Fort Jackson** (1 Fort Jackson Road, 912–232–3945), the oldest surviving brick fort in Savannah, begun in 1808 and used during the War of 1812 and the Civil War. It overlooks Five Fathom Hole, the old deepwater port on the Savannah River. The fort displays uniforms and weapons and interprets the history of coastal Georgia.

*The parlor of the Andrew Low House. The English writer and veteran traveler William Makepeace Thackeray stayed here twice and claimed that these were "the most comfortable quarters I have ever had in the United States."*

*Wassaw Island, a wildlife refuge accessible only by boat.* OVERLEAF: *The use of rifled*

# THE GEORGIA COAST

## TYBEE ISLAND

**Fort Screven** was built here in 1875 and garrisoned during the Spanish-American War. There are six batteries of the old fort to be seen, as well as the **Tybee Museum** (Meddin Drive, 912–786–4077), located in Battery Garlan. Exhibits show the history of Tybee Island from the colonial period forward, including collections of uniforms and firearms. On the fort's site is **Tybee Island Lighthouse** (912–786–5801), the bottom half of which dates from 1773. Confederate forces partly destroyed it in 1862, but it was rebuilt and put back into operation in 1867. The lighthouse is still active and is open to the public.

## FORT PULASKI NATIONAL MONUMENT

This brick and masonry fort of superb architectural qualities was designed by French military engineers and built between 1829 and

*cannon to breach the walls of Fort Pulaski in 1862 signaled the obsolescence of masonry forts.*

1847. Robert E. Lee designed the dike at the fort. The Confederates captured the fort in 1861, but less than a year later it was back in the hands of Union forces who used rifled cannon to breach the fort's defenses. Much of the fort has been restored to show the life of the soldiers who garrisoned it in the mid-nineteenth century; a small museum explains the history of ordnance leading to the rifled cannon.

LOCATION: Cockspur Islands, fifteen miles east of Savannah off Route 80. HOURS: June through August: 8:30–6:30 Daily; September through May: 8:30–5 Daily. FEE: Yes. TELEPHONE: 912–786–5787.

## RINCON

The **Salzburger Museum** is a monument to the German religious sect that was invited to settle in the new colony of Georgia in 1734. More than 150 came in all to found the town of New Ebenezer, near this site. (The British burned it during the Revolution.)

Especially adept at silk culture, the Salzburgers were skilled in handicrafts. The small museum is a replica of their orphanage building, the first orphanage in Georgia, and it contains artifacts and memorabilia relating to their skills and religious beliefs.

LOCATION: Route 275, six miles east of Rincon. HOURS: 3–5 Wednesday, Saturday, Sunday. FEE: Yes. TELEPHONE: 912–754–6333.

## ISLE OF HOPE

In addition to the many antebellum homes overlooking the Skidaway River, the Isle of Hope is also the location of **Wormsloe State Historic Site** (7601 Skidaway Road, 912–352–2548). The property was in the same family for 250 years, until it was given to the state. Noble Jones received the property in 1733, supposedly naming it Wormsloe for his plan to import silkworms and the mulberry trees they need for food. On the site are the remains of the eighteenth-century **Fort Wimbeley,** constructed of tabby, a masonry material made of lime, shells, and sand, and a much remodeled eighteenth-century house, still furnished with many Jones family pieces and surrounded by gardens.

## FORT MCALLISTER

This earthwork fortress of the Confederacy stands on the south bank of the Ogeechee River, guarding the approach to Savannah. It withstood repeated assaults in 1862 and 1863, only to fall to the fixed bayonet charge of a detachment of Sherman's army on December 13, 1864. This was to be the last resistance the Confederates would muster before Savannah was captured. A small museum has a collection of Civil War artifacts, including medical instruments. But the most impressive sights here are the well-restored earthworks and "bombproofs," defenses that were able to withstand seven sustained naval bombardments.

LOCATION: Spur 144 off Route 144, twenty-two miles south of Savannah. HOURS: 9–5 Tuesday–Saturday, 2–5:30 Sunday. FEE: Yes. TELEPHONE: 912–727–2339.

# MIDWAY

Though it is about halfway between Savannah and Darien, Midway's name may derive from the River Medway, in England. New England Puritans from Dorchester, Massachusetts, were the original settlers here, having come from an unsatisfactory colony in South Carolina in 1752. The first church in town was built in 1754, and the present **Midway Church** (Route 17) is the fourth on the site, having been built in 1792. It is a simple white clapboard structure, reminiscent of a New England meetinghouse.

When Georgia failed to send representatives to the Continental Congress of 1775, Midway's people were outraged and sent one of their own. That man, Lyman Hall, and another area resident, Button Gwinnett, were two of the three Georgians who signed the Declaration of Independence. The **Midway Museum** (912–884–5837), adjacent to the church, is a replica in the style of an eighteenth-century raised cottage, containing period furniture and documents relating to the town's history.

East of Midway, at the **Sunbury Historic Site** (Route 38, off Route 95, 912–884–5999) are the remains of Fort Morris, an earth fort built at the beginning of the Revolution and later captured by the British. During the War of 1812, another fort was built over part of the site. Today, portions of the earthworks from both forts may be viewed. A museum contains uniforms, weapons, and other relics of the forts, and special programs interpret colonial life in Sunbury, the town that once flourished here.

# DARIEN

This town on the banks of the Altamaha River was settled by Scottish Highlanders fleeing poverty and religious persecution in 1736. Oglethorpe had invited them to help protect his new settlement from the Spaniards in Florida, and Darien was indeed a check to Spanish power.

Just outside of town is a replica of **Fort King George** (Fort King George Drive, 912–437–4770), an even earlier British effort to block the French and Spanish. The fort, with its four-story

cypress blockhouse, includes a museum with relics of the region's Guale Indians, as well as olive jars, majolica, rosaries, and pieces of swords from the Spanish mission that stood nearby. The ruins of an 1818 sawmill are also on the site, a reminder of the days when Darien was an important shipbuilding center.

## Hofwyl-Broadfield Plantation Site

This site preserves the complete workings of a rice plantation that was operated by the same family from 1807 until 1973. The current plantation house, a frame house built from 1851 to 1860, was the family's fall and winter residence; the hotter months were spent in the Pine Barrens, away from the danger of malaria and yellow fever. The house is furnished much as the family left it, with heirlooms dating from as early as 1790 to as late as the early 1900s, and a small museum is on the grounds.

> LOCATION: Route 17, six miles south of Darien. HOURS: 9–5 Tuesday–Saturday, 2–5:30 Sunday. FEE: Yes. TELEPHONE: 912–264–9263.

Semitropical **Brunswick,** gateway to the Georgia islands, was once an important port and is still an important manufacturing center. The historic structures can best be seen on Union Street.

# SAINT SIMONS ISLAND

The island was once known as a high-living plantation area; after its plantations were destroyed during the Civil War, it faded into obscurity. Something of what the island once was like can be gathered by visiting the **Museum of Coastal History** (101 Twelfth Street, 912–638–4666), housed in the 1872 lightkeeper's house of the nearby Saint Simons lighthouse. The museum has a large photograph collection, some furniture and silver from the early plantation, lighthouse and Civil War memorabilia, and six fine quilts.

## Fort Frederica National Monument

This fort embraced a whole town inside its palisaded tabby walls. Founded by Oglethorpe in 1736 to protect southern Georgia from the Spanish and as a base from which to launch an attack on

OPPOSITE: *Saint Simons lighthouse. The former keeper's house contains a museum devoted to the history of the Georgia coast.*

Spanish Florida, the fort survived a Spanish attack in 1742. In 1748, England and Spain established peace with one another, and over the next ten years, the population and economy of the town declined as the troops were assigned elsewhere. A 1758 fire hastened the town's demise, although a few troops continued to be stationed there until the time of the revolution.

The ruins of a few of the old houses, barracks, and military buildings can still be seen on the site, and thirty wayside exhibits use text, pictures, and artifacts to describe the town and the lives of its inhabitants. In the summer, costumed interpreters demonstrate eighteenth-century crafts and household activities. The visitor center shows a film about the history of the fort and houses a small museum with a variety of interpretive exhibits.

LOCATION: St. Simons Island. HOURS: 9–5 Daily. FEE: Yes. TELE-PHONE: 912–638–3630.

About six miles from the fort, the **Bloody Marsh Memorial** (Demere Road) marks the site of the 1742 battle with an exhibit.

## JEKYLL ISLAND

Much of the island is covered with the "cottages" and resort buildings of the Jekyll Island Club, formed in 1886 when a consortium of millionaires from the Midwest and Northeast bought the whole island for $125,000. The Goulds, the Pulitzers, the Rockefellers, the Morgans, and the Astors rubbed shoulders here in a kind of secluded winter version of Newport, Rhode Island. A good part of Jekyll Island is now golf courses.

The **Jekyll Island Club Historic District** (912–635–2119) preserves the cottages and gardens created for these families by architects such as John Russell Pope and Horace Cleveland. All the great homes were raised between 1886 and 1928, the last year before the stock market crash. The club declined thereafter, until it finally closed in 1947. Four of the more elaborate cottages are open for tours, as is Faith Chapel, a 1904 church with a stained-glass window signed by Louis Comfort Tiffany. An **orientation center** is located in the old club stables on Stable Road.

Long before that time, in 1742, William Horton built a house on the northwest side of the island; only its four tabby walls and gaping windows remain. Horton was yet another link in Oglethorpe's chain of early-warning outposts against Spanish incursions, and after the philanthropist-soldier returned to England, Horton became commander of Fort Frederica.

# THE   COASTAL   PLAIN

The 35,000 square miles of Georgia's coastal plain were once the bed of an ancient sea. The area stretches inland from the Atlantic, its northern demarcation roughly drawn by a line from Augusta in the east to Columbus in the west. It is a surprisingly various region, ranging from wiregrass country to the longleaf, loblolly, and slash pine areas, once home to a great industry in naval stores and now important for lumber and paper, to the western lands, where the peanut, the pecan, and other newer Georgia crops are now important, and to the Okefenokee Swamp in the extreme southwest. Most of the area is sparsely populated, but at the northwest border of the plains stands Columbus, now the state's second-largest city.

## VALDOSTA

The town was first called Troupville after former governor George M. Troup, who signed the act creating Lowndes County in 1825. When the railroad bypassed it in 1860, the whole town picked up and moved to be beside it, naming the new settlement Valdosta, after Troup's country home. The railroad, lumbering, and farming have always been important to this prosperous small city.

The **Lowndes County Historical Society Museum** (305 West Central Avenue, 912–242–8646) has exhibits about the three rail lines that passed through town, the Sea Island cotton that once thrived here, and the turpentine and black pitch naval stores business. There are also a few oddities, such as a locally invented 12-gauge shotgun meant for use in World War I. Also of interest in town are the **Barber House** (416 North Ashley Street, 912–247–8100), a 1915 Neoclassical house with Mission Revival furniture and a chemistry lab in the basement. The owner was a Coca-Cola franchiser who dabbled in inventing his own soft drinks. The **Converse-Dalton-Ferrell House** (305 North Patterson Street, 912–244–8575) is a 1900 Neoclassical home noted for its elaborate detailing, ten bedrooms, and third-floor ballroom, built by one of three brothers whose homes once occupied three of the four corners of this street. **The Crescent** (904 North Patterson Street, 912–242–2196) is a remarkable 1889 to 1900 Classical Revival home with a beautiful crescent-shaped columned portico.

OVERLEAF: *A channel through the Okefenokee Swamp, lined with cypress trees and carpeted with water lilies.*

# THOMASVILLE

Thomasville sits on the highest point in southwest Georgia, approximately 273 feet above sea level. Around 1870 a doctor wrote a paper suggesting that the pine barrens around the town might make it unusually healthful, and suddenly the otherwise unprepossessing place was invaded by Northerners, building their winter resorts and living the "plantation life." The "hotel era," as the town calls it, lasted from 1870 to around 1900; during that time the winter population would swell from 5,000 to 15,000. The town never experienced the postwar poverty of so many Southern areas: There were at one time fifteen hotels and twenty-five boardinghouses; the Hannas, Goodriches, and Rockefellers all wintered here. As one citizen supposedly said, "We soon found a Yankee was worth two bales of cotton, and was twice as easy to pick."

The **Thomas County Historical Society Museum** (725 North Dawson, 912–226–7664) is a five-building complex on two-and-a-half acres. The main museum is full of photos and memorabilia of the hotel era, including a remarkable collection of women's formal wear dating from the 1820s to the 1950s. Also on the site are a one-lane private bowling alley, built in 1893, an 1850s pioneer log home, and the 1879 Joyner House.

The **visitor center** (401 South Broad Street, 912–226–9600) provides information about tours of the plantations and cottages of the town, including the 1885 **Lapham-Patterson House** (626 North Dawson Street).

On Wolf Street are the few remaining earthworks of what served briefly as a Confederate prison. When the notorious Andersonville prison was evacuated for fear that General Sherman would liberate its prisoners, 5,000 of the captured Yankees were interned here for two weeks, during which about 500 died, mainly of the ill treatment received at Andersonville.

# AGRIRAMA

Located in Tifton, an important market town in the wiregrass, this excellent living-history farm museum commemorates the last quarter of the nineteenth century in this area. It contains an 1870s log cabin, an 1890s farmhouse, a church, gristmill, printshop, drugstore, commissary, blacksmith shop, turpentine still, sawmill, tram,

OPPOSITE: *The picturesque 1885 Lapham-Patterson House is the only Thomasville resort house open to the public.*

and cotton gin on the site. Demonstrations are given at all of them. Field crops such as cotton, tobacco, and corn are grown, together with kitchen gardens.

> LOCATION: Route 75 and Eighth Street, Tifton. HOURS: June through August: 9–6 Daily; September through May: 9–5 Monday–Saturday, 12:30–5 Sunday. FEE: Yes. TELEPHONE: 912–386–3344.

## JEFFERSON DAVIS MEMORIAL PARK

Eight miles west of the town of Ocilla is the **Jefferson Davis Memorial Park** (Route 32, 912–831–2335), marking the spot where the president of the Confederacy was captured by Union forces ȯn May 10, 1865. There is a small museum of Civil War memorabilia and exhibits on Davis's flight and capture.

## FITZGERALD

Founded in 1895, Fitzgerald is named for an Indianapolis newspaperman who, together with a Georgia governor, conceived of the plan of resettling veterans of the Union army on this spot in the wiregrass region southwest of McRae. The **Blue & Gray Museum** (Old Depot Building, 912–423–5375) is a fine small local-history museum featuring Civil War memorabilia from both sides of the conflict, including General Robert E. Lee's last general orders. There are also documents and photos relating to the town's founding and a handsome mantel and desk from the town's Lee-Grant Hotel. Townspeople claim the hotel had to be built to accommodate all the Southerners who came to see a Yankee.

## SOPERTON

Soperton is proud of its position in an important lumbering district, calling itself the "Million Pines City." The first newspaper in America to be printed on pine-pulp newsprint was produced here in 1933. The **Million Pines Visitor Center** (Route 29 at Route 16, 912–529–6263) encompasses two interesting historic structures: The first is the **Curt Barwick House,** an 1840s pioneer two-room log cabin with a wraparound porch. The second is the 1888 **Blackville Post Office,** now being developed as a postal museum.

Five miles southwest of town is the ornate **Troup's Tomb** (Route 118, five miles off Route 46). On the site of Governor George M. Troup's Oconee River plantation, the tomb is surrounded with a wall of native stone and an elaborate iron gate. Both

Governor Troup and his brother are buried here. Governor Troup, who was a tireless advocate of rural life, land distribution, and Indian removal, died in 1856. Presumably, the single rosebush growing inside the enclosure was planted by a slave at the time of Troup's death.

## DUBLIN

Dublin is the center of a productive timber and farming area. Before the advent of the railroads, its position on the Oconee River made it a more important place than Macon. It was founded in 1812 on land donated by an Irishman.

The 1904 **Carnegie Library Building** (corner of Bellevue, Church, and Academy avenues, 912–272–9242) is a brick library containing a museum of local history, with antique clothing and photographs, Indian artifacts from 8000 B.C. forward, and a collection of watercolors (mainly of camellias) by a noted local artist. The library provides brochures for walking tours down Bellevue Avenue, with its fine Greek Revival and Victorian homes, some now converted to office use.

*Rows of gravestones at Andersonville National Cemetery. Some 13,000 Union prisoners of war perished at this prison camp in 1864 and 1865.*

Along Route 19 at the Oconee River is the **Fish Trap Cut,** two ceremonial mounds and a cut, about 100 yards into the bank, which was used with a weir to trap and tend fish. It was built by Indians as early as 1000 B.C. and may have been in use later than A.D. 1500. Thirteen miles north of the city on Route 441 is **Chappell's Mill,** an 1811 mill that is still operating, grinding out 15,000 bushels of corn a year by the old dry-mill process.

## ANDERSONVILLE NATIONAL HISTORIC SITE

Here are preserved the remains of the most notorious prisoner-of-war camp of the Civil War. When the Confederates felt that Richmond was threatened by Union forces, they transferred thousands of prisoners to this supposedly better-provisioned and -watered site. The camp opened in February 1864. By August of the same year it had 32,000 prisoners in what amounted to a huge pen surrounded by a high stockade. A total of 13,000 prisoners died here of disease, exposure, and malnutrition. After the war ended, the commandant of the camp, Captain Henry A. Wirz, was tried by a military court and hanged, though the real horror of Andersonville was not the brutality of the keepers but their inability to care for so many prisoners on such a makeshift site.

There is a small museum and visitor center, as well as a national cemetery. Several structures survive from the old camp, along with remains of earthworks and palisades, some showing where tunnels were made in efforts to escape.

LOCATION: Ten miles northeast of Americus on Route 49. HOURS: 8–5 Daily. FEE: Yes. TELEPHONE: 912–924–0343.

## AMERICUS

This town, founded in 1832, became and remains a prominent agricultural center and county seat. The historic district centers on Lee, Taylor, and College streets, where there are many fine Greek Revival, Victorian, and Gothic Revival homes and churches in a quiet setting. One of the earliest surviving homes is the delightful, porch-encircled **Guerry House** (723 McGrath Street), an 1833 raised cottage with mortise-and-tenon construction and elaborate woodwork and hand-blown glass. It is now a restaurant.

OPPOSITE: *Providence Canyon, known as "Georgia's Little Grand Canyon," is preserved in a state park near Lumpkin.*

West of Americus, in **Plains,** is the **Jimmy Carter National Histor-ic Site** (912–924–0343), established in 1988 and being developed as a museum on presidential campaigns, with emphasis on the Carter presidency. The downtown railroad depot, formerly the Carter campaign headquarters, is serving as the park's visitor center. Also on display are exhibits on the influence of the railroad and agricul-ture on a small rural Southern town.

## ALBANY

South of Americus, at the head of navigation of the Flint River, is Albany. Named for Albany, New York, by the Connecticut Yankee who founded it in 1836, the Georgia town is the center of the pecan- and peanut-producing region.

The **Thronateeska Heritage Foundation** (100 Roosevelt Ave-nue, 912–432–6955) sponsors a museum housed in a 1913 railway depot which features a miscellaneous collection of the cultural and natural history of the area. The foundation also operates a plan-etarium housed in a 1915 railway express office and is restoring an 1840 frame house, an outbuilding, and an 1857 railway depot on the site. The museum collection is strong in all periods of Indian artifacts, especially projectile points, an appropriate specialty, con-sidering that the Indian term for the area, Thronateeska, denotes a "place where flint is picked up."

The **Albany Museum of Art** (311 Meadowlark Drive, 912–439–8400) has some American paintings but is best known for its collection of African art, begun by Stella Davis, a local woman who served for many years as an ambassador in Africa.

The **Albany Little Theatre** (514 Pine Avenue, 912–439–7193) is housed at the back of a restored and furnished brick home built in 1855. At the turn of the century, it acquired its porch and Corinthian columns. Period furnishings include a chair where Jef-ferson Davis sat on a visit to the house.

**St. Teresa's Catholic Church** (315 Residence Avenue) is a fine example of the small-town mission church. Built in 1861 of locally made bricks, it has an elaborate tinwork ceiling.

North of the town of Blakely the **Kolomoki Indian Mounds and State Park** (off Route 27, 912–723–5296) preserves seven mounds and a ceremonial plaza dating to around A.D. 800. A museum displays artifacts from digs in the area and presents an audio-visual description of an excavated mound. Also north of Blakely is the

**Outpost Replica** (off Route 39 in Fort Gaines), a reconstruction of a palisade used to ward off Creek and Seminole attacks between 1816 and 1830.

# LUMPKIN

An old agricultural town center named for an early Georgia governor, Lumpkin contains an anthology of historic Georgia architecture. There is everything from dogtrots to the Greek Revival, along a dozen downtown streets radiating from the courthouse square. A walking-tour brochure is available at perhaps the finest house in town, the 1836 **Bedingfield Inn** (corner of Broad and Cotton streets, 912–838–4201). Built by the first doctor in the county, it served as both home and stage stop. The house combines Federal and Greek Revival influences in a very pleasing way. The interior is painted brightly, as it was in the 1840s, and the furniture is selected for that period, including some fine pieces by west Georgia artisans. The **Hatchett Drug Store Collection,** housed in an old drug-

*Red-clay streets in Westville Village, a living-history village that re-creates life in the 1850s.*

store on the courthouse square, is a remarkable group of jars and retorts and old trade items offered for sale at a drugstore in Fort Gaines during the last quarter of the nineteenth century.

## Westville Village

The motto of this living-history assemblage of old buildings is "Where it's always 1850." There are thirty-two authentic structures on fifty-seven acres, including an 1832 schoolhouse and eight pre-1850 homes in a variety of styles, all properly furnished. Craft shops include a smithy, a cabinet shop, and a bootery, all operated by the people of Westville dressed in period costume. Field crops such as corn, cotton, and sugar cane grow near the village.

LOCATION: South Mulberry Street. HOURS: 10–5 Monday–Saturday, 1–5 Sunday. FEE: Yes. TELEPHONE: 912–838–6310.

*Among the many historic buildings preserved in Columbus is this rustic log cabin, which was moved into town from the surrounding countryside.*

# COLUMBUS

Incorporated in 1828 and named for the great navigator, Columbus's two natural advantages have made it the metropolis of western Georgia. It stands at the navigable head of the Chattahoochee, making it an important supply and transport point. From the beginning it had sufficient water power to run textile mills and, later, ordnance plants, making it a natural industrial center as well. Columbus was a major supplier of both clothing and munitions to the Confederacy. Although General Sherman did not attack the city, Union General James H. Wilson did, while Georgia was still holding out for the Confederacy one week after General Robert E. Lee had surrendered at Appomattox. Columbus has since capitalized on its water resources for hydroelectric power and become the second-largest city in the state.

The headquarters of the **Historic Columbus Foundation** (700 Broadway, 404–323–7979) are in a restored and furnished 1870s Italianate villa, and tours of the town's historic district proceed from here. Among the highlights are a simple **log cabin and country cottage** moved from the surrounding countryside to 708 Broadway; the **Walker-Peters-Langdon House** (716 Broadway), an 1828 cottage and the oldest home in town; the wonderfully restored French Empire **Rankin House** (1440 Second Avenue); and the **Pemberton House** (11 Seventh Street), the residence of the inventor of Coca-Cola, between 1855 and 1860.

The 1871 **Springer Opera House** (103 Tenth Street, 404–324–5714) has been well restored and is still in use. A museum houses memorabilia of those who have appeared here, including Edwin Booth, Oscar Wilde, and Irving Berlin. The **Confederate Naval Museum** (201 Fourth Street, 404–327–9798) contains a collection of models and weapons from Confederate gunboats and, remarkably, two original Confederate warships, the ironclad ram *Jackson* and the gunboat *Chattahoochee*, both raised from the river where they had been sunk at the end of the Civil War.

At nearby Fort Benning is the **National Infantry Museum** (Baltzell Avenue, Fort Benning, 404–545–2958), with a collection of military uniforms, weapons, and artwork. Much of the museum traces American infantry history from the French and Indian War to the present, but there is substantial material devoted to the Axis powers of World War II, plus other infantry paraphernalia.

# ATLANTA
## AND
# NORTHERN
# GEORGIA

OPPOSITE: *Atlanta's Shrine of the Immaculate Conception and the gilded dome of the State Capitol.*

Almost from the start, railroads were Atlanta's pride, the reason for its eminence and the cause of its disasters. There were forts and settlements in the area from the first decade of the nineteenth century, but it wasn't until 1836 that a group of entrepreneurs realized that the area was a natural hub for railroad traffic heading in practically any direction, and the settlements turned into a town, first named Terminus, since it would be the terminus of the new Western & Atlantic Railroad. Two more railroads pushed north to meet the W & A at the new town.

The Zero Mile Post at the center of Atlanta marks the official termination of the W & A. The railroads brought wealth, and the town soon changed its name, first to Marthasville and then, in 1845 to Atlanta, in honor of its mission to carry goods to and from the Atlantic. Blessed with a comparatively equable climate—the city is at an elevation of over 1,000 feet above sea level—Atlanta grew rapidly in importance as a shipping and manufacturing center. For a short time, this preeminence was its undoing. During the Civil War, Confederate supply lines all passed through Atlanta, munitions and stores were manufactured here, and the wounded were treated here. The Federal forces could not ignore it: After months of hard campaigning General William Tecumseh Sherman's army marched into Atlanta on September 2, 1864. Sherman ordered Atlanta evacuated on the eve of his army's departure for its infamous march to the sea, and on November 15, the city burned, losing more than 90 percent of its buildings. Sherman had ordered that buildings of military importance be blown up. (The Confederate commander who had defended the city, John Bell Hood, had ordered a similar selective destruction before his troops abandoned it.) When the flames spread to stores and homes, some Union soldiers looted and danced in the streets in drunken glee, but many of them were appalled by the destruction, and Sherman himself led the firefighting brigades in a futile effort to stem the conflagration.

Appropriately, the city seal, chosen in 1887, shows a phoenix rising from the ashes, with the motto "Resurgence," or rising again. No one could burn Atlanta out of its unique place on a transportation map. Just a year after the close of the war, the city reported a population fully double that which it had enjoyed before the fire. Partly owing to its being chosen as an administrative center for the Reconstruction, it saw quick rebuilding and reinvestment. In 1867 the Freedman's Bureau established Atlanta University specifically for the education of former slaves, laying the foundations for the black middle class that would be so important to the city's life in the

*The printing press at New Echota, capital of the Cherokee nation, where the Cherokee* Phoenix *was published from 1828 to 1834 in Cherokee and English.*

twentieth century. By 1868 Atlanta had succeeded in wresting the honor of being the state capital from Milledgeville.

In recent years, Atlanta has emerged as the leading city of the Southeast, both in population and in the number of industries for which it serves as headquarters. The politics of segregation were long practiced by state governors here, but Atlanta has also been the cradle of much of the South's civil rights movement. Martin Luther King, Jr., came from the city's substantial black middle class; Julian Bond was elected to the state legislature in 1965, and in 1973, Maynard Jackson became the mayor of Atlanta, the first black to become mayor of any Southeastern city. Jimmy Carter, breaking a long tradition, spoke out against racism while he was governor of Georgia.

This chapter covers Atlanta and its environs, branches northeast to the Blue Ridge, then turns northwest, ending with New Echota State Historic Site. It was here that the Cherokee nation had their capital, and where, in 1828, they published a newspaper using an alphabet newly devised for their language.

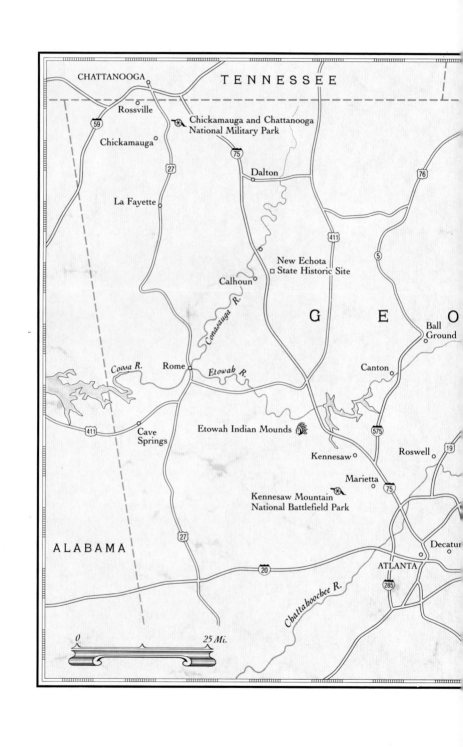

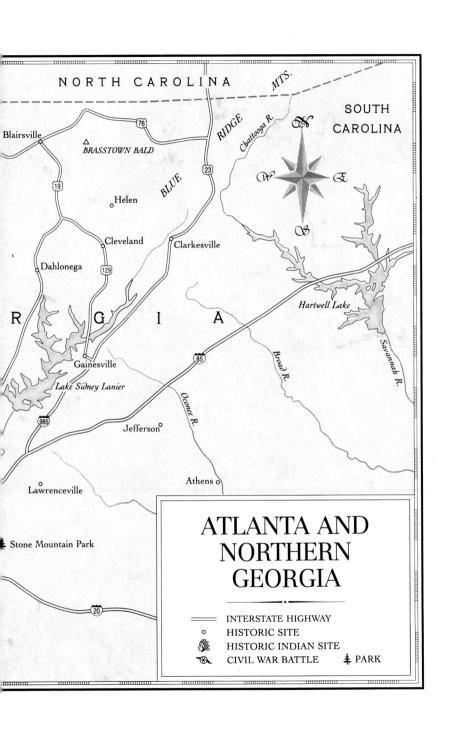

NORTH CAROLINA

BLUE RIDGE MTS.

SOUTH CAROLINA

Blairsville

76

△ *BRASSTOWN BALD*

19

23

*Chattooga R.*

Helen

Cleveland

Clarkesville

129

Dahlonega

R      G      I      A

*Hartwell Lake*

85

*Broad R.*

*Savannah R.*

Gainesville

*Lake Sidney Lanier*

985

*Oconee R.*

Jefferson

Athens

Lawrenceville

Stone Mountain Park

20

## ATLANTA AND NORTHERN GEORGIA

———— INTERSTATE HIGHWAY
∘ HISTORIC SITE
HISTORIC INDIAN SITE
CIVIL WAR BATTLE    🌲 PARK

# A    T    L    A    N    T    A

## STATE CAPITOL

Dedicated on July 4, 1889, this ornate capitol building is among the few in the nation whose dome and cupola are gilded, in this case with Georgia gold from the Dahlonega region. The city fathers brought in the Chicago firm of Edbrooke & Burnham to create the structure, on the site of the old city hall, just a block from the Zero Mile Post where the city began. The capitol is of Indiana limestone, and its dome is surmounted by a statue of Liberty; her torch is 258 feet above the ground. Parts of the first and fourth floors are occupied by the **Georgia Museum of Science and Industry,** housing a miscellaneous collection ranging from historic firearms to scale-model airplanes and Civil War items. There are also collections of flora and fauna, and the minerals collection is among the largest in the South. On the second floor of the capitol, portraits of governors and busts of signers of the Declaration of Independence and other famous Georgians make up the Georgia Hall of Fame.

LOCATION: Capitol Square. HOURS: 8–5:30 Monday–Friday, 10–2 Saturday, 1–3 Sunday. FEE: None. TELEPHONE: 404–656–2844.

The **Cyclorama** (800 Cherokee Avenue SE, in Grant Park, 404–624–1071) is a 400-foot painting-in-the-round of the battle of Atlanta, complete with sound effects.

One of the few, and splendid, survivors of old Victorian Peachtree Street is **Rhodes Memorial Hall** (1516 Peachtree Street NW, 404–881–9980). Made of Stone Mountain granite, the hall was built in 1904 at the behest of the founder of a prominent chain of furniture stores. The Romanesque Revival structure is among the finest works of Georgia architect Willis F. Denny II. Some original furnishings can be seen.

Chiefly on Auburn and Edgewood avenues just east of the city center is **Sweet Auburn,** an area that became a focal point for black urban culture in the Southeast beginning at the turn of the century. Early prominent black businessmen Alonzo Herndon and Herman Perry both came from here. On January 15, 1929, Mrs. Martin Luther King, Sr., gave birth in an upstairs bedroom at 501 Auburn Avenue to Martin Luther King, Jr., who would lead the civil rights movement of the 1960s. A ten-block stretch of Auburn Avenue is now preserved as the **Martin Luther King, Jr., National**

*Atlanta's Peachtree Street in 1865, after the departure of Sherman's Army.*

**Historic Site.** Markers identify a number of the homes and businesses important to the building of a black presence in Atlanta. The **King Birthplace** (501 Auburn Avenue, 404–331–3919) contains some family furniture and memorabilia. The three-story **Ebenezer Baptist Church** (407 Auburn Avenue, 404–688–7263) is also open for tours, and next to it is the grave site of Dr. King, now flanked by the Center for Nonviolent Change.

The 1929 **Fox Theatre** (660 Peachtree Street NE, 404–892–5685), about two miles north of the downtown center, is one of the great surviving Depression-era movie palaces, wonderfully encrusted with exotic Moorish, Egyptian, and other ornamentation.

## HIGH MUSEUM OF ART

Housed in its new award-winning building by architect Richard Meier, the High is one of the finest art museums in the Southeast. Strengths of its collections include excellent groups of nineteenth-century American painting and sculpture and a choice selection of American decorative arts embracing the periods from 1825 to

1917. The American collection includes paintings by Inman, Sargent, Bierstadt, Inness, Twachtman, and Hassam, and sculpture by Hiram Powers. Holdings in Italian painting and sub-Saharan African art are also outstanding.

LOCATION: 1280 Peachtree Street NE. HOURS: 10–5 Tuesday–Saturday, 10–9 Wednesday, 12–5 Sunday. FEE: Yes. TELEPHONE: 404–892–3600.

## ATLANTA HISTORICAL SOCIETY

Headquartered at **McElreath Hall** in the Buckhead section, the society maintains a museum, several gardens, and two restored houses on this site. The 1920s **Swan House** is the masterwork of Atlanta architect Philip Trammell Shutze. A perfectly symmetrical Palladian house, it is exquisitely detailed both inside and out with many representations of swans, a favorite bird of Mrs. Inman, who lived in the house from its completion until her death in 1965. The furnishings represent her eclectic tastes. Outside the formal gardens include a boxwood parterre and an Italianate cascade, also designed by Shutze.

The **Tullie Smith House,** imported to this site from nearby DeKalb County, provides a glimpse of mid-nineteenth-century farm life. The 1840s main house is a simple two-story wooden structure, complete with a "Parson's Room" with separate entrance. The house is furnished correctly for the period, as are the many restored outbuildings, where living-history demonstrations are held. The historical society's **museum** has the best history collection in Atlanta, including an outstanding assemblage of Civil War guns, munitions, flags, maps, medical supplies, and uniforms. There are also interpretive exhibits devoted to the civil rights movement and to the 1895 Cotton States and International Exposition, the fair that put Atlanta on the map as a major metropolis. Along with the period gardens at the two houses is the Quarry Garden, located in a former granite quarry, which is planted with native trees, shrubs, and herbaceous wildflowers.

LOCATION: 3101 Andrews Drive NW. HOURS: 9–5:30 Monday–Saturday, 12–5:30 Sunday. FEE: Yes. TELEPHONE: 404–261–1837.

OPPOSITE: *Ionic columns separate the entrance hall of Swan House from the stair hall, with its superb spiral staircase.*

*Quilting is one of the traditional crafts demonstrated at the mid-nineteenth-century Tullie Smith House.* OPPOSITE: *Behind the Tullie Smith House is the kitchen, located in a separate structure to lessen the danger of fire and to keep the main house cool.*

## DECATUR

Decatur lies at the eastern edge of Atlanta, dwarfed by its neighbor. Founded in 1823 and named for the naval hero Stephen Decatur, the town might well have grown to be what Atlanta became, except that irate citizens, unwilling to allow the noise and soot of the Western & Atlantic railroad to pollute the town, forbade the railway to stop there. So the undaunted railroad men went on to found a new town at nearby Terminus, later Atlanta.

Today, Decatur is a suburb of Atlanta, featuring a restored and rebuilt 1898 **county courthouse** (Courthouse Square, 404–373–1088). Occupying the highest point in Decatur, the cut-granite, colonnaded courthouse contains a three-room museum of local history and artifacts, including weapons, uniforms, and other memorabilia of both Confederate and Union soldiers who fought here during the struggle to take Atlanta.

## DeKalb Historic Complex

The complex contains three early homes, typical of the ordinary farm dwellings of their era. The **B. F. Swanton House** is a simple one-and-a-half-story wood-frame structure. Underlying it is an even simpler two-room cabin first raised ca. 1823, making it the oldest house in Decatur. It was occupied by Major Benjamin Swanton, who had come to Georgia in 1828. Furnished with period antiques of the 1840s, the home is notable for its hand-blown glass, decorative ironwork, and brick chimney, all made with materials fashioned on the premises. Also on the property are two 1830s log cabins, the **Biffle Cabin** and the **Thomas-Barber Cabin,** one of which is furnished with 1830s antiques.

LOCATION: West Trinity Place. HOURS: By appointment. FEE: Yes. TELEPHONE: 404–373–1088.

## STONE MOUNTAIN PARK

Like a great humped turtle back, the gray granite of Stone Mountain rises out of the trees and lakes east of Atlanta. It is the largest piece of exposed granite in the world, measuring about two miles in length and up to seven miles in circumference, reaching 825 feet above the plateau floor.

A natural landmark, the mountain served as a meeting place for Creek Indians and early settlers. The 3,200-acre park features the spectacular 90-by-190-foot-high relief sculpture of Confederate President Jefferson Davis, General Robert E. Lee, and General "Stonewall" Jackson, each astride a horse. It took over fifty years and three sculptors to finish the monument, beginning with Gutzon Borglum, sculptor of Mount Rushmore. It was finally completed in 1970.

The park's **Memorial Hall Museum** contains an excellent collection of Civil War weapons, uniforms, flags, and other memorabilia. A complex of nineteen antebellum structures is also on the site, brought from as far away as Albany and Athens, Georgia, to show the life of a working plantation. There are slave quarters and craft shops, a country store, a cook house, an overseer's house, and many other buildings typically found on a plantation, all restored and authentically furnished. Among these are the **Kingston House**

(1845), a simple wood home that was once the center of a 500-acre plantation. More elaborate is the **Dickey House** (ca. 1850), once the headquarters of a plantation that had more than 100 slaves. Both houses are furnished with fine collections of period antiques. The **Thornton House** came to the park from the High Museum of Art, and it is among the earliest houses still standing in Georgia. Built during the 1790s, it has been accurately restored and furnished.

The park also features rides around the mountain on replicas of nineteenth-century locomotives, departing from a reproduction of Atlanta's great 1853 railway depot; an antique car museum that also contains old jukeboxes and Coca-Cola memorabilia; and a laser-light show on the face of the carving.

LOCATION: Sixteen miles east of Atlanta on Route 78. HOURS: *Park:* 6 AM–12 PM Daily; *Attractions:* June through September, 10–9 Daily; September through May, 10–5:30 Daily. FEE: Yes. TELEPHONE: 404–498–5600.

# N O R T H E A S T     G E O R G I A

The southwestern spurs of the Blue Ridge Mountains cut a wedge into Georgia's northeast corner, with their true mountain country and their hardwood forests. **Brasstown Bald,** the highest point in the state at 4,784 feet above sea level, is located in this region. On its peak is an observation deck with a four-state vista.

Like northwestern Georgia, the northeast grows corn and soy in its valleys and raises chickens for the poultry industry. The northeast was until recently even more isolated than its neighboring region, since no railroad or main artery passed through this rugged area. This made for a fiercely independent mountain people, many of whom sided with the North during the Civil War.

The original inhabitants were Cherokee Indians, and it was in this Blue Ridge area that the great misfortune occurred that did so much to encourage their eventual removal in 1838–39. The name Dahlonega—given to the region's boomtown—means "yellow metal" in Cherokee; the Indians had long known of the odd metal found in the creeks of this region before the whites "discovered" the gold there in 1828, occasioning the first gold rush in the United States. The gold fields of Dahlonega would eventually yield more than $16 million in gold. Here the Cherokee first felt the dramatic pressure to cede their suddenly valuable lands; local authorities began parceling out the land to prospectors as early as 1830.

The following entries are organized in rays from Atlanta, following routes 85 and 985 up to the small roads of the Blue Ridge.

In the comparative lowlands along Route 85 heading northeast from Atlanta are several towns with sites of interest. **Lawrenceville,** where missionary Samuel Worcester and his associates were tried for giving aid to the Cherokee in 1831, contains the **Southeast Railroad Museum** (3966 Buford Highway, 404–476–2013), with a collection of antique railroad cars set in an old freight yard.

In the little county seat of **Jefferson** is the **Crawford W. Long Museum** (in the center of town, off Route 129, 404–367–5307), a museum dedicated to the doctor who here performed the first operation in which the patient was put under general anesthesia by the administration of ether in 1842. Four years later doctors in Boston used ether as an anesthetic in a widely publicized operation, after which Dr. Long, and others, stepped forward to dispute the Bostonians' claims to primacy. Memorabilia from Dr. Long's office and a diorama showing the historic operation—a cyst removal—are on display. Exhibits also outline the development of modern anesthesia and local history. An antebellum structure houses a nineteenth-century general store and a re-created 1840s doctor's office.

Eight miles south of **Carnesville,** on Route 106, is the **Cromer's Mill Covered Bridge.** Built in 1906, it stretches 132 feet in a single span.

## GAINESVILLE

Gainesville, incorporated in 1821, is a gateway to the Blue Ridge region. Standing in the foothills, it was not so isolated as the higher towns. A brief gold rush in 1829 fizzled, but the town laid the foundation for more lasting prosperity when a railroad laid its track through here during the last quarter of the nineteenth century. About the same time, poultry and eggs became an important industry in the surrounding area, and today Gainesville bills itself as the "Poultry Capital of the World."

The evidence of Gainesville's prosperity can be seen in the **Green Street Historic District,** whose stately Victorian and Neoclassical homes (inspired by the Chicago Exhibition of 1893) neatly

OPPOSITE: *Two trim Neoclassical houses, the legacy of late-nineteenth-century prosperity in Gainesville, Georgia.*

date the town's rise from obscurity. The **Green Street Station** (311 Green Street, 404–536–0889) contains a fine introductory museum relating to the culture and crafts of the northeastern mountains.

## DAHLONEGA

West into the mountains, Route 60 leads to Dahlonega, whose name derives from the Cherokee word meaning "yellow metal," and which was the center of the first great gold rush in the United States, beginning in 1828. A U.S. mint was established here between 1838 and 1861. The **Dahlonega Courthouse Gold Museum** (Public Square, 404–864–2257) is located in the 1838 brick Greek Revival building that served as a courthouse for the county until 1965. The museum shows a film about the gold rush and displays such artifacts as a five-and-a-half-ounce gold nugget, a collection of coins minted at Dahlonega, mining tools, a stamp mill, and the restored chambers of the judge and jury of the old district court.

**Cleveland** is another county seat once prominent as a gold town. The **Old White County Courthouse** (Public Square, 404–865–5356) is a small-scale imitation of Philadelphia's Independence Hall, constructed between 1857 and 1859.

East of Cleveland is the town of **Clarkesville**, a county seat in a mountain-ringed valley. Three miles west of town on Route 115 is the **Big Holly Cabin** (404–255–3583), an 1820s cabin that had been inhabited by members of the same family from its construction until 1980.

The town of **Helen** was not incorporated until 1913, when a St. Louis lumber company located a mill here (it was promptly named for an official's daughter.) But tourism soon beat out logging, and the town was transformed in 1969 into a replica of a Bavarian village. The **Museum of the Hills** (Main Street, Castle Complex, 404–878–3140), located in a simulated castle, contains photos and memorabilia of early-twentieth-century Helen, with dioramas and reconstructed building fronts, a barbershop, and period rooms.

The fifty-two-acre **Track Rock Archaeological Area** (southeast of Blairsville on Town Creek Road, 404–745–2384) preserves pre-A.D. 1500 Indian petroglyphs, depicting animals, crosses, circles, and other geometric designs.

OPPOSITE: *The Dahlonega Courthouse Gold Museum contains artifacts from America's first gold rush. Dahlonega gold was used to gild the dome of Atlanta's State Capitol.*

# NORTHWEST GEORGIA

Northwestern Georgia is mountainous ridge and valley country, covered with pine and oak woodland and linked to the Cumberland Plateau and the Alleghenies. Water from its rivers flows to the Gulf of Mexico, not to the Atlantic, and the climate is cooler than in most of the rest of Georgia. The valleys yield corn and soybeans; the hills yield timber.

Here was the ancestral home of the Cherokee nation, and here the tribe created its capital of New Echota, operating as a true independent nation during the early 1820s. White settlers and gold prospectors, however, were anxious to claim Cherokee lands, and in 1828 the Georgia legislature asserted sovereignty over the Cherokee. When the latter applied for relief to the federal government, President Andrew Jackson refused them, only to have John Marshall's Supreme Court annul the Georgia law and reinstate Cherokee sovereignty. The president nevertheless refused to enforce the court's order, and the state proceeded with the forced removal of the Cherokee between 1832 and 1838. The trek west to the Indian territories in present-day Oklahoma was a hard one, and many died on what became known as the Trail of Tears.

The following entries proceed generally northwest from Atlanta, branching out to towns of import for the Indian and white settlement of the area, and ending at the Chickamauga and Chattanooga National Military Park, on the Georgia/Tennessee border.

## MARIETTA

Just northwest of Atlanta, this important industrial town was for many years a sleepy county seat. Since it was in the line of Sherman's march on Atlanta, the central district suffered terribly during the Civil War, but a driving tour available from the **Marietta Welcome Center** (4 Depot Street, 404–429–1115) provides an unusually well prepared guide to the surviving early homes of the city, in a variety of styles, paying particular attention to the changes and additions that have been made to many of them.

Nearby, just two-and-a-half miles southwest of Smyrna, is the **Concord Bridge,** an 1848 queen-post bridge that is 133 feet long.

OPPOSITE: *The Kennesaw Mountain National Battlefield Park commemorates a Confederate victory that stalled but did not halt General William Tecumseh Sherman's offensive against Atlanta.*

# KENNESAW MOUNTAIN NATIONAL BATTLEFIELD PARK

This 3,000-acre park commemorates the Battle of Kennesaw Mountain, a key confrontation on the road to Atlanta. General Joseph E. Johnston's 65,000 Confederate troops held the high ground against General Sherman's 100,000 federal troops between June 19 and July 2, 1864. In the bloody frontal attack on June 27, the Union lost 3,000 men to only about 500 on the Confederate side. The South was heartened by the "victory," but General Johnston continued his policy of retreat before a numerically superior force until he was relieved by General John Bell Hood. At that point Sherman already stood at the gates of Atlanta. The park preserves the entrenchments and redoubts used by both sides at key moments in the battle.

LOCATION: Three miles north of Marietta. HOURS: 8:30–5 Daily. FEE: None. TELEPHONE: 404–427–4686.

# BIG SHANTY MUSEUM

This museum of Civil War artifacts, such as medals, weapons, and uniforms, also displays one of the war's most celebrated relics— The General—the actual locomotive whose theft by Union saboteurs touched off the "Great Locomotive Chase." In April 1862 a band of soldiers, dressed in civilian clothes and led by the spy James J. Andrews, boarded the train in Marietta. At the breakfast stop in Big Shanty, they uncoupled the passenger cars, commandeered the locomotive, and took off for Chattanooga, intending to destroy bridges and tunnels on the way. But they were hotly pursued in a handcar by an enraged conductor, who managed to commandeer another locomotive and gather volunteers for the chase. When The General ran out of steam at the Tennessee border the would-be saboteurs were captured. Andrews and seven of his men were hanged, but his entire band was awarded Congressional Medals of Honor, posthumously.

LOCATION: 2829 Cherokee Street, Kennesaw. HOURS: March through November: 9:30–5:30 Monday–Saturday; December through February: 12:30–5:30 Monday–Saturday. FEE: Yes. TELEPHONE: 404–427–2117.

OPPOSITE: *Roswell's graceful Bulloch Hall was built in 1840 by Major James S. Bulloch, Theodore Roosevelt's grandfather.*

# ROSWELL

Set on the northern edge of the Piedmont and on a bluff overlooking the Chattahoochee River, Roswell is one of the loveliest old towns in Georgia. In other respects it is far from typical, having been settled by Roswell King and his relatives and friends, who were natives of Connecticut. Originally King was seeking a more healthful climate than the malarial areas of Darien and Savannah where he had earlier settled; he fell in love with the site of Roswell, and by 1839 he and his partners had a cloth-manufacturing facility thriving there. Modeled as much on a New England mill town as on any southern place, the town featured workers' housing built by King, some of which still survives. General Sherman had the productive mills burned to the ground during the Civil War, but he spared the palatial Jeffersonian homes of the town's founders.

Three of these remarkable homes survive today—**Bulloch Hall, Barrington Hall, and Mimosa Hall**—all built by Willis Ball during the 1840s and all fine examples of the Greek Revival style in Georgia. Simple, stately, and symmetrical, they express the notion of civilization that these transplanted New Englanders expected to bring to the Georgia highlands. The house would be as appropriate to central Massachusetts as they are to central Georgia. Of the three, only Bulloch Hall is open on a regular basis, but tour information for a walk-by of all of them can be obtained at the **Roswell Historical Society** (227 South Atlanta Street, 404–992–1665).

# ETOWAH INDIAN MOUNDS

Just west of Route 75 in the Etowah Valley is an aboriginal site of considerable interest. It is the largest of numerous mound sites in the vicinity, embracing at least six large mounds and two open squares. The largest of the mounds covers three acres and rises 63 feet high. Artifacts discovered in the mounds show that the Indians who peopled this city of several thousand between roughly A.D. 1000 and 1500 had dealings with their fellows as far north as the Great Lakes and as far south as the Gulf of Mexico. A small museum displays idols, shell ornaments, weapons, and a particularly interesting group of effigy figures.

LOCATION: Three miles south of Cartersville off Route 113. HOURS: 9–5 Tuesday–Saturday, 2–5:30 Sunday. FEE: Yes. TELEPHONE: 404–387–3747.

*The prehistoric Etowah Indians buried their nobility—dressed in elaborate costumes—in these burial mounds.*

A fine 1886 **covered bridge** spans Euharlee Creek two miles north of Cartersville off Route 113. It is of town lattice design, and the numbers on the members indicate that it was cut elsewhere and assembled on the site.

Southwest of Rome, near the Alabama border, is the tiny and quiet town of **Cave Springs,** named for the fresh spring water that still wells from a nearby cave, providing the town with its water. The town dates from 1826, and it boasts some ninety historic buildings, the majority of them from the 1850s.

## ROME

Standing near the hills at the head of the Coosa Valley, Rome has been an important manufacturing center since before the Civil War. Founded in the 1830s on the site of a former Cherokee Indian settlement and reportedly named in a drawing-of-lots among the five founders, the town came to boast the important Nobles' Foundry, a factory that manufactured cannon for the Confederacy. Union Colonel Abel Streight, with more than one thousand soldiers, was eager to capture the place in 1863; but he was outmaneuvered by Confederate General Nathan Bedford Forrest's roughly 400 soldiers, who succeeded in convincing the Yankee general that he was outnumbered. Nevertheless, Rome was by October 19, 1864, in the hands of Sherman's army, which eliminated its industrial contributions to the Confederacy.

In spite of the war and the disastrous floods of the Coosa during the 1880s (during which riverboats floated through the town), Rome is once again the most important manufacturing town in northwestern Georgia. The 1871 **Old Town Clock** sits atop a 104-foot-high water tower that occupies the crown of one of Rome's hills. The clock's bell was cast in Troy, New York.

The **Chieftains Museum** (501 Riverside Parkway, 404–291–9494) is located in the white clapboard home built over the frame of a 1794 log cabin erected by the Cherokee leader Major Ridge. The small museum contains items relating to Cherokee history, but the house is most notable as the home of the man who signed the treaty that led to Cherokee removal from the area. Once an ally of John Ross, Ridge later changed his mind and in 1835 at New Echota, he assented to the "treaty" under which the Cherokee were forced to emigrate to Oklahoma. Ridge went west with his fellow Cherokee, only to be executed there for selling off tribal lands.

## CANTON AND BALL GROUND

The county seat at Canton was named, enthusiastically, after the ancient Chinese city by early settlers who unsuccessfully attempted the production of silk here. The **Gazaway Indian Museum** (three miles off Route 20 on Route 372, 404–887–8760) contains a miscellaneous assemblage of minerals and of Indian artifacts from all over America. The nearby town of Ball Ground, essentially just a railroad stop, comes by its name through its place in Indian culture. It is certain that the Cherokee and Creek here played a game similar to lacrosse, and legend has it that one game was played as a mock battle to decide how hunting lands would be divided. The Cherokee won.

# CHICKAMAUGA AND CHATTANOOGA NATIONAL MILITARY PARK

Here, covering over 8,000 acres in both Georgia and Tennessee, is the nation's first military park, established in 1890. The Georgia part of the park—the Chickamauga Battlefield—was the site of one of the Civil War's bloodiest battles, fought on September 19 to 20, 1863. The Union army under General William S. Rosecrans had swept the Confederates from middle Tennessee and was intent on capturing Chattanooga. Instead of attacking the city directly, Rosecrans headed southeast of the city to cut off its rail line to Atlanta. The Confederate army under General Braxton Bragg abandoned Chattanooga in an attempt to trap Rosecrans in northern Georgia. The armies met at Chickamauga Creek. By luck, Confederate General James Longstreet was able to break through a gap in

*The Florida Monument is one of five Confederate memorials erected at Chickamauga Battlefield, part of the first National Military Park.*

*Monument to the 1st Ohio Cavalry, in the Chickamauga and Chattanooga National Military Park.*

Union lines—Federal units had been removed from the line at that point through a mix-up in communications. Longstreet's cavalry sent half of Rosecrans's army fleeing in dismay. His advance was stopped on Snodgrass Hill by the heroic stand of General George H. Thomas, whose exploits that day earned him the nickname "Rock of Chickamauga." It was a crucial moment for the Confederacy. Had General Bragg heeded the pleas of his subordinates, Longstreet and Forrest, to destroy Rosecrans's army before it could be reinforced, the war might have turned out differently. As it was, Rosecrans was able to retreat to Chattanooga, where Bragg, with reinforcements, besieged him, threatening to starve the army into submission. President Lincoln placed General Ulysses S. Grant in charge of the relief of Chattanooga. The Federals eventually broke the siege, with the result that General William Tecumseh Sherman was able to use Chattanooga as the base for his attack on Atlanta the following year.

The fighting at Chickamauga took place largely in woodlands. Some 16,000 Union troops and 18,000 Confederates were killed, wounded, or captured in the battle. Monuments and markers along a tour road in the park trace the events of the battle; there is also a visitor center with a fine collection of weaponry, including many types of light artillery.

LOCATION: Seven miles south of Chattanooga on Route 27. HOURS: 8–4:45 Daily. FEE: None. TELEPHONE: 404–866–9241.

The only structure that survived the battle in the village of Chickamauga was the **Gordon-Lee Mansion** (217 Cove Road, 404–375–4728), an 1847 Greek Revival house with brick walls fourteen inches thick. It is now furnished with antebellum antiques. The house was used first as the headquarters of General Rosecrans, then the site of a Union army hospital. Twenty-five Union medical officers remained in the house after the Union retreat, submitting to capture rather than leave their patients.

## JOHN ROSS HOUSE

Northernmost of the Cherokee landmarks in Georgia, the John Ross House is located in Rossville, the town named for him, near the Tennessee border. Like many Cherokee leaders of the time, he was of mixed blood. As president of the Cherokee nation, he fought to the end against their removal, and when it proved inevitable, he accompanied his people into exile. His wife died on the march.

Ross's ancestors were prominent people in the frontier history of this borderland. His grandfather, John MacDonald, raised the original cabin on the site; his father was Daniel Ross, whose trading post was the original building in what became Chattanooga. In 1797 the cabin was expanded into a two-story dogtrot split-log home. It was here that Ross lived until the removal, and the restored house has been refurnished in part with furnishings from the Ross estate, including his bed.

LOCATION: Off Route 27, Rossville. HOURS: May through September: 1–5 Thursday–Tuesday. FEE: None. TELEPHONE: 404–861–3954.

## THE CHIEF VANN HOUSE

In the little Appalachian town of Spring Place is the brick Federal style house of Chief James Vann, the leading citizen of the Cherokee nation. Vann invited Moravian missionaries onto his plantation here in 1801; with their help and with slave labor, he built this

*Chief James Vann's brick house, called "the showplace of the Cherokee Nation" when it was constructed in 1805.*

comfortable dwelling in 1805. President James Monroe was entertained here by Vann's son. The interior painting has been beautifully restored, and the house is furnished with period antiques. The younger Vann was unceremoniously evicted from the house in 1834 by a captain of the Georgia militia, just in time for the captain's brother to take up residency. Vann was eventually paid a sum of almost $20,000 for his home, outbuildings, and 800 acres. Vann's gold signet ring and his portrait are among the personal artifacts on display in the home.

> LOCATION: In Spring Place, at the junction of routes 225 and 52. HOURS: 9–5 Tuesday–Saturday, 2–5:30 Sunday. FEE: Yes. TELEPHONE: 404–695–2598.

Northwest on Route 75, **Calhoun,** incorporated in the 1850s, suffered severely during the Civil War. **Oakleigh** (335 South Wall Street, 404–629–1515), a plain symmetrical wood-frame plantation house, survived, perhaps because it served briefly as General Sherman's headquarters. Today it is home to the local historical society.

*The interior woodwork in the Chief Vann House, carved by Moravian artisans, has been restored to its original color scheme.*

Five miles north of Calhoun, off Route 75, is the **Resaca Confederate Cemetery.** From May 5 to 15, 1864, the armies of generals Sherman and Johnston met here at the Battle of Resaca, one of the first confrontations on the road to Atlanta. Each lost about three thousand men; the Union dead were removed from the field, but the Southerners were not, until a farmer and his slave dug graves for them, creating the first Confederate cemetery. More than 400 of the Confederate fallen are buried here, with a poignant plaque that lists their names. Some are identified only by a first name, some by initials and hometowns; and there are many unknowns.

## NEW ECHOTA STATE HISTORIC SITE

For a little more than a decade, New Echota—the word means "town" in Cherokee—was the capital of the Cherokee nation. The site at the confluence of two rivers had been selected in 1819. An assembly meeting on the site in 1820 created a Cherokee republic, with John Ross as its president. By 1829 the town had a courthouse,

ABOVE: *New Echota's reconstructed 1829 Cherokee Supreme Court building, where the Cherokee Nation established a government patterned on that of the United States.* LEFT: *Sitting at this elevated judge's bench, a three-judge panel heard the legal proceedings.*

a school, and other permanent buildings; three years later, the *Cherokee Phoenix*, a newspaper using the alphabet newly devised for the language by the Cherokee Sequoyah, began publishing. It issued the biblical book of Genesis in the Cherokee tongue. In the same year, the Georgia state legislature started its own decade-long process of wresting control of northern Georgia from the Cherokee. In 1838 General Winfield Scott set up camp at New Echota with his troops, marshaling the disenfranchised Cherokee—13,000 of them—for their long walk to Oklahoma.

Most of the buildings now on the site are reconstructions of New Echota buildings, including the Cherokee Supreme Court building and the *Cherokee Phoenix* printing office. The **Worcester House** is the 1828 home of Moravian missionary Samuel Worcester, which was used as church and post office for the town. It is furnished as it was when Worcester occupied it.

LOCATION: Northeast of Calhoun on Route 225. HOURS: 9–5 Tuesday–Saturday, 2–5:30 Sunday. FEE: Yes. TELEPHONE: 404–629–8151.

# HEART
## OF THE
# PIEDMONT

OPPOSITE: *The splendid entry hall of the Gordon-Banks House in Newnan. The house originally stood in Milledgeville, where it survived unscathed its occupation by a detachment of Sherman's invading troops.*

The sandy loams and the red clay hills of the Georgia Piedmont plateau stretch in a broad sash diagonally across the state, bordered on the north by the mountain ranges and on the south by the extensive coastal plain. When these were the ancestral lands of the Creek Indians, the hills were covered with mixed oak and pine woodland, now much reduced by deforestation and farming. The westward march of Georgia's succession of state capitals marks the white settlers' penetration of this interior heartland and its rapid conversion to the plantation system. From the original colonial capital at Savannah, the seat of government moved just after the American Revolution to Augusta, on the eastern edge of the Piedmont. In 1795, the capital was moved deeper into the region, settling at Louisville on the Ogeechee River; in 1805, it moved farther west to Milledgeville on the Oconee River, where it remained until after the Civil War.

Settlement spread up the fingers of rivers that extend northwest from the Atlantic coast. As the farmers moved in, the Creek were moved farther and farther west. As early as 1763 the Creek ceded the first of their lands in the interior; in 1790 they yielded Piedmont lands soon to be made valuable by the invention of the cotton gin. In the first decades of the nineteenth century, former Indian lands were distributed to white settlers in a lottery system that granted property in 202-acre blocks. Indicative of this change, the non-Indian population of the state more than quadrupled between 1800 and 1840, reaching 691,000.

Cheap land, slaves, and cotton produced great wealth for a planter oligarchy and for smaller operators as well. Although many of the towns were in the line of Sherman's march to the sea, a large number of historic homes and public buildings remain, giving a remarkable flavor of the plantation system.

As late as 1911, cotton was the driving force in the Piedmont economy, but thereafter the boll weevil forced abandonment of the monoculture that had endured a full century. Today, the agriculture of the region is more varied: Soy, corn, wheat, and peanuts all outrank cotton in acres planted. The area's two main cities, Macon and Augusta, lie at opposite edges of the Piedmont, making them natural distribution and manufacturing centers.

The itinerary of this chapter forms a loop starting at Athens, proceeding southwest through Monroe to towns south of Atlanta, turning east to Macon, then heading northeast to Augusta.

*Artifacts excavated at Ocmulgee National Monument include plain Mississippian vessels dating from A.D. 900 to 1100 and decorated pots of the Lamar culture from ca. 1300.*

## ATHENS

General Sherman's army passed south of Athens. This is one reason that this small city set on a beautiful high bluff above the Oconee River was able to preserve such a large number of historic homes and buildings set among stately oaks and elms.

The town, incorporated in 1801, was named in a fever of classicism associated with the University of Georgia, chartered in 1785. The first building of the new university was a log hut, but that was no handicap to the vision of educators who, until the Civil War, instituted and maintained a system of higher education based on the study of the classics and of rhetoric and oratory.

Many students went off to fight in the war between the states, causing the university to close in 1863. Nonetheless, a town had sprung up around it, owing to the original need to sell off parcels of the 40,000-acre land grant that had funded the university.

The symmetrical **Church-Waddel-Brumby House** (280 East Dougherty Street, 404–353–1820) was built in 1820 for Alonzo Church, later the president of the University of Georgia. It is the oldest surviving house in Athens and has been restored as the city's Welcome Center, furnished with period antiques.

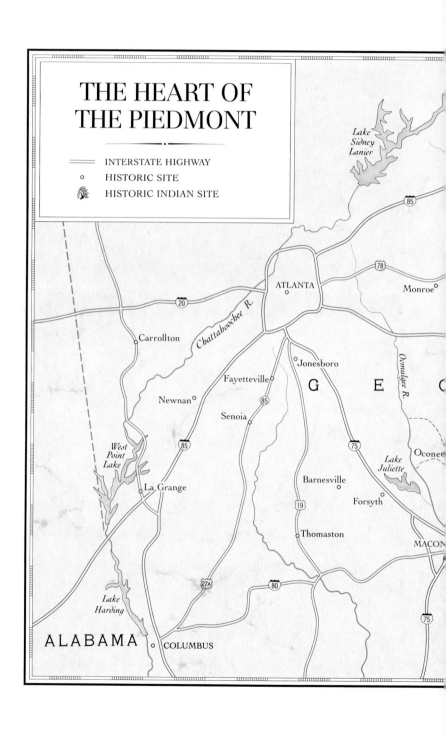

# THE HEART OF THE PIEDMONT

=== INTERSTATE HIGHWAY
○ HISTORIC SITE
🪶 HISTORIC INDIAN SITE

*Lake Sidney Lanier*

ATLANTA

*Chattahoochee R.*

Monroe

Carrollton

Jonesboro

Fayetteville

G       E

*Oconee R.*

Newnan

Senoia

Oconee

*West Point Lake*

Barnesville

*Lake Juliette*

La Grange

Forsyth

Thomaston

MACON

*Lake Harding*

ALABAMA

COLUMBUS

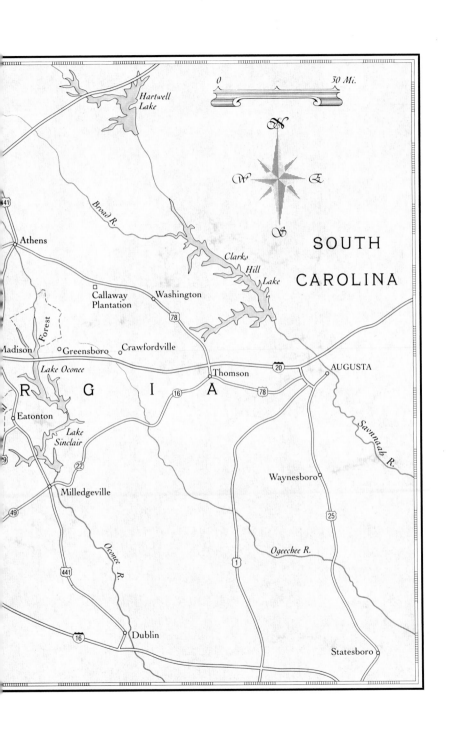

*Athens, site of the University of Georgia, is known as the "Classic City" because of its many surviving Greek Revival buildings. Among them are, clockwise from left, the 1857–1858 University President's House, the last great Georgia house built in the Greek Revival style; the 1845 Taylor-Grady House; and the 1832 University chapel.*

In the center of the downtown area is the **First Presbyterian Church** (185 East Hancock Avenue), raised in 1855. Its hand-hewn pews are of particular interest. Nearby, on the City Hall lawn, is an odd experimental **Double-Barreled Cannon.** Created in 1863, the unique cannon was intended by its Confederate inventors to fire two cannonballs linked by a chain. It didn't work.

Several interesting houses survive along Prince Avenue. The **University of Georgia President's Home** (570 Prince Avenue, open by appointment, 404–354–4096) is a very imposing ornate late–Greek Revival mansion, built in 1857 to 1858 by a railroad magnate. The front colonnade is in a Composite mode, with more elaborate capitals than the Corinthian order. Inside, rooms are furnished with an eclectic but very fine selection of European furniture and decorative arts of the eighteenth and nineteenth centuries. The **Taylor–Grady House** (634 Prince Avenue, 404–549–8688) was built by a prominent cotton planter and factor in 1845 in the Greek Revival style. Thirteen Doric columns compose a colonnade that embraces three sides of the house. The builder moved his family here so his sons could attend the university. Henry Grady's father bought the house in 1863, and the young Henry—who would become the revitalizing editor of the Atlanta *Constitution*—lived here for three years until his own graduation from the university. The house is furnished appropriately for the period. The **Stephen Upson House** (1022 Prince Avenue, 404–353–1801) is a large, two-story mansion with Greek Revival elements, built in 1847. The woodwork of the interiors is particularly finely carved and detailed, and the brick walls are eighteen inches thick. The house has been restored and is used as a bank.

Protecting all this Prince Avenue glory is **Fire Hall No. 2** (489 Prince Avenue, 404–353–1801). The 1901 Victorian firehouse is a wedge-shaped little building that serves as headquarters for the local heritage foundation and still contains its original fire pole.

On the southwestern edge of the downtown area at Pulaski Street is the **Ross Crane House** (247 Pulaski Street, private), now a fraternity building. The boxwood garden was designed in the formal style popular at the time the house was built, in 1842. The **Lucy Cobb Institute** (200 North Milledge Avenue, 404–542–2736), located in a three-story stucco building with wonderful lacy ironwork detailing, was the brainchild of General Thomas R. R. Cobb, who had read a pseudonymous article about the education of women in the local newspaper. It inspired him to found a college for Southern women in this building in 1858.

On the southern edge of the downtown blocks, near the University of Georgia campus, is the **Franklin Hotel** (480 East Broad Street), an 1845 Greek Revival structure used in its early years as a hotel and then for more than a century as the headquarters of a hardware company. It has recently been renovated for office space.

## University of Georgia

The campus preserves a number of early structures, including the 1832 **Chapel,** the earliest, and most genuine example of the Greek temple style in Athens. The 1824 **Demosthenian Hall** is a two-story Palladian structure housing the oldest literary society on campus. The Federal style **Old College,** built 1801 to 1805, is an imitation of Yale's Connecticut Hall and the oldest building on campus.

Near the southern edge of the campus is the **Founders Memorial Gardens** (325 South Lumpkin Street, private). The brick house on the site was built as a professor's residence in 1857; later it was used, among other things, to house rats for experiments. Now restored and furnished by the Garden Club of Georgia with interesting period antiques, the home is noted for its spectacular gardens, particularly the authentically patterned and designed parterre and knot gardens.

At the end of the South Campus is the **Governor Wilson Lumpkin House,** a stone house with two-foot-thick walls.

# MONROE

The county seat of Monroe has long been identified with cotton and textile manufacturing. The latter has made it busier and more prepossessing than its sleepier surroundings. The town has a wealth of older homes, many in an amalgam of Greek Revival elements upon a raised cottage style. A highlight is the turn-of-the-century **Davis Edwards House** (238 North Broad Street, 404–267–6594), an L-shaped home that mixes traditional and Greek Revival elements in an intriguing melange. Some of the rooms have period furniture. Three more imposing houses of note are located on McDaniel Street: the **McDaniel–Tishner House,** built in 1887, the **Walker Home** right across the street, and the nearby **Selman-Pollack-Williams Home,** whose basic structure dates from 1812. All three are private. A walking tour of town is available from the Walton County Chamber of Commerce (323 West Spring Street, 404–267–6594). North of Monroe on Route 11, Kilgore Mill Bridge Road leads to a covered bridge that is still in use.

# JONESBORO

As do many towns in the area, this small county seat of Atlanta claims to be the real model for Margaret Mitchell's *Gone with the Wind*. Of particular note are the **Stately Oaks Mansion** (Lake Jodeco Road, at the southeast edge of town) and the **Ashley Oaks Mansion** (College Street between Main and Fayetteville streets). The former, an 1839 Greek Revival manse with double porches, was originally located north of town and served as a guidepost to Sherman's troops as they circled Atlanta in an effort to break its defenses. The latter is an elegant brick townhouse built between 1879 and 1880. Both are restored and furnished and are open by appointment through Historic Jonesboro, in the town's **visitor center** (404–478–6549), located at 9712 Tara Boulevard.

# FAYETTEVILLE

Just ten miles southwest of Jonesboro, Fayetteville houses the oldest **courthouse** still in use in Georgia. Built in 1825, just four years after the founding of Fayette County, it contains a steepled bell tower on its south side, added in 1888. The stucco-over-brick edifice sits in the middle of the town square (200 Courthouse Square, 404–461–6041). One block west of the courthouse is the **Holiday-Fife House,** an unaltered 1855 Greek Revival home, built by Dr. John Stiles Holiday, uncle of "Doc" Holiday of Wild West fame. The house is renovated and open by appointment. The **Fayetteville Academy,** Scarlett O'Hara's school in *Gone with the Wind,* was built the same year, and students and faculty lived in the Holiday house for two years. Author Margaret Mitchell did research in the county and befriended five ladies who were in the process of constructing a library building, named **The Margaret Mitchell Library** when it opened in 1940. The library is now located at 165 Johnson Avenue (404–461–8841); the old library building is currently the home of the **Fayette County Historical Society** (195 Lee Street, 404–461–8493) and houses a small museum as well as research material on genealogy in Fayette County and Civil War materials.

# SENOIA

The town is named for the mother of Creek Indian leader William McIntosh, Jr., who signed the Treaty of Indian Springs that resulted in a further cession of Creek lands to the state of Georgia. A

*A wartime ball in* Gone With the Wind, *the 1939 film that romanticized the Confederate cause and fed nostalgia for the antebellum South.*

driving tour available at the city hall contains twenty-four stops, the oldest sites dating from the 1850s but the majority from the turn of the century, when Senoia boomed as a railroad town. The Steamboat Gothic–style **Culpepper House** (Broad at Morgan Street, 404–599–8182) dates from 1871 and is now an inn. The 1907 **Veranda** (252 Seavy Street, 404–599–3905) is a Classic Revival structure built as a hotel to handle railroad traffic.

## NEWNAN

Named for a War of 1812 soldier, Newnan is a very prosperous textile and farming town that preserves a large number of fine old residences and public buildings. During the 1820s and 1830s, it was an important cotton shipment center. There are twenty-three sites included on a driving tour of the town, copies of which may be obtained at the **Male Academy Museum** (30 Temple Avenue, 404–251–0207). The museum occupies the 1873 quarters of a boys' secondary school and has a very strong collection of textiles, including clothing and cloth made in the local area, as well as Civil War artifacts.

One of the many homes of note is the **Parrott-Camp-Soucy House** (155 Greenville Street, 404–253–4846), built in 1842 by one of the early white settlers of the county and Victorianized into a mansard-roofed French Second Empire mansion in 1885, with fine scrollwork and gingerbread ornamentation. The house is furnished with Victorian pieces and serves as a bed-and-breakfast inn. Another distinguished house, the 1820s **Gordon-Banks House** (784 South Highway 29, private), was originally constructed west of Milledgeville. This finely detailed residence was designed by Daniel Pratt, an architect and builder from Temple, New Hampshire who established a style called "Milledgeville Federal." The house was moved to its current location in 1969 and completely restored. It is included in Newnan's annual October house tour.

## LA GRANGE

La Grange owes its modern prosperity to its textile industry, particularly the mills run by the Callaway family. The patrons of the town are remembered in the 1929 **Callaway Memorial Tower** (Truit and Fourth avenues), based upon the campanile of St. Mark's Square in Venice and erected by Callaway's employees. Beginning in 1900, when the family's first textile mill opened, they were the largest employers in town.

An earlier generation of wealth is remembered at **Bellevue** (204 Ben Hill Street, 404–884–1832), the 1852 to 1854 Greek Revival mansion once inhabited by statesman Benjamin Hill. The home was once the center of a 12,000-acre plantation and is furnished with period furniture. Of particular note are the black marble mantelpiece, the walnut staircase, and the decorated ceilings with plasterwork medallions.

The **Chattahoochee Valley Art Association** (112 Hines Street, 404–882–3267) is housed in a 1892 brick Victorian former county jail. The collection includes crafts and fine arts by regional and national artists. The **Troup County Historical Society Archives** (136 Main Street, 404–884–1828) exhibits local historical and genealogical materials in a 1917 bank building.

## THE LITTLE WHITE HOUSE

Nestled into the slopes of Pine Mountain, this is the house Franklin Delano Roosevelt built for himself in 1932, its simplicity a testimony to the life he enjoyed here. Roosevelt first came to Warm Springs in 1924, looking for relief from polio, and bought the old resort on the site, plus over 1,000 acres of surrounding land. The home is maintained today as it was when Roosevelt died here on April 12, 1945, with his two hand-operated automobiles and many personal effects are on display.

LOCATION: Route 85 West, south of Warm Springs. HOURS: 9–4:30 Daily. FEE: Yes. TELEPHONE: 404–655–3511.

## FORSYTH

Named for the secretary of state under presidents Jackson and Van Buren, Forsyth got its first big boost when the railroad from Macon reached here in 1834. The **Courthouse Square** is a harmonious and peaceful place, with most of its many fine historic structures dating from the end of the nineteenth century and the beginning of the twentieth. The 1896 Victorian courthouse is known for its painted pressed-tin ceilings. Tour brochures of the district are available at the **Whistle Stop Museum** (Train Depot, 912–994–0534), a local history museum with turn-of-the-century antiques such as the desk belonging to the writer Joel Chandler Harris. It is housed in a handsome brick Victorian station built in 1899.

A nearby small town of interest is **Barnesville,** named for the man who operated a tavern here in the early nineteenth century. In town is **Barnesville Hardware** (116 Main Street, 404–358–0250), a hardware store that has been operating in this building since 1876, prior to which it was the showroom of the Jackson G. Smith Buggy Company. The door to the big corner store is six feet wide, big enough to pull a buggy through. The hardware store maintains a wonderful collection of wares, both old and new, including trace chains, horse collars, rope, and stovepipe.

## THOMASTON

Thomaston is a center for textiles, livestock, and peach farming. The ca. 1835 **Pettigrew-White-Stamps House** (South Church Street and Andrews Drive, 404–647–9691) is a typical middle-class six-room home, furnished with antiques of a variety of periods. Some of the furniture was made by itinerant craftsmen in the local area. One room is a museum of local history, featuring a good collection of old surgical and dental instruments. About twelve miles south of town on Allen Road is the 1898 **Auchumpkee Covered Bridge,** preserved but no longer in use.

*The Italianate Hay House, built by William Butler Johnson on his return from a three-year European trip.* OPPOSITE: *A statue in the Hay House's ornate ballroom.*

# MACON

Named for Nathaniel Macon, a North Carolina senator, presumably by the immigrants from that state who helped incorporate the town in 1823, Macon has been important both as a river-shipping and a railroad center. Its location on the fall line between the Piedmont and the southerly coastal plain provided power for its mills. The town was used by the Confederacy as an arsenal, gold depository, and as a shipment point and manufacturing center. Macon resisted two Union attacks in 1864 but capitulated in April 1865, after generals Sherman and Johnston had already agreed to an armistice.

Macon is rich is historic structures. **City Hall** (700 Poplar Street), though remodeled in 1935, is based on an 1836 Greek Revival bank building. The last session of the Confederate Congress was held here during 1865, when Macon served as temporary capital of Georgia. The imposing 1925 **Municipal Auditorium** (Cherry and First streets) is notable for its gigantic copper-covered dome and for its mural depicting the history of Macon from 1540, when de Soto is said to have passed this way, to World War I.

Three homes in the downtown area are open to the public and of particular interest. The **Old Cannonball House** (856 Mulberry Street, 912–745–5982), a Greek Revival mansion built in 1853, now houses period rooms and a Confederate museum with a collection of uniforms, weapons, and items relating to Macon. The house is so called because one of General George Stoneman's cannonballs went through one of its columns, entered the parlor, and landed, unexploded, in the hall. The **Hay House** (934 Georgia Avenue, 912–742–8155) is a very unusual and elaborate Italianate structure built between 1855 and 1861. The house is restored and refurnished, but some of the most impressive items were built in, such as the nineteen Carrara marble mantelpieces. The Italianate detailing is splendid—in scale and opulence of detail, this is the grandest Italianate villa in the South. Overlooking the city of Macon from atop Coleman Hill, the **Woodruff House** (988 Bond Street, 912–744–4187) is a fine Greek Revival mansion with colonnades on

*Woodruff House, in Macon, built ca. 1836 by a banker and railroad financier. He soon found himself in financial difficulties and sold it to one of the city's major cotton planters.* OPPOSITE: *Woodruff House's massive hand-carved oak door.*

three sides, built in 1836 for a banker. Owned by Mercer University, the refurbished house is named for a university benefactor, George Woodruff of Atlanta.

Sidney Lanier, Georgia's best-known poet, was born in the **Sidney Lanier Cottage** (935 High Street, 912–743–3851) in 1842. It is a Victorian home, furnished to reflect that period. Here too are the offices of the local historical society.

*A Mississippian effigy, originally the top of a bottle, found in a burial site at Ocmulgee.*

## Ocmulgee National Monument

This important archaeological site has been occupied continuously over the last 10,000 years. Its period of greatest development came between A.D. 900 and 1100, when a farming people known as the Mississippians created the elaborate and large mounds now found here. A reconstructed earthlodge—probably originally a temple or council house—is on the site, and excavations of the funeral mound have turned up an unusual number of fine pottery vessels, effigy figures, and shell and copper jewelry, all on display.

LOCATION: East of Macon on Route 80. HOURS: 9–5 Daily. FEE: Yes. TELEPHONE: 912–752–8257.

# MILLEDGEVILLE

Between 1804 and 1868, Milledgeville, named for early Georgia governor John Milledge, was the fourth capital of Georgia. For two days in November 1864 it was occupied by Sherman's army. The Yankees looted the state house, but Sherman ordered that cotton stockpiles and a flour mill be spared. Milledgeville suffered little from the invaders, despite the Northerners' rage at the emaciated condition of some newly arrived escapees from Andersonville's Confederate prison.

Milledgeville is known today for its outstanding nineteenth-century houses including the ca. 1825 **Stetson-Sanford House** (corner of Jackson and Hancock, 912–452–4687). It is a structure in transition, managing to blend vernacular eighteenth-century and Classical Revival styles with such decorative touches as the parlor's pine wainscoting that has been feathered and stained to resemble mahogany. It is furnished with Empire and Victorian antiques. The architect of this house, John Marlor, an Englishman working in Georgia, is also responsible for the fine Italianate 1830 **Masonic Building,** also on Hancock Street.

The so-called **Old State Capitol** (912–453–3481), a Gothic Revival structure which is now the main building of Georgia Military College, is a replica of the 1807 structure that stood here until destroyed by fire in 1941. It contains a museum with Civil War relics, uniforms, period costumes, pictures, and documents.

Milledgeville is also known as the home of Flannery O'Connor for many years before her death in 1964. The author of the novel *Wise Blood* and other novels and short stories, she is regarded as one of the finest American fiction writers of the twentieth century.

*The 1838 Old Governor's Mansion in Milledgeville, today the office of the president of Georgia College.*

## The Old Governor's Mansion

This unusually fine Palladian house was built in 1838 to designs by Charles Cluskey. It is the most ambitious structure in the Renaissance tradition in Georgia, with an interior dome and portico that set the trend for the many "Greek Revival" colonnades in the area. The stately pink stucco mansion served as home to ten governors—and briefly to General Sherman too—and has been elegantly restored and furnished predominantly in the English Regency style, in vogue at the time of construction.

LOCATION: 120 South Clark Street. HOURS: 10–5 Tuesday–Saturday, 2–5 Sunday. FEE: Yes. TELEPHONE: 912–453–4545.

## EATONTON

This town was founded in 1808 and named for a Connecticut general. Author Joel Chandler Harris, of Uncle Remus fame, was born here in 1848. The **Uncle Remus Museum** (Turner Park, 404–485–6856), a simple log cabin made out of two slave cabins, commemorates Harris's life and work. Many of Eatonton's fine nineteenth-century homes are to be found on Madison Avenue, including the 1822 to 1852 **Bronson House** (404–485–4532), one of those mansions that began in the frame, vernacular style of the Piedmont and gradually accreted Greek Revival elements. The house is restored and furnished.

Nine miles north of town on Route 441 is an unusual site, the **Rock Eagle Effigy,** a great bird figure made of quartz boulders laid out on the ground. Rising 10 feet high and with a wingspan of 102 feet, the effigy mound is over 6,000 years old.

## MADISON

Like most of the other towns in this area, Madison was spared destruction in the Civil War, and remains relatively unchanged. Virtually the whole town is a historic district, featuring thirty-two different sites, dating from the 1830s to the turn of the century. **Heritage Hall** (277 South Main Street, 404–342–4454) is an 1835 Greek Revival residence converted into the Morgan County Historical Society headquarters. The **Madison-Morgan Cultural Center** (434 South Main Street, 404–342–4743) is in an 1895 Romanesque Revival public schoolhouse, one of the first graded brick schools in the South. The historical museum here includes artifacts, decorative arts, and interpretive information relating to the Piedmont area in the early 1800s, along with a restored classroom of the period.

## GREENSBORO

Greensboro, laid out in 1786, was named in honor of the great Revolutionary War general Nathaniel Greene, a Rhode Island native who commanded the American forces in the South and was given extensive tracts of land by a grateful Georgia legislature. It was a town that grew around the mansions of the owners of the surrounding plantations; the monoculture bled the soil nearly to death, before wiser planning and the boll weevil encouraged a less damaging approach to agriculture. The **Greene County Historical Society Museum** (201 Greene Street, 404–453–7592) gives a good overview of local history, with collections of clothing and textiles, Creek artifacts, and photographs.

Two noteworthy sites in town are the **Greene County Courthouse** (Main Street), an 1848 brick Greek Revival building with Doric columns, and behind it, the 1807 **Old Greene County Gaol,** a dimly lit granite blockhouse jail. A trapdoor from the second floor was used as a scaffolding for hanging.

## LIBERTY HALL AND CONFEDERATE MUSEUM

This house, now restored, was the home of the vice-president of the Confederacy and, later, governor of Georgia, Alexander H. Stephens. A diminutive man who, despite his unusually high-pitched voice, was praised for his oratorical abilities by fellow congressman Abraham Lincoln, he opposed the secession but bowed to the will of his fellow Georgians. His sole desire while in a federal prison in Boston in 1865 was to be back at his Crawfordville home, Liberty Hall. Stephens first moved here in 1845, but with the exception of the rear ell, the present structure dates from 1875. The house is done in a classic, conservative style with little embellishment but an elegant sense of proportion, and is filled with Stephens's furniture. The adjacent Confederate Museum contains Civil War artifacts, uniforms, cannon, and guns.

This well-preserved home is a fine tribute to a man who had not only courage and loyalty, but a ready wit. It is said that when a congressman tried to bully the young Stephens by threatening to swallow him whole, he quipped, "If you did, sir, you would have more brains in your stomach than in your head."

LOCATION: Route 22, Crawfordville. HOURS: 9–5 Tuesday–Saturday, 1:30–5:30 Sunday. FEE: Yes. TELEPHONE: 404–456–2221.

## WASHINGTON

North of Crawfordville on Route 47 is Washington, a town settled in 1773 by a family who apparently named it after their former neighbor in Virginia, George Washington, making it the second town in the nation to take Washington's name (the first was Washington, Virginia, of 1756).

Washington is a treasure trove of historic homes, with more than forty Greek Revival structures alone. Among the earliest homes is the **Robert Toombs House** (216 East Robert Toombs Avenue, 404–678–2226), originally built between 1794 and 1801, and remodeled with a portico and Doric columns by Toombs in 1852. Toombs was a U.S. representative, a senator, briefly the Confederate Secretary of State, a Confederate general, a prominent postwar exile in Paris, and finally an influential post-Reconstruction politician. The house is restored with period furnishings and exhibits about Toombs's career. The **Mary Willis Library** (Liberty and Jefferson streets, 404–678–7736) is an 1889 public library building notable for its fine windows by Tiffany & Company. The **Washington-Wilkes Historical Museum** (308 East Robert Toombs Avenue, 404–678–2105) is housed in an eighteen-room "cottage" that dates to 1835. Along with its collection of Confederate weapons, the museum features a furnished bedroom, dining room, and parlor. Information on walking tours of Washington is available here.

Just off Route 44, eight miles southwest of town, a **marker** commemorates the Revolutionary War Battle of Kettle Creek, where militia under Andrew Pickens, John Dooly, and Elijah Clarke defeated a detachment of 700 Tories on February 14, 1779.

## CALLAWAY PLANTATION

Just west of Washington is a complete working plantation that was in the hands of a single family from ca. 1785—when the Callaways arrived from Virginia—until it was donated to the town as a living history museum. Among the authentic and furnished structures on the site are a 1785 log cabin, a simple house of 1790 similar to the Federal houses of Virginia, and a late Greek Revival mansion built by the family in 1869. Barns, a blacksmith shop, hog pens, a well shelter, and every other structure needed to run the plantation are also on site. It is said that the Callaways were able to weather the Civil War and build a big house just afterwards because of the good fortune of Parker Callaway, who got out the last shipment of cotton past the Union blockade at the outset of the war and found himself with a fortune in British money safely stored in a London bank.

LOCATION: Five miles west of Washington on Route 78. HOURS: April through mid-December: 10–5 Tuesday–Saturday, 2–5 Sunday. FEE: Yes. TELEPHONE: 404–678–7060.

## THOMSON

Thomson was settled in the 1850s and named for J. Edgar Thomson, the surveyor who planned the Georgia Railroad's route through the town. The downtown district dates mainly from the turn of the century. There is a **monument** to the women of the Civil War era at Railroad and Main streets.

The **Hickory Hill** estate (Route 223, private) once belonged to Populist Thomas E. Watson, a congressman and senator who championed rural causes in the late nineteenth and early twentieth century. He was William Jennings Bryan's running mate on the Populist ticket of 1896, and that party's presidential candidate in 1904. He introduced the legislation that led to Rural Free Delivery.

Four miles outside of Thomson is the **Rock House** (Rock House Road, off Route 223, 404–595–5584), the oldest dwelling in Georgia with its design intact. The stout stone structure was built in 1785 by Thomas Ansley (an ancestor of former President Jimmy Carter). It has been restored and furnished correctly for its period. Rock House is the only surviving dwelling associated with the **Wrightsborough Settlement,** the first settlement above Augusta, in up-country. It was established in 1768, mainly by Quakers from North Carolina, who had originally come from Delaware. (The Ansley who built Rock House was not a Quaker.) The stone architecture in this area is similar to that in Northern Quaker areas such as Chadd's Ford, Pennsylvania. The Quakers soon moved on to the Midwest and West—the last had left Wrightsborough by 1805.

## CLINTON

Clinton was settled by New Englanders in about 1808 and named in honor of Governor DeWitt Clinton of New York. It has an unusual number of early wood-frame homes, fully a dozen of them built before 1830. The town suffered in the Civil War, but since then it has been comparatively unchanged. A walking tour is available at the 1809 **McCarthy-Pope House** (off Route 129), a simple New England saltbox house furnished with period pieces. Among the other white wooden beauties are the 1830 **Lockett-Hamilton House** and the low-steepled 1820 **Old Clinton Methodist Church.**

## AUGUSTA

Named for the mother of King George III of England, Augusta was founded by James Oglethorpe in 1735, making it the second city in Georgia, behind Savannah. It stands at the navigable point farthest upstream on the Savannah River and was from the beginning an important trading post. Like Macon to the southwest, it also stands astride the fall line that separates the Piedmont from the coastal plain, giving it the advantages of both regions: an equable climate and water power for running mills, together with fertile and easily worked soil.

OPPOSITE: *Augusta's Old Medical College, built in 1835. It was the first medical school in Georgia and one of the first in the nation.*

During the Revolutionary War control of Augusta shifted back and forth amid brutal fighting between local Tories and Patriots. In June 1781, American troops under General "Light-Horse Harry" Lee captured the Tory stronghold, Fort Cornwallis, after a siege. In the postwar period, Augusta served as the state capital (from 1785 to 1795), while the newly chosen site at Louisville was being prepared, and Milledgeville waited in the wings.

At this time, newcomers from Virginia and the Carolinas brought to Augusta the tobacco culture that would dominate local agriculture until the turn of the nineteenth century. For the next century, however, Augusta, the Piedmont, and the Coastal Plain planted cotton, cotton, and more cotton, thanks to the revolution brought by the cotton gin—Eli Whitney's 1793 invention that mechanically shucked the lint off the seeds of upland cotton, replacing hours of manual labor. At Augusta and all up and down the rivers of the area, textile mills and cotton-processing operations began to spring up, creating an industrial base.

Augusta consolidated her position as the second city of the state with the building of roads to Savannah and the interior and the construction of the Georgia Railroad in 1837 and a canal in 1845. Outbreaks of yellow fever were damaging during the 1850s, but General Sherman did spare Augusta during his march to the sea. Augusta recovered slowly after Reconstruction, hampered in part by disastrous floods, but today it is a thriving industrial and transportation center.

By the riverside in old Augusta is **St. Paul's Episcopal Church** (605 Reynolds Street), the fourth on this site, where the original was built in 1750 under the shadow and protection of Fort Augusta. The fort and church were destroyed when captured from the British, who occupied Augusta during the American Revolution. The church was rebuilt after the war, and retains its original baptismal font. The cemetery contains the graves of early colonists and patriots and of William Longstreet, one of the first men to operate a steamboat successfully, and William Few, signer of the Constitution. A Celtic cross at the rear of the property marks the site of the colonial fort built by General Oglethorpe in 1737.

Down Reynolds Street at Eighth is the **Cotton Exchange Building,** an 1886 Victorian structure situated beyond the levee,

OPPOSITE: *The corner doorway of Augusta's 1886 Cotton Exchange, the center of its then-booming cotton trade.*

near where endless bales of cotton embarked downriver. In Augusta it is said that a child could walk a mile here on bales of cotton without ever touching the ground.

Farther down Reynolds is the **Springfield Baptist Church,** home of one of the oldest black congregations in America, transplanted here in 1787 but originally established in South Carolina in 1773. The present brick church is from 1910, but the little white frame house behind it served as the church during much of the nineteenth century, having been moved to this site in 1844.

One block back on Broad Street, once the commercial hub of Augusta, are two important monuments to the old city. The **Confederate Monument** (Broad between Seventh and Eighth) is unmistakable, rising seventy-two feet high and dedicated in 1878. The life-size figures at the base are of generals Lee, Jackson, Walker, and Cobb. At the corner of Broad and Fifth streets is the **Old Market Column,** on the site of the slave market. A preacher is said to have cursed the old market of which the column was once a part, resulting in the destruction of all but this lone column.

At Greene and Gwinnett streets is the 1848 **Signers' Monument,** a fifty-foot obelisk of granite quarried at Stone Mountain. It commemorates the three Georgians who signed the Declaration of Independence, two of whom, George Walton and Lyman Hall, are buried here. The third, Button Gwinnett, was supposed to have been buried here too, but he was killed in a duel and his body ended up in the Colonial Park Cemetery in Savannah.

The **Old Government House** (432 Telfair Street) is a brick building of simple square design, stuccoed to mimic stone. It was raised in 1801 and served as the county courthouse.

## Gertrude Herbert Institute of Art

Known locally as Ware's Folly, the Institute, which sponsors shows of regional art, is an upland example of Regency architecture. The house got its nickname because the builder, Mayor and later Senator Nicholas Ware, spent $40,000 on its construction in 1818. The house is perfectly symmetrical, with two projecting bays embracing two semicircular colonnaded porches, one on the entrance level and one above. Inside, the home is equally daring yet restrained. Particularly notable are the elliptical staircase, the "Adam style" mantles, and the elegant fanlights.

LOCATION: 506 Telfair Street. HOURS: 10–5 Tuesday–Friday. FEE: Yes. TELEPHONE: 404–722–5495.

## Augusta-Richmond County Museum

The museum, founded in 1937, is housed in a former school building, built in 1802. Its collection is wide ranging, including dioramas with models, period clothing, weapons, and household items from the Revolutionary period through the Civil War. There are also exhibits of prehistory, early man in Georgia, aboriginal artifacts, a World War II cruiser, the USS *Augusta*, a 1930 railroad complex, and a DC-3 airliner.

LOCATION: 540 Telfair Street. HOURS: 10–5 Tuesday–Saturday, 2–5 Sunday. FEE: Yes. TELEPHONE: 404–722–8454.

## Meadow Garden

At the edge of the old downtown is a house important for both its architectural and historical interest. Meadow Garden is a ca. 1794 cottage that was occupied until 1804 by George Walton, a signer of the Declaration of Independence and two-term Georgia governor.

*Meadow Garden, the home of George Walton, one of the three signers of the Declaration of Independence from Georgia.*

Originally standing alone on 121 acres and now part of the city, Meadow Garden has been restored and furnished with antiques.

LOCATION: 1320 Independence Drive. HOURS: 10–4 Tuesday–Saturday, 1–4 Sunday. FEE: Yes. TELEPHONE: 404–724–4174.

The **De Chaffee Cottage** (914 Milledge Road, private) is one of the oldest houses in Augusta; the earliest portion was constructed ca. 1780, with additions in 1810, 1840, and 1890. The one-and-a-half-story wood frame dwelling, with its high basement and central hall, is one of the earliest and finest examples of a type called the Sand Hill cottage, which is common in this area.

The area upriver from the old downtown, now a part of West Augusta, was originally the town of Harrisburg, named for the tobacco merchant Ezekiel Harris around 1800. Here along the site of the **Augusta Canal,** the city's first important industrial mills were established. The 176-foot chimney standing alone in front of **Sibley Mills** (1717 Goodrich Street) is all that is left of a factory of a different sort: the Confederate Powder Works  The factory made more than two million pounds of gunpowder for the Rebel cause.

## Harris House

The finest eighteenth-century house surviving in Georgia, this beautifully detailed three-story frame house is notable for its vaulted hallway and excellent interior and exterior woodwork. It is the second-oldest residence in Augusta, dating to about 1797. The house was built for Ezekiel Harris, a tobacco merchant who had immigrated from South Carolina. Magnificently restored and furnished, it stands as an emblem of the first wealth tobacco cultivation brought to Georgia.

LOCATION: 1840 Broad Street. HOURS: 10–4 Daily. FEE: Yes. TELEPHONE: 404–733–6768.

Up on the sand hills is the neighborhood called Summerville, an elevated site where, beginning in 1800, residents made their summer homes on the heights, away from the malarial miasmas of the riverside. Many families moved here permanently before the Civil War; after it, they often rented rooms to vacationing Yankees, and the area became a prominent Victorian winter resort. Many beautiful homes and hotels are to be seen here in the large historic

*Rear piazza of the Harris House, with an exterior stairway to the second and third floors.*

district. One of the oldest is **Appleby House** (2260 Walton Way, 404–736–6244), an 1830s Greek Revival home that was later the winter home of a New York businessman and now serves as a public library.

## WAYNESBORO

Waynesboro was laid out in 1783 and named for the Revolutionary War General "Mad Anthony" Wayne. The **Burke County Historical Museum** (536 Liberty Street, 404–554–4889) is housed in a four-room cottage built ca. 1858. It is a small, eclectic, and very well organized museum, with everything from Indian burial urns and huge oyster fossils to a survey of local farming with displays of farm implements and tools. There is a good collection of Victorian furniture, and the Revolutionary and the Civil War exhibits are particularly strong.

# NORTHERN FLORIDA

OPPOSITE: *Pensacola Bay, seen from the porch of Pensacola's 1825 Barkley House.*

Florida is the southernmost of the continental United States, its shape so distinctive that the continent would be nearly unrecognizable without it. But for millions of years, while North America was forming, the plates colliding and thrusting rock upward and downward, the land that would become Florida lay at the bottom of the sea, accumulating marine sediments. About 20 million years ago, the bulk of it was thrust up to an elevation just slightly above sea level. Some time later, the southernmost part of the new peninsula—the area covered by the Everglades and the Big Cypress Swamp—built up a big enough barrier of coral and sand to begin forming hummocks and developing terrestrial vegetation.

Florida's highest point—in the far north near Lakewood—is only 345 feet above sea level. A spine of relatively high ground leads down the center of the peninsula, but most of the state is flat, cut with 1,700 rivers and creeks and dotted with 200 springs and 30,000 lakes, ponds, and swamps. A bed of limestone, on which most of Florida rests, reaches a depth of 18,000 feet in some places and is honeycombed with subterranean streams and caverns that sometimes produce the surprising spectacle of lakes that dry up overnight, then fill again as the underground waters shift.

The state divides easily into northern and southern regions, differing not only in degrees of latitude but in the character of their distinctive histories. When the aboriginal peoples arrived in Florida some 12,000 years ago, they lived on the bounty of the land, harvesting game, wild plants, and especially shellfish. But by around 500 B.C., the northern tribes—the largest among them being the Timucua and the Apalachee, along with smaller groups such as the Pensacola, the Chtot, and the Apalachicola—began to cultivate corn. Their southern Florida neighbors continued on as hunter-gatherers. The tribes that inhabited aboriginal Florida are now no more than names and sketchy histories. Those who were not killed by European diseases or guns were sold off as slaves for West Indian plantations.

European peoples first settled in northern Florida, where they struggled to establish an industrious colonial life. Mixed farming remains important throughout the Panhandle and the north, and the distinction between rural and urban in cities such as Pensacola, Tallahassee, and Jacksonville and the surrounding countryside preserves a comfortable, nineteenth-century feel. Southern Florida, on the other hand, is a creature of this century. Its economy rocketed to prosperity during the 1880s and then bounced to the

*Timucuan Chief Saturiba greeting René de Laudonniére, who established a French colony near present-day Saint Augustine in 1564.*

jerky rhythms of the tourist trade and influxes of retirees and other immigrants (only 35 percent of Floridians are native born).

The north of Florida tends to be conservative, resembling the rest of the Deep South far more than does Miami or Palm Beach or even Key West. It has the longest history of continuous European occupation in the United States. For the better part of the sixteenth century, the Spanish, the English, and the French all struggled to obtain a toehold upon this region that most regarded as an island. It was probably John Cabot, sailing for the English, who was the first European to see Florida in 1498, but he did not land. The first to explore Florida was Juan Ponce de León, a Spaniard who came with Christopher Columbus on his second voyage and who had secured a patent as *adelantado* (governor and general) of "Bimini," thought to be an island north of Hispaniola that was rich in gold and contained a spring where men might recover their youth.

On April 2, 1513, Ponce landed on the shores of a land that seemed much larger than the Bimini he had been seeking. Since the place was lush with flowers and since it was Easter time (*Pascua Florida,* in Spanish), Ponce christened the new land Florida. He then sailed around the cape and probably as far as present-day

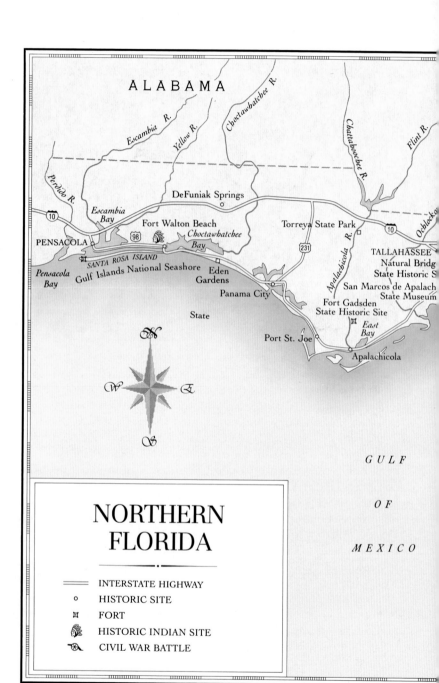

ALABAMA

*Perdido R.*

*Escambia R.*

*Yellow R.*

*Choctawhatchee R.*

*Chattahoochee R.*

*Flint R.*

DeFuniak Springs

Escambia Bay

Fort Walton Beach

*Choctawhatchee Bay*

Torreya State Park

*Ochlockon...*

PENSACOLA

98

SANTA ROSA ISLAND

Gulf Islands National Seashore

*Apalachicola R.*

TALLAHASSEE

Natural Bridg
State Historic S

Pensacola Bay

Eden Gardens

Panama City

San Marcos de Apalach
State Museum

Fort Gadsden
State Historic Site

State

Port St. Joe

*East Bay*

Apalachicola

GULF

OF

MEXICO

# NORTHERN
# FLORIDA

INTERSTATE HIGHWAY
HISTORIC SITE
FORT
HISTORIC INDIAN SITE
CIVIL WAR BATTLE

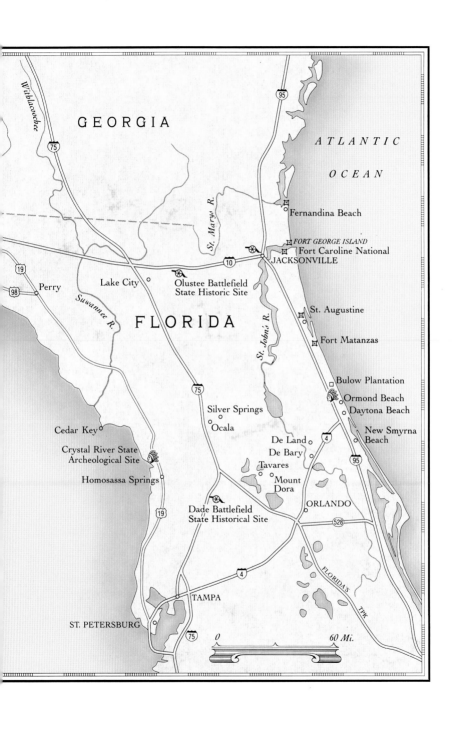

GEORGIA

ATLANTIC

OCEAN

*Withlacoochee*

75

*St. Marys R.*

Fernandina Beach

FORT GEORGE ISLAND
Fort Caroline National
JACKSONVILLE

10

19

98    Perry

Lake City

Olustee Battlefield
State Historic Site

*Suwannee R.*

FLORIDA

*St. Johns R.*

St. Augustine

Fort Matanzas

75

Bulow Plantation

Silver Springs

Ormond Beach
Daytona Beach

Ocala

Cedar Key

De Land
De Bary

New Smyrna
Beach

Crystal River State
Archeological Site

4

Tavares

Homosassa Springs

Mount
Dora

95

19

Dade Battlefield
State Historical Site

ORLANDO

528

*FLORIDA'S TPK*

4

TAMPA

ST. PETERSBURG

75

0                    60 Mi.

Apalachicola before he turned back to make a brief stop at Charlotte Harbor (near Fort Myers) and head for Hispaniola.

In 1521 he returned with 200 men to establish a colony at Charlotte Harbor. He had taken Indian slaves on his first "visit"; now he met with fierce Indian resistance. In the ensuing battle, Ponce was wounded. His fledgling colony abandoned, the *adelantado* of the new land reached Cuba before dying of his wound.

Then came a succession of other luckless Spaniards. Pánfilo de Narváez led a party that landed at Tampa Bay in 1528, then set out for the lands of Apalachee in the Panhandle, where his informants claimed there was gold. Failing to rendezvous with his ships in the north, he tried to set sail for Mexico in five rickety homemade boats. Only four of his men ever reached Mexico City, and they did it by traveling overland, arriving eight years later.

In May 1539, Hernando de Soto landed in the vicinity of Tampa Bay and set off north after gold with several hundred followers. He died on the banks of the Mississippi River three years later, no closer to the golden cities he had sought. In 1559, Tristán de Luna y Arellano brought more men—about 1,500—to establish a Florida colony on Pensacola Bay. His colony lasted two years.

It took the French to make the Spanish set root in Florida. Jean Ribault explored the mouth of the Saint Johns River in 1562, claiming the region for France with the aim of making it a Protestant refuge. Ribault was generous in his praise of the site, calling it "the fairest, frutefullest and pleasantest of all the worlds. The sight of the faire-meadows is a pleasure not able to be expressed with tongue." This paean may establish Ribault as Florida's first great real-estate promoter. His second-in-command, René de Goulaine de Laudonniére, who returned to the Saint Johns River in 1564, built triangular Fort Caroline and established a colony of French Protestants—Huguenots—numbering 300 men and 4 women.

Alarmed at this French intrusion into their territory, the Spanish dispatched Pedro Menéndez de Avilés to found a settlement. The Spanish commander landed at a point south of the Huguenot fort on September 8, 1565, the day of the feast of San Augustin. He named the settlement to honor Saint Augustine, and the city has retained the name for more than 400 years.

Ribault sailed against the Spanish—and Roman Catholic—settlement, intent on exterminating it. He might have done so had

OPPOSITE: *Castillo de San Marcos, one of the finest examples of military architecture in the New World.*

*Laudonniére's party exploring one of the rivers that empty into the Atlantic along the Florida coast. An Indian village with beehive-shaped houses is on the shore at left.*

not a storm forced his ships away. Meanwhile, Menéndez quickly marched to Fort Caroline, capturing the lightly garrisoned fort and executing all but women and children. When he fell upon Ribault's shipwrecked force later, the Frenchmen suffered the same fate, at a place known ever after as Matanzas (Spanish for "killings"). In retaliation the French sent an expedition across the Atlantic in 1568 that captured Fort San Mateo (the Spanish name for Fort Caroline) and executed its male inhabitants.

Regardless, Saint Augustine was firmly established as a settlement, in spite of periodic raids by buccaneers and privateers. Sir Francis Drake burned the town in 1586. In the seventeenth century, the Spanish extended their tenuous control over the north. By the end of the century, there were settlements at San Marcos de Apalache and Pensacola, along with a network of thirty-eight Franciscan missions for the education and conversion of Indians. To stave off attacks from the British and their Creek allies, the Spaniards built a magnificent fortress, the Castillo de San Marcos, at Saint Augustine, so strong that it survives (somewhat restored from time to time) to this day. In fact, the fort is the only Spanish structure that survives in Florida from the sixteenth and seventeenth centuries. The extensive system of Franciscan missions—a larger network than those the Spanish built in the Southwest and in California—has disappeared.

Spanish power was waning as the eighteenth century began. The English and the Creek destroyed the missions, carrying off many Catholicized Indians into slavery. Elements of the Creek nation drifted into Florida from present-day Alabama and Georgia, forming a new tribal group that was dubbed the Seminole, from the Spanish word *cimarrones,* meaning "runaways." Over the next century, the plantation system first sought to enslave Indians and then brought African slaves to the cotton belt. Many escaped slaves made for Florida and lived among the Seminole.

Throughout most of the eighteenth and the first quarter of the nineteenth century, Florida was a marker in a game of colonial hopscotch. First the French captured Pensacola from Spain in 1719, but immediately gave it back to thwart the British, whose Georgia representative James Oglethorpe laid siege—unsuccessfully—to Saint Augustine in 1740. In 1763, after the French and Indian Wars, the Spanish ceded Florida to England in exchange for the return of captured Havana, and the British promptly split their new colony into two parts, East Florida with its capital at Saint Augustine and West Florida with its capital at Pensacola. (At that time West Florida stretched clear to the Mississippi.) The British were friendly with the Seminole, and their liberal land policies helped attract plantation owners to northern Florida. As a result, neither part of British Florida was inclined to rebel during the American Revolution, and Florida's wealth was increased by an influx of prominent Tories fleeing the rebellious colonials. A Spanish armada succeeded in capturing Pensacola in 1781, toward the end of the war, and Britain gave Florida back to Spain in 1783 in exchange for the Bahamas. Most of the Florida Tories, sensing which way the wind was blowing, followed the British flag to the islands.

In the meantime, American plantation owners and speculators began to agitate for the acquisition of Florida, and many took stakes in the area. The Seminole resisted these new invaders, and twice, in 1814 and 1818, Andrew Jackson made forays into the Spanish-owned Panhandle. The first incursion, during the War of

OVERLEAF: *Saint George Island, separating Apalachicola Bay from the Gulf of Mexico.*

1812, was purportedly launched to punish the British. In 1818, Jackson went after the Seminole. In 1817 a band of American pirates, in league with the Laffites in Texas, captured Amelia Island in the northeast. At last, through byzantine negotiations between 1819 and 1822, the United States forced Spain to sell it Florida. Andrew Jackson was named military governor, a post he held briefly before returning to Tennessee.

With the issue of ownership decided among the Europeans and European-Americans—though not with the agreement of the Native Americans—planters from the United States poured into northern Florida, establishing cotton and sugarcane cultivation, or rather, reestablishing what the British had ably begun. The capital of the new territory was created in the forest at Tallahassee by an act of the legislature in 1824, and a road connecting the major settlements was begun.

The Seminole continued to resist the influx of settlers, and the latter began vociferously to demand the removal of the former. In 1835, Seminole warriors surprised and wiped out a detachment of

*Saint Augustine's González-Alvarez House. Originally built in the 1720s, it has been extensively remodeled. Its rooms are furnished with Spanish and British pieces.*

soldiers under the command of Francis L. Dade, and the Seminole War (the Second Seminole War, if Jackson's 1818 incursion is counted as the first) had begun. Tenacious fighters, the Seminole were not defeated until 1837, when their charismatic leader, Osceola, was betrayed and captured as he went to a parley under a flag of truce. On Christmas Day 1837, forces under General Zachary Taylor defeated the Seminole on the shores of Lake Okeechobee in the last major battle of the war. Most of the surviving Indians were removed to present-day Oklahoma, but a branch of the tribe hung on deep in the Everglades, never surrendering. It was not until 1934 that a treaty was signed with them.

Prior to the Civil War northern Florida consolidated its plantation economy, and by the time of the war the number of black slaves roughly equaled the number of white settlers. The territory had declared itself ready for statehood in 1839 but was not admitted until 1845. It joined the Union as a slave state concurrently with Iowa, a free state. Florida's first east–west railroad link—from Fernandina on the East Coast to Cedar Key on the West Coast—had just been completed in 1860 when the state prepared to secede from the Union. During the Civil War Florida served as a larder for the Confederacy. Federal troops succeeded in occupying Fernandina, Saint Augustine, Pensacola, and Jacksonville by 1863, but their efforts to cut off central Florida were blocked at Olustee in 1864, and in 1865 the home guard succeeded in resisting the attack on Tallahassee, making it the only uncaptured Confederate capital east of the Mississippi.

Reconstruction was as painful to former slave holders in Florida as elsewhere, but its rigors were cut short when Hamilton Disston, a northern capitalist, bought 4 million acres of swampland in central Florida at twenty-five cents per acre, wiping out the state's onerous debt. In the last quarter of the nineteenth century, Florida's development shifted to the center and south, where the citrus and tourist industries boomed, but the center of government has remained in the north at Tallahassee, amid ground fertile for farming and timber.

The following entries cross the historic north of Florida, roughly from west to east, beginning in Pensacola and ending south of Saint Augustine on the East Coast, with one intermediate detour down the West Coast of the peninsula to the vicinity of Cedar Springs.

# P E N S A C O L A       A R E A

The largest city of the Panhandle, Pensacola has the distinction of predating Saint Augustine as the first European settlement in Florida. Somewhere on Pensacola Bay, the Spaniard Tristán de Luna established a small colony in 1559. When supply ships were wrecked in a storm, however, the settlement was abandoned in 1561. (The question of whether two years of occupancy qualifies a site as established is much debated. Many scholars refer to Santa Elena, on the South Carolina coast, as the first European settlement on the coast of North America. It lasted longer.)

Many cities in the Southeast can count numerous national flags that have flown over their rooftops, but Pensacola has perhaps more reason to count than most. The Spanish established a second settlement here in 1698, which the French captured in 1719. European standards of title bounced back and forth until the town officially returned to Spanish rule in 1722. The Spaniards decided to move the settlement to Santa Rosa Island for better protection, but a hurricane devastated this effort in 1752, so the city finally moved to its present site in that year. A decade later, in 1763, the whole of Florida came under British rule, and Pensacola's Spaniards went to Mexico. The town, filled with Tories fleeing the American Revolution, became very prosperous, with particularly strong ties to the Creek Indians. In 1781 the Spanish recaptured the town in the Battle of Pensacola and evacuated the British; two years later the Treaty of Paris ceded all of Florida to the Spanish.

Pensacola remained a thorny problem for the United States during the War of 1812, for, though it was nominally Spanish, a British detachment began to drill there. Thereupon, Andrew Jackson attacked the "neutral" town, forcing the British to withdraw. In 1818, Jackson took Pensacola, ostensibly in retribution for Seminole raids into Georgia but also to assure certain land investments made in the area. It is perhaps little wonder, then, that Pensacola became the place where Florida's first territorial legislature under American jurisdiction met in 1822, naming Jackson himself the provisional governor.

In 1825, Pensacola entered the business that has been a city mainstay ever since, establishing a navy yard on the well-sheltered bay. By the time of the Civil War, Pensacola was the largest city in Florida. Confederate Pensacola fell to Union forces in 1862, early in the war, and the town sank into a lethargy from which it recovered only in the last quarter of the nineteenth century. The revitalized naval industry depended on supplies of naval stores that were shipped by new railroad lines into Pensacola from Alabama, Georgia, and the Panhandle. With better rail connections and a well-developed network of river steamboats, the city also became an important international port of call. The navy again helped boost Pensacola's economy in 1914, when the Pensacola Naval Air Station became the navy's first flight-training center. The navy is still important in the area today.

## PENSACOLA

This city of about a quarter million people stands on the north shore of fifteen-mile-wide Pensacola Bay. The old downtown is flat, but residential areas climb the North Hill and East Hill, from which there are fine views over the bay.

The bayside heart of Pensacola is still built around the old Spanish plaza, that is, around the two halves into which that square has been divided: Plaza Ferdinand VII and Seville Square. In the center is the **Pensacola Historical Museum** (405 South Adams, 904–433–1559), housed in the 1832 Old Christ Church, the oldest Protestant church in Florida. Used by Union forces as a prison, barracks, and hospital during the Civil War, it was remodeled later in the nineteenth century, acquiring its current Gothic arches and stained glass. The museum comprises a wide-ranging collection of Indian and Civil War artifacts, Victorian clothing, art glass, photographs, and memorabilia of the city's shipping industry.

In the same **Seville Square Historic District,** as the old downtown is known, there are a number of smaller museums and important historic house museums. In neighboring restored fish warehouses are the **Museum of Industry** (200 East Zaragoza Street, 904–444–8905) and the **Museum of Commerce** (201 East Zaragoza Street, 904–444–8905), the former including a Hispanic museum displaying such items as sixteenth-century Spanish armor and household furnishings, the latter including a collection of antique buggies and other conveyances. Beside this museum complex is the **Julee Cottage** (210 East Zaragoza Street, 904–444–8905), the dwelling of a free black woman, which dates from the early 1800s. It now contains an exhibit on the history of blacks in the area.

Three fine old houses, restored and furnished in the style of their heyday, recall the days when the neighborhood around

Seville Square was Pensacola's fashionable residential district. The **Charles LaValle House** (205 East Church Street, 904–444–8905) is a well-restored Creole cottage. LaValle moved here from New Orleans with his mistress and built this one-story frame house in 1815. It is furnished in the Creole-French taste of the period. The original design of these houses—once the most common type in the downtown district—came from the Caribbean via New Orleans. **The Quina House** (204 South Alcaniz Street, 904–434–3050) provides a look at a furnished Creole cottage of the second quarter of the nineteenth century, while the 1871 **Clara Barkley Dorr House** (311 South Adams Street, 904–444–8905) is the late–Greek Revival residence of a lumber magnate's family, filled with mid-Victorian furnishings. At the corner of Garden and Alcaniz streets is **Saint Michael's Cemetery,** the oldest surviving cemetery in town, dating back to the 1780s. There are old Spanish graves here, as well as that of Dorothy Walton, whose husband, Judge George Walton, was a signer of the Declaration of Independence.

More houses built by the late-nineteenth-century lumber barons of Pensacola can be seen in the **North Hill Historic District,** Pensacola's first elegant suburb, located within the box formed by LaRue, Palafox, Blount, and Reus streets. There are more than 400 historic houses, all of them private, in these blocks, including examples of the Queen Anne, southern vernacular, Tudor, and Mediterranean Revival styles.

## Pensacola Naval Air Station

This air station was the first naval aviation training base in the nation, founded in 1914. It is currently the home of the Blue Angels flying squadron and of the USS *Lexington,* a World War II carrier now used for training. The **Naval Aviation Museum** is one of the most comprehensive air museums in the nation, containing a collection of fifty-five aircraft, ranging from a replica of the navy's first plane, purchased in 1911, to an actual Skylab command vehicle. The museum also features missiles, bombs, and hands-on training simulators, and several films. On the base itself are a number of historic structures, including an 1845 octagonal armory and chapel and some seaplane hangars from the first years of the base.

OPPOSITE: *Julee Cottage, the home of a free black woman named Julee Patton. It is one of Pensacola's oldest surviving houses.*

*Fort Barrancas, Pensacola's Confederate military outpost.*

Also inside the naval air station are the restored **Fort Barrancas** and batteries and redoubts erected by Pensacola's various possessors (mainly the Spanish) to defend the harbor entrance. The fort itself and the advance redoubt date from the Civil War period, but below Barrancas, the **Bateria de San Antonio**—or Spanish Water Battery—dates from 1797 and was the last Spanish fortification built in Florida. This fort was held by the Confederates in 1861. They bombarded Fort Pickens across the bay on Santa Rosa Island but were unable to capture it. Barrancas was evacuated by the Confederates in 1862. The fort is now run by the National Park Service as part of the Gulf Islands National Seashore.

LOCATION: Pensacola Naval Air Station, southwest of Pensacola on Route 295. HOURS: 9–5 Daily. FEE: None. TELEPHONE: 904–452–3604.

## Fort Pickens

On Santa Rosa Island, part of the Gulf Islands National Seashore, is the fort built by the Americans between 1829 and 1834 to defend the naval shipyard in Pensacola. This moated pentagonal brick fort has walls forty feet high and twelve feet thick. The big guns on

*Fort Pickens remained a Union stronghold despite several Confederate attempts to capture it.*

display in the batteries date from the 1890s to the 1930s. Fort Pickens was the prison—one might say cage—in which the Apache chief Geronimo was confined between 1886 and 1888, attracting many tourists to the area.

LOCATION: Route 10, west of Pensacola Beach. HOURS: 10–4 Daily. FEE: Yes. TELEPHONE: 904–934–2600.

## INDIAN TEMPLE MOUND MUSEUM

East of Pensacola in the town of Fort Walton Beach is a twelve-foot-high Mississippian-period temple mound. A fine associated museum houses more than 4,000 artifacts taken from mounds in the area, ranging from 10,000-year-old paleo-Indian projectile points to artifacts of the Mississippian period. Especially notable are the effigy vessels, including a burial urn depicting a man with pierced ears sitting in a chair with a cloak around his shoulders and a number of figural animal vessels. Pottery dating from the apex of this site—around A.D. 1200—is known as "Fort Walton period."

LOCATION: 139 Miracle Strip Parkway, Route 98. HOURS: May through August: 9–4 Monday–Saturday; September through April: 11–4 Monday–Saturday. FEE: Yes. TELEPHONE: 904–243–6521.

*Indians hunting alligators, as depicted by Jacques Le Moyne, an artist who accompanied de Laudonniére's expedition. Le Moyne wrote that the Indians regarded alligators as "such a menace that a regular watch has to be kept against them night and day."*

## DE FUNIAK SPRINGS

This town is named for an official of the Louisville & Nashville Railroad and for the perfectly round lake that sits in the center of it. The spring-fed lake is eighty feet deep and about a mile in circumference. Here, during the 1880s, an L & N official thought to create a winter wateringhole for northerners. New York's Chautauqua Society began making excursions to this spot in 1885. The surviving Neoclassical **Chautauqua Auditorium** (Circle Drive) served as Chautauqua headquarters from 1910 until the Great Depression. The **Walton-De Funiak Public Library** (Circle Drive, 904–892–3624) is one of the oldest public libraries in the state, having opened in 1886. A surprising feature of the library is its armor—some pieces date back to the Middle Ages.

## EDEN STATE GARDENS

Farther east along the Panhandle coast, overlooking Choctawhatchee Bay, is a lonely, white-columned mansion that once commanded a prospering sawmill community. The house was built by William Wesley in 1897, at the height of the lumber boom in the Pensacola region. It has been restored with eighteenth- and nineteenth-century furnishings. The house is surrounded by gardens of camellias and azaleas sheltered by moss-draped oak trees.

LOCATION: One mile off Route 98, at Point Washington. HOURS: 8–Dusk Thursday–Monday. FEE: Yes. TELEPHONE: 904–231–4214.

## JUNIOR MUSEUM OF BAY COUNTY

Panama City is known more as a jumping-off place for fine Gulf Coast beaches than for its historic sites, but this small museum features exhibits on local history and a reconstructed cabin and cane mill, a reminder of how important sugarcane plantations once were in the area.

LOCATION: 1731 Jenks Avenue, Panama City. HOURS: 9–5 Tuesday–Friday, 10–4 Saturday. FEE: Yes. TELEPHONE: 904–769–6128.

# T A L L A H A S S E E   A R E A

The name Tallahassee, meaning "old town" or "old fields," originally referred to an Apalachee Indian village that de Soto had passed on his way northwest in the early sixteenth century. When the legislature of the newly created territory of Florida sought a capital city, they split the difference between the two major cities—Pensacola and Saint Augustine—agreeing to install the capital at a hilly wooded site in the Appalachian foothills about halfway between the two. So was born the capital of Florida in 1823.

Ralph Waldo Emerson, who visited the raw town in 1827, had little good to say about it. "A grotesque place," he wrote, ". . . rapidly settled by public officers, land speculators and desperadoes." From the 1830s through the Civil War, Tallahassee served as a center for the distribution of cotton grown on Florida, Georgia, and Alabama plantations. A railroad built to the coast at Saint Marks in 1834 was the first in the state and cemented the town's commercial position.

Since the Civil War, the focus of Florida culture has moved inexorably south away from Tallahassee, but it is still an important city, not only as the seat of government but as the location of Florida State and Florida A & M universities.

# CONSTITUTION CONVENTION STATE MUSEUM

This museum commemorates Florida's first state constitution, drafted here in 1838. At the time, this area was part of the town of Saint Joseph, among the most populous in Florida. Railroads ran to it, and cotton poured out of its port to destinations around the world. Then, in 1841, yellow fever killed three-quarters of the citizens. The epidemic caused real-estate values to collapse; the townspeople could no longer meet their financial obligations, and the banks foreclosed their mortgages. In August 1843 the people of Apalachicola bought the homes and hotels, dismantled them, and brought them by barge to Apalachicola. The remnants of the town were swept away by a hurricane in September 1844.

The museum tells the story of the town and the convention, complete with a re-creation of one wing of the convention hall. There is a model of the first steam locomotive and a plaque commemorating the early railroad line that once terminated here.

LOCATION: 200 Allen Memorial Way, Port Saint Joe. HOURS: 9–5 Daily. FEE: Yes. TELEPHONE: 904–229–8029.

# APALACHICOLA

Named for a tribe of Indians who long ago occupied the area, this town was once a cotton port and is now the oyster capital of Florida. It was from Apalachicola Bay that Pánfilo de Narváez's men set out in self-made boats to try to reach Mexico; only four of his crew made it, and they traveled mostly overland. The bay was also the favored haunt of pirate William Bowles during the last quarter of the nineteenth century.

The **Trinity Church** (Gorrie Square at Sixth Street), with its twin Ionic columns and its tall, narrow, green-shuttered windows, was erected here in 1839, making it the third oldest Episcopal church in the state. It was shipped partly assembled from New York. The **John Gorrie State Museum** (Avenue C and Sixth Street, 904–653–9347) commemorates a pioneer in the development of air-conditioning and refrigeration. Dr. Gorrie invented the first artificial ice-making machine in the early 1830s when he was trying to alleviate the suffering of his malaria and yellow fever patients. A replica of his machine is on display, along with exhibits on local industries such as shipping, turpentining, lumbering, oystering, and cotton.

# FORT GADSDEN STATE HISTORIC SITE

Here can be seen the ruins of a British fort built in 1814 as an assembly point for the Seminole and to give shelter to runaway slaves. It was destroyed by United States forces in 1816 but was rebuilt as a supply depot two years later at the orders of Andrew Jackson. Confederate forces occupied it briefly during the Civil War. A few earthworks remain, and an interpretive center displays some artifacts, along with a small-scale replica of the fort.

LOCATION: Route 129, off Route 65, twenty-four miles northeast of Apalachicola. HOURS: 8–Dusk Daily. FEE: None. TELEPHONE: 904–670–8988.

# TORREYA STATE PARK

The park is set on a beautiful wooded bluff above the Apalachicola River, more reminiscent of the Appalachians than of most of Florida. Here is the only native habitat of one species of the evergreen genus *Torreya*, also known as "stinking cedar" for the smell it emits when bruised. Inside the park is the 1849 **Gregory House,** a restored plantation house open to visitors. At Battery Point the remains of Confederate earthworks guard a splendid view over the river basin.

LOCATION: Route 271, off Route 12, in Bristol. HOURS: 8–Dusk Daily. FEE: Yes. TELEPHONE: 904–643–2674.

# TALLAHASSEE

Government and education have sustained Tallahassee since its founding as territorial capital in 1823, but the wealth that built the older sections came from cotton and then timber. The greatest influx of settlers came between 1823 and the Civil War, with many prominent families relocating from Virginia and the Carolinas. Descendants of Thomas Jefferson, George Washington, and John Adams all settled in Tallahassee, and the downtown blocks along Park Street and Calhoun Street still reflect the frontier opulence of those antebellum days.

Florida's gleaming 1977 capitol building stands across a plaza from the **Old Capitol** (400 South Monroe Street, 904–487–1902), whose central block, with pediment and colonnade, dates from 1845 (wings and a dome were added in 1902). Inside, the old legislative chambers have been restored. The first state legislature

*In 1839, Florida territory declared itself ready for statehood and began work on a state capitol, which was completed in 1845.*

met in this building when Florida was admitted to the Union in 1845. A museum examines the history of the capital area from aboriginal times through the territorial period and statehood, the Civil War, Reconstruction, and up to 1960. Among the artifacts displayed are the original Florida Constitution and uniforms and weapons from the territorial period and the Seminole War.

Just east of the capitol is the 1841 **Union Bank Building** (corner of South Carolina Street and Apalachee Parkway, 904–487–3803), the oldest commercial building in Florida. Its interior detailing and vaulted ceiling have been restored, and there are exhibits of Florida currency and banking history. The original bank had already overextended itself when the structure was raised, and it failed in 1844. Later, from 1867 to 1874, the building was the headquarters of the Reconstruction-era Freedman's Bureau Bank, the second black bank in the state.

Four blocks west, housed in the R.A. Gray Building, is the **Museum of Florida History** (500 South Bronough Street, 904–487–1902), a good miscellaneous collection containing a re-created steamboat, a citrus-packing house, a turpentine exhibit, and a collection of artifacts from Spanish shipwrecks.

The **First Presbyterian Church** (Adams Street at Park Avenue, 904–222-4504), completed in 1838, is the oldest house of worship in Tallahassee. Like so many old Protestant churches, it was Gothicized in the nineteenth century, but it has recently been restored to its original Neoclassical design. Except for a small extension at the west end, and a 1932 apse and portico, it is substantially the same church that once served the affluent citizens of the city and their slaves.

The offices of Tallahassee's chamber of commerce are in the two-story brick townhouse called **The Columns** (100 North Duval Street, 904–224–8116), a building that once served both as a residence and as the first office of the Union Bank. Built in 1830, the structure is the oldest house still standing in Tallahassee. It was built by an early Florida banker whose nickname was simply "Money." When he sold out in 1833, the house became part residence, part bank office. It has been restored and furnished appropriate to the period of its building.

Another notable house is **The Grove** (First Avenue and Adams Street, private), located near what was once the northern edge of the city and still in the hands of the family that built it back in 1824. The Greek Revival structure features a portico with Doric columns. The owner and builder, flamboyant Florida territorial governor Richard Keith Call, built this substantial house to provide his Tennessee bride with a suitable home in the wilds of northern Florida, a task made urgent by the fact that the couple had eloped. Close friends of Andrew Jackson, they were married at The Hermitage, Jackson's Tennessee home.

Radiating around the city proper are several important archaeological and historic sites. The **Lake Jackson Indian Mounds** (four and a half miles north of Tallahassee, off Route 27, 904–562–0042) represent the largest Fort Walton–period ceremonial center in Florida, active from A.D. 1100 to 1500. The site includes six temple mounds and a burial mound; the largest is 36 feet high and more than 78 feet long. Some of the artifacts discovered here are breathtaking, particularly a copper breastplate showing a dancing falcon figure in a style that seems distinctly Mesoamerican.

The **San Luis Archaeological and Historic Site** (2020 Mission Road, 904–487–3711) shows digs-in-progress of the ruins of San Luis de Talimali, once the largest of the sixteen Franciscan missions in the Apalachee Indian province. In a 1655 census of the province, San Luis was listed as the capital, and in 1675 there were said to be 1,400 Indians and Spaniards living at the mission,

growing corn and beans to feed themselves and the Spaniards of
Saint Augustine. A palisaded blockhouse fort was built here in
1696 to hold off English and Creek raiders who were terrorizing
the missions. As a result, the marauders never attacked San Luis,
but they wreaked such havoc elsewhere in the province that Spanish authorities ordered the mission abandoned and razed in 1704.
Exhibits on the site feature drawings showing reconstructions of
the mission's buildings, such as the Indian council house and the
fort, together with a sampling of the artifacts found here.

The **Tallahassee Junior Museum** (3945 Museum Drive, on
Lake Bradford, 904–575–8684) is largely composed of a working
1880s "Cracker" farm, complete with gristmills, schoolhouse,
church, smithy, and farm animals. Also on the site is **Bellevue,** a
simple one-and-a-half-story vernacular cottage that was the home
of George Washington's great-grandniece, Princess Catherine Murat, between 1854 and 1867. She had married Prince Napoleon
Achille Murat, one of two sons of the Napoleonic-era king of
Naples to come to America. Napoleon Achille was crown prince; he
owned plantations in Florida and Louisiana. They were married in
1826 over the objections of her relatives. After his death in 1847,
she received recognition as a princess of France from Napoleon III
and a sum of money that allowed her to purchase Bellevue. The
cottage is restored and furnished with antebellum antiques.

## Natural Bridge State Historic Site

This pleasant rural park was the scene of the battle where 650
Union troops were routed by an equal number of Confederates,
many of them boys and old men—Tallahassee's home guard of
cadets and grays—who surprised the Federal troops on March 6,
1865. As a result, Tallahassee remained the only uncaptured Confederate capital east of the Mississippi.

LOCATION: Nine miles south of Tallahassee on Route 363 to Woodville, then six miles east on Route 354. TELEPHONE: 904–925–6216.

# SAN MARCOS DE APALACHE STATE MUSEUM

Saint Marks—or San Marcos—at the confluence of the Wakulla
and Saint Marks rivers, was an important coastal access point for
Tallahassee, but its history goes deeper still. The Spanish first built
a fort here around 1660, and stonework from the third fort of the

*A regiment of black soldiers advancing in the face of heavy artillery fire during the Battle of Olustee, February 20, 1864. Entrenched Confederate militia turned back the Union column, inflicting heavy losses.*

Spanish period (1739) can still be found on the site. The British, the French, the Americans, and the Confederates have also occupied this important crossroads. The museum contains relics of the colonial and Civil War eras.

LOCATION: Twenty-four miles south of Tallahassee on Route 363. HOURS: 8–12, 1–5 Thursday–Monday. FEE: Yes. TELEPHONE: 904–925–6216.

## PERRY

East from Saint Marks on Route 98, in the bend of the Panhandle, is Perry, the heart of northern Florida timber and turpentine country and a crossroads for travelers heading to Tampa. The **Forest Capital State Museum** (off Route 98, just south of Perry,

904–584–3227) is a dome built of Plexiglas and Florida timber and furnished with exhibits on everything from turpentine making to the cultivation of the longleaf pine. One curiosity is a map of Florida made from sixty-seven different Florida hardwoods, one for each county in the state. Adjacent to the museum is a **Cracker Homestead,** representing a typical 1860s rural dwelling in this pine-hummock corner of the state. It features a furnished dogtrot log cabin together with a smokehouse, corncrib, chicken coop, barn, and other outbuildings that made a "Cracker's" self-sufficient life possible. The term *Cracker* is derived not from eating habits, nor from "cracking" corn, but from the occupation of these rugged folk during the early logging boom. Many joined the lumber camps as drivers of the ox teams that hauled huge trunks out of the forest, and their skill at signaling to their animals by means of a crack of the whip—usually without actually touching the animal—gave the people the nickname that they retain today.

## LAKE CITY

Heading eastward from Tallahassee on Route 10, about halfway to Jacksonville, is Lake City, an important center for the mixed farming belt of north-central Florida. At 207 South Marion Street is a Queen Anne house from 1894, the **T. G. Henderson House** (private).

Just north of Lake City is the **Stephen Foster State Folk Culture Center** (Route 41, in White Springs, 904–397–2733). It is on the Suwanee River, which Foster made famous in his "Old Folks at Home," now the state's official song. The center offers an antebellum mansion and carillon that peals out Foster tunes. Curiously enough, Foster never saw Florida or the Suwanee. He wrote the famous lyrics in Pittsburgh, finding that "Suwanee" had just the right rhythm to fit between "Way down upon the" and "river."

East from Lake City at Olustee is the **Olustee Battlefield State Historic Site** (Route 90, two miles east of Olustee). There is little here today but a trail along the battle lines and a small museum telling the story of Florida's largest Civil War battle. Here, on February 20, 1864, Confederate militia beat back a force of more than 5,000 Union troops, killing or capturing 700 of them in a five-hour battle. As a result, the Federal troops were unable to accomplish their objective of splitting Florida in half.

# THE   NORTHEAST   COAST

Centerpiece of this much-visited coast is the oldest continuously occupied town in the United States, Saint Augustine. Nearby Amelia Island claims that it is the only place in the country to have flown eight different flags, though the count includes an 1812 battle flag and the Mexican flag briefly flown by freebooters in order to surpass the claims of settlements on Florida's northwestern Gulf Coast. Nonetheless, while the northwestern Gulf Coast traded hands frequently between the sixteenth and nineteenth centuries, Florida's northeastern Atlantic Coast did so even more often. As a result, many of the surviving monuments are either forts or the remains of some group that settled on the coast in pursuit of their particular dream. It should also be recalled that the northeast coast was a popular winter resort in the last quarter of the nineteenth century, on the eve of Henry Plant's and Henry Flagler's push southward.

## FERNANDINA BEACH

A Spanish town and mission stood near this site in the 1680s, but in 1702, British governor James Moore of South Carolina and his Creek allies swept down on Amelia Island, destroying both. Georgia's James Oglethorpe occupied the island in 1735, only to return it to the Spanish in 1748. Americans fought Tory Loyalists here during the Revolutionary War but returned the land to Spain in 1783. A land grant at this time gave the town its name, the grantee being a Señor Fernandez. Pierre and Jean Lafite and other pirates worked out of the sheltered estuary during the first years of the nineteenth century; then, with the complicity of the U.S. government, a band of Americans captured the island at the outset of the War of 1812, only to return it to Spain again. In 1817 a Scottish adventurer, Gregor MacGregor, took Fernandina in partnership with a French pirate who raised the Mexican flag.

The **Amelia Island Museum of History** (233 South Third Street, 904–261–7378) is an excellent local-history museum that also offers tours of nearby historic districts and archaeological sites. The museum has oral-history materials plus prints of the work of French artist Jacques LeMoyne, who accompanied the Huguenot party that sailed these waters in the sixteenth century. LeMoyne's portraits of coastal Indian life are invaluable portraits of a vanished people. The museum also displays nineteenth-century lithographs and photographs, showing the island as it was, along with laminated newspaper pages from the early days of the town. Artifacts from the ongoing digs at the 1683 Spanish-era Dorian Mission are on display, including the priest's seal, rosaries, mirrors, potsherds, olive jars, and the like.

The Centre Street area is a district of historic houses, spanning all Victorian styles and recalling the heady days when Fernandina Beach was a favorite winter wateringhole of sunseekers. The museum offers walking tours that include visits to such notable structures as the 1895 **Bailey House** (28 South Seventh Street), with its corner turrets, gables, bay windows, and wraparound porch. (The house is now a bed-and-breakfast.) Across the street is the wonderfully eclectic 1885 **Tabby House** (private), designed by New York architect Robert Schuyler. The stick style arched porches are particularly attractive.

## Fort Clinch State Park

The masonry of the fort is impressive, and cannon are mounted on its ramparts, but Fort Clinch never saw action. It was begun in 1847 and desultory work continued until 1860, when two bastions facing the Saint Marys River were completed. The Confederates took it without a struggle in 1861 and abandoned it to the Union in 1862. Thereafter, work continued under U.S. jurisdiction, but the invention of the rifled cannon—first used in 1862 against Fort Pulaski at Savannah—made masonry forts instant dinosaurs.

Among the sights at the fort, in addition to the bastions themselves, are barracks, a bakery, a blacksmith's shop, an infirmary, and other necessary outbuildings, all restored.

LOCATION: Enter off Route A1A, on Atlantic Avenue. HOURS: *Park:* 8–Dusk Daily; *Fort:* 9–5 Daily. FEE: Yes. TELEPHONE: 904–261–4212.

# JACKSONVILLE

Given the number of times Andrew Jackson marched into Florida and his occupancy of its first territorial governorship, it is no wonder that Florida's largest city—in size—was named for him. (The city has embraced most of the surrounding county within its city limits.) Set on either side of the Saint Johns River, a little inland

*Jacksonville's lavish Florida Theater, where such diverse entertainers as Eddie Cantor and Elvis Presley have performed.*

from the coast, Jacksonville is the state's industrial and shipping center, having first risen to prominence before the Civil War as a port for cotton, timber, and the then-thriving citrus industry along the river. Occupied four times by Union forces during the war, the city recovered its maritime business slowly thereafter, adding its first rail connections in 1883. The Riverside-Avondale Historic District contains a large number of distinctive houses from the first quarter of the twentieth century, along with a smattering of older structures. A 1901 fire destroyed many of Jacksonville's buildings.

The **Cummer Gallery of Art** (829 Riverside Avenue, 904–356–6857) occupies a 1961 building, but it preserves a furnished room from the 1907 Cummer house, a fine example of the Tudor style in Jacksonville. The formal gardens of the original mansion also remain. The eclectic collection dates from a 1280 B.C. relief of Ramses II up to the present century, and fills eleven galleries. It is especially strong in early-eighteenth-century Meissen porcelain.

The **Museum of Science and History** (1025 Gulf Life Drive, 904–396–7062) comprises a planetarium and natural history museum and many hands-on science exhibits, but it is also strong in the archaeology of Florida Indians, with artifacts from the mound cultures and Seminole canoes, clothing, and chickee houses. The pioneer section contains a log cabin furnished with spinning wheels, looms, a pegged cradle, while a separate work shed contains the kettle and implements used for refining sugar. A photographic exhibit traces the rebirth of Jacksonville after the 1901 fire.

## KINGSLEY PLANTATION HISTORIC SITE

South toward Jacksonville on Fort George Island—now actually in the northern part of that expansive city—is this early-nineteenth-century frame plantation house and the adjoining 1791 Don Juan McQueen House, its first floor in tabby (a handmade concrete composed of mortar and crushed oyster shells) and its second in frame. Also on the property are the ruins of two dozen slave cabins, plus a brick and tabby barn. The older house was deeded to McQueen by the Spanish, but when Zephaniah Kingsley acquired the island in 1817, he built a white nine-room frame house more appropriate to the image of an early-nineteenth-century business-man growing sea island cotton, dabbling in politics, and trading slaves. His wife, Anna Jai, was a black woman from Madagascar who spoke French, Spanish, and English and was in charge of house-servant training. The house is furnished with antebellum and Victorian furnishings, some of them brought to the house when a later owner, who also pioneered in citrus culture here, turned the property into a resort.

LOCATION: Off Route A1A at Hecksher Drive, Fort George Island. HOURS: 8–5 Thursday–Monday. FEE: Yes. TELEPHONE: 904–251–3122.

## FORT CAROLINE NATIONAL MEMORIAL

Here is a model of the triangular earthworks-and-palisade fort built in July 1564 by a party of 300 French Huguenots with Timucuan Indian help, four miles from the mouth of the Saint Johns River. They hoped to create a French presence in the New World and find the wealth it promised. The colony was rent by dissension, some members mutinying and raiding Spanish shipping against the orders of René de Laudonniére, their nominal leader. The

French, who had narrowly escaped starvation and had alienated
many of their Indian allies, were on the brink of abandoning the
fort and returning home when Jean Ribault arrived with reinforcements in August 1565. Right behind him, however, was the great
Spanish admiral Pedro Menéndez de Avilés, who guessed correctly
that Ribault's forces were moving to attack him at his newly established settlement of San Augustin. With 500 men he marched on
Fort Caroline, forty miles to the north, while the French ships were
caught in a storm. More than 140 French Protestants died when
the Spanish took the fort on September 20. Two weeks later,
Menéndez turned on the shipwrecked Ribault party, killing half of
them. Two and a half years later, with Fort Caroline renamed San
Mateo by its captors, the Frenchman Dominique de Gourgues
successfully carried out a surprise counterattack, burning the fort
and executing the Spanish garrison.

The museum and visitor center have some Indian and European artifacts of the period, but the real attraction is the reconstructed fort itself.

LOCATION: 12713 Fort Caroline Road. HOURS: 9–5 Daily. FEE:
None. TELEPHONE: 904–641–7155.

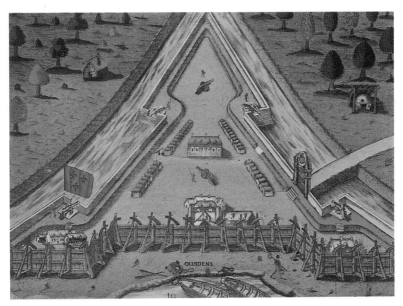

*Fort Caroline, named to honor French King Charles IX, was the site of many bloody encounters
between the French and the Spanish in their struggle for control of Florida.*

# SAINT AUGUSTINE

On September 8, 1565—forty-two years before the settlement of Jamestown in Virginia—Don Pedro Menéndez de Avilés established the Florida outpost he called San Augustin (Saint Augustine) in honor of the saint's day, August 28, when he first sighted the Florida coast. He chose the location for military reasons, with three sides flanked by rivers and the fourth to be protected by a fort. Menéndez was intent on punishing the freebooting Huguenots of Fort Caroline, but he realized the need for a permanent fortress to protect Spanish shipping in the area.

Despite the fort's strength, Sir Francis Drake was able to take Saint Augustine in 1586 and put it to the torch. The rebuilt town was attacked repeatedly as it shifted from Spanish to British and finally to American hands, but many of the older parts of the city have survived. It was an important shipping center for the northern Florida plantation culture before the Civil War and, beginning in the 1880s, for the tourist boom, when Henry M. Flagler established resort hotels here and drove his railway empire from Saint Augustine. Old Saint Augustine stands directly on the dividing line between the old plantation Florida and the new tourist Florida. Today the old city is a living history museum, much of it built from a material called coquina, a sort of natural aggregate of seashells embedded in a lime mortar. Strong and easily worked, the material was naturally suited for the forts and other structures of the Saint Augustine area.

The **Restored Spanish Quarter** (entrance on Saint George Street, 904–824–6383), bordered by Saint George, Hypolita, Cordova, and Orange streets, is a group of mostly reconstructed eighteenth-century Spanish buildings, "inhabited" by costumed "Spaniards." These comprise a museum that includes the one-room **Gomez House,** refurbished as a 1740s residence and general store; a working blacksmith shop and eighteenth-century weaver and spinner in the **Gonzalez House;** and a carpenter working under a thatched-roof pole shed. The **De Mesa–Sanchez House** is one of the few original structures in the area, dating from the early to

OPPOSITE: *A gallery of the Ximenez-Fatio House, which was operated as a boardinghouse in the nineteenth century.*

mid-eighteenth century with a number of nineteenth-century additions. Unlike the other houses in the district, this one is fitted out with furniture from the 1840s. The **Gallegos House** is a substantial structure made of tabby (a handmade concrete composed of mortar and crushed oyster shells) and containing an indoor kitchen, unusual for the mid-eighteenth century.

Also in the restored Spanish Quarter is the **Old Wooden Schoolhouse** (14 Saint George Street, 904–824–0192), a ca. 1778 clapboard house built to be a residence but later used as a school. It is the oldest wooden building that survives in Saint Augustine and has been restored to its appearance as a school, with period furnishings; the Spanish style kitchen also survives. Farther out Saint George Street is the **Sanchez House** (number 105, 904–824–8247), a substantial 1809 coquina house with a courtyard built by a Spanish merchant who married an Englishwoman. Now owned by an insurance company, the two-story white structure is furnished with early-nineteenth-century English and American antiques.

An especially fine residence in the downtown area is the **Dr. Peck House** (143 Saint George Street, 904–829–5064), named for the Connecticut doctor who moved his family here in 1837 and added a second, frame story to the existing coquina house. The original structure is among the oldest in the city of Saint Augustine, having been built for the Spanish royal treasurer prior to 1764. The house fronts the street and contains an interior courtyard with an arcaded loggia. Constructed in a U shape, the building was built to serve as a fortress in time of need: The livestock could be driven in the open end of the U and the whole house sealed off. One of the Peck House's notable features is its collection of eighteenth-century American antiques from the Connecticut River area, all of them the documented dowry of Dr. Peck's wife.

On narrow, one-lane Aviles Street is the **Ximenez-Fatio House** (number 20, 904–829–3575), a two-and-a-half-story coquina and frame house built for a Spanish merchant between 1797 and 1802. Originally, the house served simultaneously as a general store and tavern with living quarters above. In 1830 it was purchased by Margaret Cook, who added a large wing and ran a very successful boardinghouse here. She was followed by two more landladies, the last of whom made a specialty of renting accommodations to the rich northerners who were among the early tourists to Florida. The structure is an interesting combination of Spanish and English styles, with plastered walls and a wooden balcony and gabled roofline. The Colonial Dames of America maintain it as a boarding-house museum of the 1830s–1860s period. Rooms are furnished and arranged complete with such accoutrements as glove stretchers and hatboxes, as though the guests had just checked in.

West on King Street from the junction with Aviles are a series of structures that illustrate the history of late-nineteenth-century Saint Augustine. Just off the thoroughfare is the **Oldest Store Museum** (4 Artillery Lane, 904–829–9729), an overstuffed re-creation of a turn-of-the-century general store with more than 100,000 items. At the junction of King and Cordova streets are two of the three grand hotels built by Henry M. Flagler between 1887 and 1889, the first such tourist extravaganzas in Florida. The indefatigable Flagler hired New York architects Carrère & Hastings to design the buildings, sending them to Spain to study Spanish and Moorish architecture before setting them to the task of creating these elaborate Hispano-Moorish style hotels. The first, **Flagler College** (74 King Street, 904–829–6481), once the Hotel Ponce de León, features a central dome and corner towers, Tiffany glass, and murals depicting the history of Saint Augustine. The second, the **Lightner Museum** (75 King Street, 904–824–2874), once the Alcazar Hotel, was scarcely less elaborate and today features a museum of nineteenth-century decorative arts, including a large collection of American cut glass, a Tiffany room, an Oriental room, cloisonné, fine china and porcelains, and a Victorian village re-creation. Just beyond the two hotels is the building that may have inspired Flagler: **Zorayda Castle** (83 King Street, 904–824–3097), a brightly colored coquina and cement Moorish-style residence built in 1883. Today it houses the eclectic collections of its second owner, including Far Eastern vases and Oriental rugs.

South and east of the castle is the **Oldest House** (the González-Álvarez House, 14 Saint Francis Street, 904–824–2872), which was begun in 1723, although it has been extensively remodeled over the centuries. The simple vernacular dwelling was once a one-story coquina house; later, the second floor was added with a wood frame. The tabby floors, hand-hewn cedar beams, and huge hearth of the old house are an impressive sight. The house is furnished room by room, according to the period in which it was built: There are rooms showing the first and second Spanish period and the British period. Next door is the **Webb Museum** (904–824–2872), containing artifacts from the Menéndez to the Flagler period and an exhibition on the Saint Johns Railway.

## Castillo de San Marcos National Monument

The oldest building in Saint Augustine is also the largest: the Castillo de San Marcos, begun in 1672 and substantially completed by 1756. The great coquina fort has walls twelve feet thick at the bottom, thinning to a mere seven feet on the upper ramparts. It was the tenth fortification built on the site, the nine previous wooden ones having succumbed to salt, wind, poor construction, and, in 1586, to fire set by the victorious troops of Sir Francis Drake. The strong stone castillo itself withstood a number of attacks and two major British sieges, in 1702 and 1740, never surrendering or being captured. Even when the raiders burned the whole town down, the inhabitants of Saint Augustine remained safe inside their fortress.

The castillo, renamed Fort Saint Mark, served the British as a staging base for attacks on Georgia and South Carolina during the Revolutionary War. Captured Yankee soldiers were also imprisoned here. In the American period, some artillery was added and minor changes made, but for the most part the fort looks the same now as it did during the eighteenth century.

LOCATION: Junction of Castillo Drive and Avenida Menendez. HOURS: 9–5 Daily. FEE: Yes. TELEPHONE: 904–829–6506.

In north Saint Augustine, beyond the castillo, is a 208-foot cross marking the beginning of the Spanish settlement and the site of the first Mass said in what is now the United States, on September 8, 1565. Thereafter, the **Mission of Nombre de Dios** (101 San Marco Avenue, 904–824–2809) was established here, though the current church on the site is a modern structure.

# FORT MATANZAS NATIONAL MONUMENT

Fourteen miles south of Saint Augustine, Fort Matanzas was built as an outpost of the Castillo de San Marcos in 1742 to guard the southern entrance to the inland waterway. The fort is on Rattlesnake Island, a short ferry ride from the visitor center on Anastasia Island. The exhibits commemorate the end of Ribault's Huguenots, who after surrendering to Pedro Menéndez de Avilés's smaller Spanish force in two groups (on September 29 and October 12,

OPPOSITE: *Castillo de San Marcos. During the Revolutionary War three signers of the Declaration of Independence were imprisoned here by the British.*

1565) were brutally executed, not so much because they were Frenchmen, as Menéndez put it, but because they were Protestants. Rangers lead visitors through the old stone bastions.

LOCATION: Anastasia and Rattlesnake islands, fourteen miles south of Saint Augustine via Route A1A. HOURS: 8:30–4:30 Daily. FEE: None. TELEPHONE: 904–471–0116.

## BULOW PLANTATION STATE HISTORICAL MONUMENT

This burned-out hulk of a pioneer sugar mill tells the story of Seminole resentment of the encroachment of white planters into this area during the first half of the nineteenth century. The now-destroyed two-story wood-frame plantation house was built in 1821 and controlled a large sugar-growing area complete with its own processing facilities. Plantations like these were prime targets of the Seminole during the Second Seminole War. The troops of Major Putnam were quartered here at the beginning of 1835 and lost a battle just south on an adjoining plantation. With many wounded, and fearing themselves outnumbered, they withdrew from the plantation, and the Seminole burned it on January 31, 1836.

LOCATION: Route A1A, twelve miles north of Ormond Beach. HOURS: 9–5 Daily. FEE: Yes. TELEPHONE: 904–439–2219.

## ORMOND BEACH AND DAYTONA BEACH

Once this was rural sugar-plantation country. Then came the hotel and winter-house builders of the 1880s, and cities and resort communities began to spring up. Henry M. Flagler bought and enlarged an 1875 hostelry, the **Hotel Ormond** (15 East Granada Street, Ormond Beach), in 1888 as he was extending his railroad and hotel empire south. John D. Rockefeller bought his comparatively modest Shingle-style winter place, **The Casements** (25 Riverside Drive, Ormond Beach), in 1918 and spent much time there late in his life.

Daytona Beach was named for Mathias Day, an 1870s immigrant from Ohio. The real influx of settlers came after Flagler's hotel in Ormond Beach began to boom. The 500-foot-wide white sand beaches, beaten hard, were an ideal place for the idle rich—and soon for automobile companies themselves—to test the speed and maneuverability of new motor vehicles, giving birth eventually to the Daytona Speedway. The **Halifax Historical Society** (252 Beach Street, 904–255–6976) operates the Halifax Historical Museum in Daytona's first bank building, the 1910 Merchants Bank. In addition to exhibits on local history, the society maintains a research library and collection of historic photographs.

Two miles north of Ormond Beach is a monument of much greater antiquity, the site of the Timucuan village of Nocoroco located at **Tomoka State Park** (Beach Street, off Route 40, 904–677–9463), a set of excavated burial mounds with a small museum. The burial mounds are not open to the public, but the museum in the visitor center has exhibits on the history of the Timucuan Indians and on the natural history of the region.

In Ormond Beach is the **Birthplace of Speed Museum** (160 East Granada Avenue, 904–672–5657), with a collection that includes historic photographs and loving cups, plus four cars: a Model T, a Model A, a Stanley Steamer, and a "rocket car" about the size of a go-cart that was capable of reaching speeds of 160 miles per hour.

Sugar—the product that once gave this area its wealth—is remembered at the **Sugar Mill Gardens** (Route 1, three and a half miles south of Daytona Beach, then one mile west on Herbert Street, 904–767–3812), the remains of yet another sugar plantation that was destroyed by the Seminole in the 1830s. It was renovated in 1848 by John F. Marshall, who converted the refining process to steam power, and by 1851 it was producing 200 tons of sugar each year. During the Civil War, the Confederates used its vats to produce salt. Visitors can see the walls and chimneys of the old mill, as well as a good deal of the old steam-driven machinery, a botanic garden, and nature trails.

About twenty miles south of Daytona Beach is the **Ponce de León Inlet Lighthouse** (4931 South Peninsula Drive, Ponce Inlet, 904–761–1821), a 175-foot structure built in 1887. The keeper's and two assistant keepers' cottages have been restored, with displays on the keeping of the light, as well as local marine biology and the shipwrecks that occurred on this dangerous strip of coast.

OVERLEAF: *Vacationers at Daytona Beach, one of Florida's earliest resorts. The broad expanse of hard, smooth sand also attracted automobile racers early in the century: In 1903, Alexander Winton set a world's speed record here—68 miles per hour.*

## NEW SMYRNA BEACH

There had already been an Indian village and a Spanish mission on this site when Dr. Andrew Turnbull, a Scotsman, appeared here in 1767 with 1,500 colonists bent on growing indigo. The colonists were mainly Minorcan, with a scattering of Greeks and Italians, all of them supported by grants from the British government. Briefly prosperous, the colony nevertheless failed due to internal dissension, and its members moved away, many of them to Saint Augustine. (There are still a significant number of people of Minorcan descent in the city.) Still extant in town are the foundations of a fort (Riverside Drive, north of Canal Street), probably Spanish and predating the colony. Old bits of canal and disused wells can also be found around the town.

West of New Smyrna is another Seminole-ravaged sugar plantation, the **New Smyrna Sugar Mill Ruins State Historic Site** (two miles west of Route 1, off Route 44, 904–428–2126). Built of coquina in 1830, it was burned five years later. Some of the machinery and refining kettles, along with ruins of the house and mill, are still visible.

# THE    LAKE    COUNTRY

From here, the entries move inland, describing an arc that begins on Route 92 at Daytona Beach, then heads west to De Land and wanders through north-central Florida lake country before emerging on the Gulf Coast and proceeding north to Cedar Key.

## DE LAND

De Land was founded in 1876 by a baking powder magnate of the same name. One of its most noted citizens was a Chinese named Lue Gim Gong who developed strains of orange and grapefruit that were crucial to the development of the citrus industry in central Florida. It is also the location of Stetson University, the oldest private university in Florida. There one can find the 1884

OPPOSITE: *Remnants of nineteenth-century sugar mills—rollers for crushing sugar cane, top, at Yulee Sugar Mill ruins, and large cooking kettles, bottom, at the New Smyrna Sugar Mill ruins.*

De Land Hall, restored to its original "Carpenter Gothic" appearance, and several other buildings from the late nineteenth and early twentieth centuries.

Nearby is **Hontoon Island State Park** (six miles southwest of De Land, off Route 44, 904–736–5309), a lovely and secluded island in the middle of the Saint Johns River, reached only by ferryboat. The island is the site of a 300-foot-long Timucuan Indian mound, along with a number of shell middens and a replica of one of three intriguing owl totem poles recently unearthed here.

To the south, on Lake Monroe, is **DeBary,** a small town named for Baron Frederick DeBary, a wine merchant who built his winter place here in 1871. **DeBary Hall** (210 Sunrise Boulevard) is the chief landmark, a remarkable frame house with a wraparound two-story verandah. The house is now a senior citizen's center.

## MOUNT DORA

This quiet recreational town is set beside Lake Dora, a popular yachting center. The **Seaboard Coast Line Railroad Station** is a pretty wood-frame structure, with its original 1915 cabinetry and signaling equipment intact; it now serves as headquarters of the chamber of commerce. The **Donnelly House** (Donnelly Avenue, private) is an elaborate Queen Anne house built by one of the town's founders in 1893.

## TAVARES

Tavares was founded in 1880 by Alexander St. Clair Abrams, who hoped to make it the capital of Florida. He named the town for a supposed Portuguese ancestor and built the Peninsular Hotel, which burned in 1888, and later the Osceola Hotel, which now serves as City Hall.

The history of Tavares and the surrounding county is told in the **Lake County Historical Museum** (402 West Main Street, 904–343–1987). There are a few local Indian artifacts, together with a large number of historic photographs of early industries and methods of transportation, a small country store, a parlor, and a rotating exhibit room.

# DADE BATTLEFIELD STATE HISTORIC SITE

Southwest along Route 301 at Bushnell is this monument to the so-called Dade Massacre. Here, on December 28, 1835, a party of Seminole led by chiefs Micanope and Jumper ambushed Major Francis Dade and 107 troopers, killing all but three of them. An organized invasion of American troops replaced the incursions, and the Second Seminole War began. A concrete reproduction of the breastworks thrown up by the soldiers marks the fight.

LOCATION: Off Route 476, just south of Bushnell. HOURS: 8–Dusk Daily. FEE: Yes. TELEPHONE: 904–793–4781.

# HOMOSASSA SPRINGS

Central Florida is full of small towns named for nearby freshwater springs. This one is very near to the Gulf Coast on Route 19, west of Bushnell. The **Yulee Sugar Mill Ruins State Historic Park** (on Route 490, west of Route 19, 904–795–3817) preserves the remains of the sugar mill established here in 1851 by David Levy Yulee, a large plantation owner and the first U.S. senator from Florida. The site includes a boiler, chimney, cane-crushing rollers, and large cooking vats, all with plaques explaining sugar-refining.

# CRYSTAL RIVER STATE ARCHAEOLOGICAL SITE

Here is an important pre-Columbian mound site, with both temple and burial mounds set around a large plaza area. The on-site museum contains pottery, projectile points, and other artifacts from the site.

LOCATION: Off Route 19, five miles northwest of Crystal River. HOURS: *Museum:* 9–5 Daily; *Grounds:* 8–Dusk Daily. FEE: Yes. TELE-PHONE: 904–795–3817.

# CEDAR KEY STATE MUSEUM

Three miles offshore in the Gulf of Mexico, Cedar Key was, from 1860, the western terminus of a railroad that ran from Fernandina in the northeast corner of Florida, and it became a resort community before such activities shifted south to Tampa in the late 1880s.

Lumbering, shipbuilding, and pencil manufacturing were also economic mainstays of the area. The museum contains artifacts that reflect the shifting fortunes of the island.

LOCATION: Museum Drive, Cedar Key. HOURS: 9–5 Thursday–Monday. FEE: Yes. TELEPHONE: 904–543–5350.

## OCALA

An important crossroads town on Route 27 northwest of Tavares, Ocala was a citrus-growing center during the nineteenth century until the freezes of 1894 and 1895 forced the industry to move farther south. The rolling hills of the vicinity are also an important breeding ground for thoroughbred horses. It was near this site that Fort King was established in 1827; in 1834 the Seminole leader Osceola put a knife through a treaty that would have removed his people to Oklahoma; the next year, he killed the local Indian agent and an officer of the fort. The same day, Major Francis Dade's troops were ambushed and destroyed by a Seminole war party, initiating the Second Seminole War.

Ocala features many Victorian residences built during the town's citrus-growing heyday. A fifty-five-block historic district centered on Watula Avenue, Eleventh Avenue, and Southeast Sixth Street contains most of the houses of note. Three attractive private homes, all on Southeast Fort King Street, are the 1888 **Burford House** (number 943), the **Seven Sisters Inn** (number 820), and the 1895 **Rheinauer House** (number 603).

About twenty-six miles northeast of Ocala, at **Silver Springs,** is the **Orange Springs Community Church,** a simple but impressive 1818 country church with a back door that allowed settlers to escape Indian raids and a slave balcony. The cemetery is full of Civil War–era gravestones.

OPPOSITE: *Beginning in the late 1800s, Florida citrus growers used colorful paper crate labels to promote their products. Many labels emphasized the scenic charms of the state. Growers in Plymouth, Florida, made use of a renowned New England landmark, Plymouth Rock, to promote their fruit.*

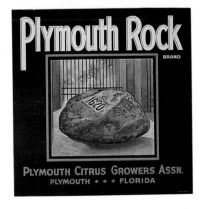

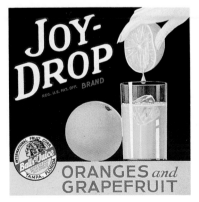

# CENTRAL
## AND
# SOUTHERN
# FLORIDA

OPPOSITE: *The hispanic origins of Tampa's Ybor City, the cigar-making district, are evident in this tiled doorway.*

The cities of northern Florida were already old when today's great metropolis of Miami was a tiny village. In spite of government efforts to convince people to live in the south— anticipating the Homestead Act by offering more than 100 acres to any settler willing to occupy his land for five years running—the pre–Civil War settlement of the region was minimal. Even after the Civil War and Reconstruction, Miami was still a small town on Biscayne Bay, a bay too well protected by the Florida Reef for any serious sea traffic, and it was served by a mailman who walked barefoot down the beach from the town of Jupiter, far up the coast.

Sixteenth-century Spaniards were the first Europeans to try to conquer southern Florida. Ponce de León landed near present Charlotte Harbor on the southwest coast in 1521; the Spanish had killed and kidnapped natives on the coast before, and the Calusa Indians were forewarned and hostile. They attacked Ponce and his 200 invaders, driving them back to their ships. Ponce died later that year of an arrow wound received in this encounter. Next came Pánfilo de Narváez and his 300 stalwarts who landed at Tampa Bay in 1528 and marched northward. In 1539 Hernando de Soto did much the same on a larger scale, leading his 600 soldiers northwest from Tampa Bay; de Soto died near the Mississippi River, and the remains of his party reached Mexico in 1542.

Pedro Menéndez de Avilés, who as founder of Saint Augustine in 1565 became the first European to establish successfully a settlement in Florida, spent the next seven years helping to establish a Spanish presence on the peninsula, creating missions as far south as Tampa Bay and Charlotte Harbor on the Gulf Coast. None prospered, however, and later Spanish missionary efforts were focused on the northeastern region and the Panhandle.

It would be three more centuries before southern Florida was effectively occupied by Europeans. American efforts to settle southern Florida in the 1820s proceeded slowly. The "Indian problem" was as severe as it had been for Ponce de León: Though the Calusa and allied southern tribes had been largely destroyed 200 years before, the Seminole—most of them members of the "Creek" nation who had migrated south from Georgia and Alabama—were, if anything, fiercer in their resistance to white efforts to remove them. An 1823 treaty limited them to an interior area north of Lake Okeechobee, but it wasn't long before would-be settlers were clamoring for the removal of the Indians to the Arkansas Territory. Though several fraudulent treaties were pushed through, the

*A busy Miami real estate office in the 1920s.* PAGES 406–407: *Big Cypress National Preserve, northwest of the Everglades. This swamp is a habitat of the endangered Florida panther, a subspecies of the mountain lion.*

Seminole refused to budge, resulting in the prolonged conflict known as the Second Seminole War (1835 to 1842). Only by tricking the leader Osceola into capture and by one decisive American victory by General Zachary Taylor in the Battle of Lake Okeechobee on Christmas Day, 1837, were the majority of the Seminole brought to heel. Even so, some small bands never surrendered, melting into the depths of the Everglades, where the fear of them stalled further invasion long after almost 4,000 Seminole had been shipped west to what is now Oklahoma.

With the "removal" of the Seminole, the U.S. Congress passed the Armed Occupation Act of 1842, encouraging settlers with the promise of 160 acres to anyone who would occupy the land for five years. A number of families took up holdings in what is now Miami; eight years later only one of them remained. The new Florida state legislature took matters into its own hands in 1855. Assuming that improved transportation would attract residents, the legislature promised vast land grants to anyone who would build a railroad. Here was the first hint of the miracle that later transformed southern Florida, but its realization was delayed by the coming of the Civil War.

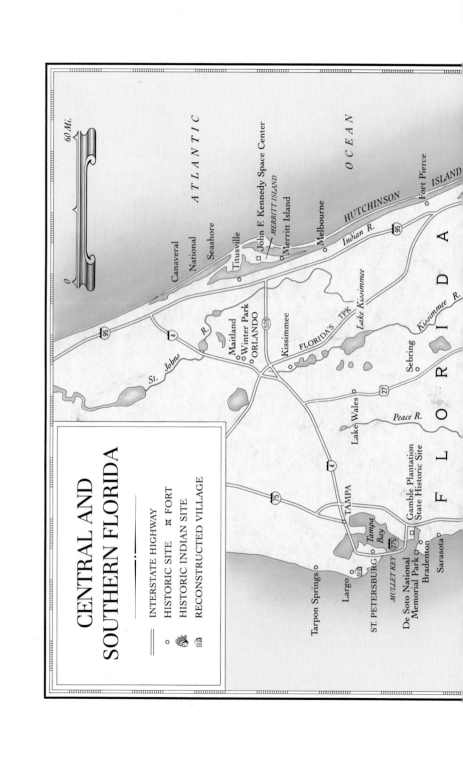

# CENTRAL AND
# SOUTHERN FLORIDA

INTERSTATE HIGHWAY

○   HISTORIC SITE   ⊟ FORT

🌸   HISTORIC INDIAN SITE

🏠   RECONSTRUCTED VILLAGE

*ATLANTIC*

*OCEAN*

60 Mi.

0

Canaveral
National
Seashore

Titusville

John F. Kennedy Space Center

*MERRITT ISLAND*

Merritt Island

Melbourne

*Indian R.*

HUTCHINSON

Fort Pierce

ISLAND

95

St. Johns R.

Maitland
Winter Park
ORLANDO

Kissimmee

528

*FLORIDA'S TPK*

*Lake Kissimmee*

*Kissimmee R.*

Sebring

95

4

Lake Wales

27

*Peace R.*

F   L   O   R   I   D   A

4

75

TAMPA

Gamble Plantation
State Historic Site

Tarpon Springs

Largo

*Tampa
Bay*

ST. PETERSBURG

*MULLET KEY*

275

De Soto National
Memorial Park

Bradenton

Sarasota

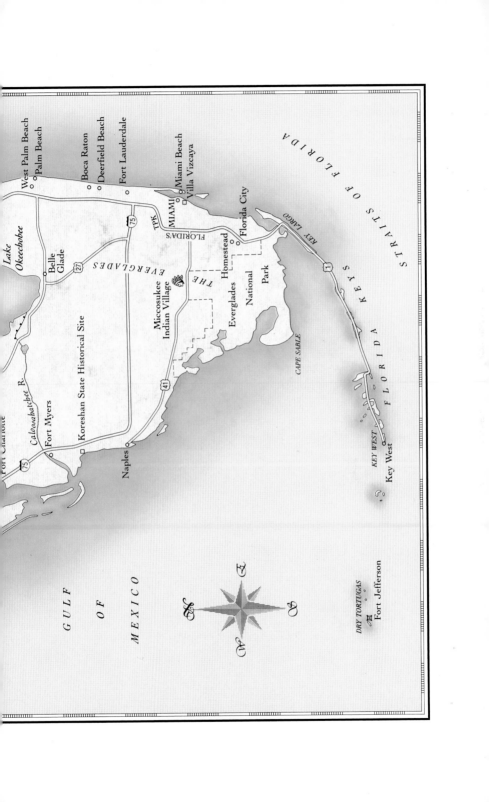

Key West, the island town 100 miles from the mainland of the peninsula and only about 90 miles from Cuba, was long a home to pirates and freebooters. But when Commodore David Porter suppressed the buccaneers during the early 1820s, the town of Key West began to earn a remarkable livelihood salvaging the many vessels that ran aground on the Florida Reef. The culture of the "wreckers" brought wealth to the town and even influenced its architecture—wood, fixtures, and even portholes from stranded vessels were incorporated into local homes. By 1830, its residents claimed the highest per-capita income in the United States. Beginning in the 1850s the construction of lighthouses made navigation safer and cut into the wreckers' business. A cigar-packing industry—begun with Cuban workers in 1831 and fed thereafter with a steady stream of expatriates—helped diversify the local economy, as did the establishment of the U.S. naval station and construction of nearby Fort Jefferson. By 1880, Key West had 10,000 inhabitants and was the largest town in Florida.

*Henry Flagler's 1894 Royal Poinciana Hotel, Palm Beach, with a special railroad spur and service tracks for private railroad cars. Railroads and hotels transformed rural Florida into a winter resort paradise.*

A year later, modern Florida was, in effect, launched by a single man. The Reconstruction had returned the state to self-government in 1877, and the Internal Improvement Fund—the land bank created back in 1855 to encourage railroad construction—was in danger of seeing its assets sold off at bargain prices to pay the state's debts. Then, in 1881, a Philadelphia investor, Hamilton Disston, bought 4 million acres (6,250 square miles) of south-central Florida real estate from the fund at the attractive price of twenty-five cents per acre. The state could pay its debts, the fund was saved, and Disston got the then-marginal lands of the Kissimmee and Caloosahatchee valleys, which he proceeded to drain for farming. Florida's benefactor himself came to a sorry end in 1896. After losing a fortune in the 1893 panic, Disston was unable to continue his ambitious plans, and one night after attending the theater, he drew a warm bath, got into it, and shot himself in the head.

This might have been a cautionary tale for the generations of promoters who followed Disston into southern Florida, converting a sleepy backwater into a booming land of pleasures, attractions, developments, and speculation. Here was one of the few cases in history when pioneers have been able to make their living serving tourists. Indeed, the two Henrys—Henry Plant and Henry Flagler—whose railroads and hotels transformed the southland, both first visited Florida as Yankee tourists in search of a healthful winter climate for their ailing wives.

Connecticut Yankee Henry Plant was the prominent southern agent of the Adams Express Company who remained in Atlanta to manage the firm as the Southern Express Company during the Civil War, in spite of his refusal to become a Confederate citizen. His friendly competitor Henry Flagler had been the partner of John D. Rockefeller in the creation of the Standard Oil Company. Taking advantage of the generous land-grant provisions of the Internal Improvement Fund, Plant and Flager began to buy up railroad charters at a fantastic rate, establishing networks of rail lines that extended to Tampa in the west and to Key West in the southeast. (In addition, Plant controlled steamship lines that worked Florida's rivers and the trade with Cuba.) Through the 1880s and the 1890s—and in Flagler's case up until his death in 1913—the two men built luxurious resort hotels and transportation empires. The Plant System virtually created the city of Tampa, whose centerpiece was the astounding Tampa Bay Hotel with its thirteen silver minarets. Flagler's Florida East Coast Railroad expanded from Saint Augustine, to Ormond, to Palm Beach, to Miami, and finally, via a 100-mile string of arched bridges over the Florida Keys, to Key West. At each stop, Flagler created great resort hotels that served as the foundations for resort communities, and in the case of Miami, a major city.

Southern Florida, then, was "rediscovered" during the last decades of the nineteenth century. Not all the discoveries were resorts: A disastrous fire in 1886 moved the cigar industry from Key West to Tampa, making Tampa an important center for revolutionists bent on freeing Cuba of Spanish domination. José Martí spoke to crowds of sympathizers here, and surreptitious aid campaigns were organized. During the Spanish-American War, Tampa was the base for the American expeditionary force.

The 1880s and 1890s also saw the awakening of the south-central peninsula. Phosphate had been discovered on the Peace River during the early 1880s and was soon a major extractive industry. Then, after a disastrous freeze that destroyed 90 percent of the crop in 1894, the citrus industry moved from its centers around the St. Johns River in the north to the south-central farmlands.

Southern Florida accelerated into the twentieth century at blinding speed. Efforts to drain parts of the Everglades began in 1905, and a large-scale sugarcane industry developed. Tampans pioneered night flying and in 1914 briefly operated the first scheduled airline in the world. (In 1955, Florida kept its air travel distinction by inaugurating the world's first passenger jet service, between Miami and New York.) Military bases in Florida were key training posts for World War I soldiers and airmen.

The most spectacular sign of growth, however, was the land boom of the early 1920s. Between 1920 and 1925, the population of Miami alone went from 30,000 to 100,000, and more than a quarter million visitors sampled the shores of sunny Florida. Great numbers invested in land, at first prudently and then wildly, selling and reselling parcels of land that ranged from fine lots in authentic developments like George Merrick's Coral Gables to marginal parcels in abandoned stone quarries and even to underwater land. Between 1924 and 1925, banks in Florida saw their deposits shoot from $41 million to almost $130 million, as investors poured money into real estate, depleting the funds in northern banks so severely that several of them failed.

The land boom itself went bust in 1926. First, the railroads proved unable to handle the volume of freight needed to build all the mock Moorish castles being erected across the state. Then one of the fleet of near-derelict ships pressed into service to replace the railroads overturned, blocking the entrance to Miami's harbor and bankrupting those who anxiously awaited delivery of materials. Finally, on September 17, a disastrous hurricane damaged almost half the homes in Miami and ruined numbers of boomtowns. Florida entered the Great Depression three years in advance of the rest of the nation.

World War II brought the vanguard of returning prosperity, since Florida was able to convert from a year-round playground to a year-round training field for the military. Resort hotels became barracks, and thousands of young men got a look at the "paradise" to which they might return after the war.

Technology that spun off from the conflict seemed tailor-made to benefit Florida. The process for creating frozen concentrates—first developed as a way to package and preserve medicines for the front lines—was applied to orange juice in 1950, paving the way for Florida to become the number one citrus producer in the United States. Improved road and air transportation converted the land south of Lake Okeechobee into the nation's winter vegetable capital. And in 1950, a captured German V-2 rocket took off from a place called Cape Canaveral on the East Coast, inaugurating the U.S. space program that nineteen years later would launch *Apollo 11* to a landing on the moon.

This chapter divides central and southern Florida into two groups: the East and the West coasts. The former begins at Orlando, then moves east to the coast and follows it through Miami to Key West and beyond to the Dry Tortugas. The second group of entries begins at Naples, the entrance to the Tamiami Trail, proceeds north to the Tampa Bay area, and then moves inland, back toward Orlando.

# T H E   E A S T   C O A S T

## ORLANDO

Orlando was born out of the Seminole Indian Wars, when settlers appeared near Fort Gatlin, an 1837 stockade created to protect whites from Indian raids. The first settlers raised cattle; despite periodic problems with raiding Seminole the ranchers stayed when the fort closed in 1848, eventually forming their own village. Orlando wasn't incorporated as a town until 1875 and, as late as 1880, there were only 200 residents.

Then came the railroad. On October 2, 1880, the South Florida Railroad ran its first train through from Mellonville; when the train failed to make it up a grade, the honorary passengers leapt off to help push. Within three years, the railroad had been incorporated into the Plant System, and Orlando was off on the spurts of dramatic growth that characterize it even today. Only six years after the railroad first arrived, the population had catapulted from 200 to 4,000. In the interim, the local area has switched from cattle ranching and pine woods to vast citrus groves and urban sprawl.

Still, **Orange Avenue** preserves several examples of Orlando's earlier boom architecture, including the Art Deco **McRory's Five and Dime** (1909) and the Egyptian Revival **First National Bank Building** (1929). Among the most handsome and best preserved Victorian eclectic buildings in this part of Florida is the 1886 **Rogers Building** (37–39 South Magnolia Avenue, private), a sheet-metal building embossed with louvers, spirals, acanthus leaves, and other ornamentation. The second floor served as a meeting place for the English Club, a group of British residents who had moved to the area during the 1880s boom and established a polo club and orange groves.

The **Orange County Historical Museum** (812 East Rollins Street, 407-898-8320) contains reconstructions of a pioneer kitchen, a hot-metal-type newspaper office, an 1880s parlor, and other period rooms. There are also Indian artifacts—including a Timucuan canoe—and exhibits about the real-estate boom of the 1920s and the freeze of 1894–1895 that wiped out the local citrus industry. Behind the museum proper is **Fire Station No. 3,** furnished with firefighters' gear and featuring the 1885 steam pumper purchased by the town's first fire department.

OPPOSITE: *Lift-off of the Space Shuttle* Discovery *at Kennedy Space Center on September 29, 1988—the first shuttle flight after the loss of the* Challenger.

## WINTER PARK AND MAITLAND

Essentially northern suburbs of Orlando, these two towns have been centers for the early citrus industry, and more recently, for the sunseekers who have settled here. They are both known for interesting and unusual museums, including the **Maitland Art Center** (231 West Packwood Avenue, Maitland, 407–645–2181), a complex of Mayan style buildings, polychromatic and highly ornamented, created in 1937 by artist and set designer André Smith as an artist's colony. The museum offers changing exhibits of local and regional paintings, graphics, sculpture, and crafts.

The **Charles Hosmer Morse Museum of American Art** (133 East Welbourne Avenue, 407–645–5311) contains one of the finest collections of ceramics and Tiffany glass in the world, many of the pieces of which were salvaged from the artist's summer estate in New York. There is also a fine assemblage of Rookwood pottery and American painting, including works by John Singer Sargent and Rembrandt Peale.

## JOHN F. KENNEDY SPACE CENTER

More than 1.5 million people visit the home of the U.S. space program every year. The first U.S. space satellite rose from this base in 1958, and in 1961, Alan Shepard and Gus Grissom became the first and second Americans to fly into space, both on suborbital flights. Less than a decade later, in 1969, *Apollo 11* lifted off from the space center for the first manned landing on the moon. In 1981, the first Space Shuttle flight rose from Pad A. The Kennedy Space Center remains the heart of the American space program; rocket assembly, mission planning, and development of an American space station are all ongoing projects.

The visitor center, named **Spaceport U.S.A.,** has a collection of actual Mercury, Saturn, and Gemini rockets, as well as models of rocket engines and the Lunar Module, Lunar Rover, and the flight deck of a Space Shuttle. Also displayed are the recovered capsules of a number of manned flights.

Bus tours take visitors past the gigantic Vehicle Assembly Building—among the largest buildings by volume in the world—the nearby Launch Control Center, the crawler-transporter that carries the shuttle to the pad, and Pad A itself, the site of shuttle

*Louis Comfort Tiffany's 1906* Ornamental Window in Rose Design *is one of forty Tiffany windows in the Morse Museum collection.*

launches. An especially interesting stop on the tour is the Flight Crew Training Building, where visitors can experience a simulation of the *Apollo 11* launch and see an actual lunar module.

LOCATION: Route 405, NASA Causeway, forty-seven miles east of Orlando. HOURS: 9–Dusk Daily. FEE: For bus tour. TELEPHONE: 407–452–2121.

North of the space center is the **Merritt Island National Wildlife Refuge** (Route 1, 3 miles south of Titusville, 407–867–0667), an important wildlife and bird sanctuary with nature trails and a visitor center. To the east, bordering Merritt Island on the Atlantic Ocean, is **Canaveral National Seashore** (407–267–1110), the site of the fifty-foot-high **Turtle Mound,** an Indian shell mound so prominent that it appeared on sixteenth-century Spanish maps. It still offers a wonderful view of the surrounding area.

## FORT PIERCE

On Florida's East Coast, at the beginning of the "Gold Coast" section leading to Miami, is Fort Pierce, named for the 1838 palmetto-log fort that was built here against the Seminole. The town was not incorporated until 1901. Active as a citrus and vegetable shipping center, Fort Pierce is also known for its ocean beaches.

The **St. Lucie County Historical Museum** (414 Seaway Drive, 407–468–1795) is an unusually fine local-history museum. It features coins and other artifacts from a 1715 Spanish shipwreck; a reconstructed Seminole Indian encampment; a restored 1907 "Cracker" house; military artifacts from the Seminole Wars; exhibits on local cattle and pineapple industries; and a remarkable collection of 1,500 glass-plate negatives taken in the area between 1890 and 1920 by Harry Hill. Nearby is the **U.D.T. Seal Museum** (3300 North A1A; North Hutchinson Island, 407–464–3764), with exhibits and artifacts relating to the Navy Underwater Demolition Teams who trained on Fort Pierce beaches during World War II.

## HUTCHINSON ISLAND

Across the Saint Lucie and Indian rivers from the town of Stuart, Hutchinson Island contains one indigenous and one imported monument of interest. The former is the restored **Gilbert's Bar House of Refuge** (MacArthur Boulevard, five miles east of Stuart, 407–225–1875), a three-story frame house built by the U.S. Coast

Guard in 1875 to shelter shipwrecked sailors who might come ashore here. (The government acted after an actual shipwreck in 1873, when the survivors found no shelter on the island.) The main house is furnished with Victorian antiques, and its boathouse exhibits early lifesaving equipment and a reconstructed 1875 surfboat constructed with nails and clinkers, or wooden screws.

The nearby **Elliott Museum** (Route A1A, 407–225–1961) is a complex devoted to the memory of inventor Sterling Elliott, who invented address-stamping and knot-tying machinery and the steering system used in automobiles before the advent of power steering. Elliott's son assembled the museum, which contains a miscellany of his father's inventions, collections of early cars, sulkies, bikes, period rooms, needlepoint objects, tools, and toys.

## JUPITER

At the junction of the wild Loxahatchee River and the Jupiter Inlet is the town of Jupiter and its **Jupiter Inlet Lighthouse** (407–747–6639), built between 1854 and 1860, making the 105-foot conical brick structure one of the oldest lighthouses still operating on the Atlantic seaboard. A small museum is attached.

The nearby **DuBois House** (DuBois Park, 407–747–6639) is a house built in 1898 by an early white resident named Harry DuBois. When he bought the land in 1896 it contained an 800-by-40-foot Indian shell mound. DuBois sold off the shell rock for twenty-five cents a pound, and much of it ended up as the base for local roads. The house sits atop the remnants of the mound and is furnished with DuBois's possessions and other period items.

The **Loxahatchee Historical Museum** (805 North Route 1, 407–747–6639) preserves and presents the history of the area, from the Hobe Indians of 500 B.C. to the present. Exhibits display Indian artifacts (including a Seminole dugout canoe), railroad and steamboat memorabilia, and other items of local history.

## PALM BEACH

The first settler on the skinny twenty-two-mile-long island that would become Palm Beach was A. O. Lang, a horticulturist and former assistant keeper at the Jupiter Lighthouse, who may have been making himself scarce to avoid serving in the Confederate army. It would be another quarter-century before the place turned into one of the premier watering holes for the wealthy in America.

Palm Beach is named for its palms, and the story goes that the first of these came ashore in 1878, when a Spanish ship, the *Providencia*, bound from Trinidad to Cádiz, ran aground, giving up a cargo of coconuts. The coconuts were planted, and the theretofore scrubby strip of sand took on its exotic character.

Henry Morrison Flagler did the most important planting in Palm Beach, however, when he erected the immense Royal Poinciana Hotel (now demolished) in 1894, another link in the railroad-and-resort chain that would eventually reach Key West. It had 1,150 rooms and a staff of 1,400; the workers alone made a larger population than that of any town around, and the thoughtful Flagler built West Palm Beach, on the mainland side of Lake Worth, as a city "I am building for my help." The more than 2,000 guests—Wanamakers and Wideners and Vanderbilts and Goulds—were pampered on Palm Beach island. No cars were allowed; guests were transported in rickshawlike contraptions by servants.

## Henry Morrison Flagler Museum

Flagler followed the great success of his resort by building his own home here on the shores of Lake Worth in 1902. The immense

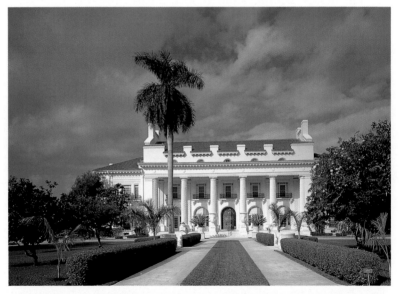

*Henry Flagler's massive Whitehall, an eclectic Carrere & Hastings design that incorporates a traditional Spanish red tile roof with the columns and porches of Southern plantation houses.*

fifty-five-room marble mansion, originally called Whitehall, was designed for Flagler by the firm of Carrère & Hastings, whose careers he had helped by commissioning them to design the Ponce de León Hotel in Saint Augustine. The 71-year-old Flagler spent $4 million gratifying the opulent tastes of his third wife, Mary Lily Kenan. The foyer alone contains seven kinds of rare marble. The guest bedrooms were decorated to represent epochs in world history, and the Flaglers' own boudoir mimicked Versailles directly. Now a museum, the home contains not only Flagler furnishings and memorabilia of the empire he created on Florida's East Coast but also collections of decorative arts and clothing of the period. Flagler's own private railway car is restored and parked outside.

LOCATION: Cocoanut Row. HOURS: 10–5 Tuesday–Saturday, 12–5 Sunday. FEE: Yes. TELEPHONE: 407–655–2833.

In its early days, Palm Beach was a hotel resort. With the arrival of globe-trotting architect Addison Mizner in 1918, the age of the posh winter residence began. Mizner's pastel-colored, elaborate, Spanish-Moorish fantasies—for which he fabricated much of the tile, materials, and even furniture himself—were well planned for

*Whitehall's entrance foyer, with benches and urns made of Carrara marble.*

the site and climate and became enormously popular during the 1920s. A surviving house, now turned into condominiums, is the **William Gray Warden Residence** (112 Seminole Avenue, private), a Mediterranean Revival structure that shows Mizner's talent at turning "the Spanish inside out like a glove."

Certainly the most opulent mansion in all Palm Beach is the towered, tiled, arched, and fantastic **Mar-A-Lago** (1100 South Ocean Boulevard, private), built between 1923 and 1927 for cereal heiress Marjorie Merriweather Post. Its tower and some of the house can be seen from the road.

## BELLE GLADE

Inland from Palm Beach, about three miles from the southeastern shores of Lake Okeechobee, is Belle Glade, a town built by the boom in 1925, then largely destroyed in 1928, when a hurricane whipped water from Lake Okeechobee over the southern lowlands, killing 2,000 people. The **Lawrence E. Will Museum** (530 South Main Street, 407–996–3453) tells the story of the flood and the local sugarcane industry and contains exhibits on the Seminole Indians and their predecessors on the land, the Calusa, who so fiercely opposed Spanish explorers during the sixteenth century.

## BOCA RATON

Today Boca Raton is one of the fastest-growing areas on the coast. The name, which means "mouth of the rat," may have been originated by Spanish pirates, who feared this inlet along the coast for its jagged rocks. The town was spawned in 1925 as a planned community of 1,600 acres by Addison Mizner, the architect who had already done considerable work in Palm Beach, and his brother Wilson. The land boom busted before the Mizners could build their posh little city where "mere existence is a joy." Still, Mizner did manage to build the Cloister Inn, now called the **Boca Raton Hotel and Club** (500 East Camino Real), which, though much remodeled, still shows the beautiful lines and color of Addison's finest Mediterranean Revival work. Also surviving in the town is the **Administration Building** (Camino Real and Dixie Highway, private), built by Mizner in imitation of El Greco's house in Spain.

OPPOSITE: *Addison Mizner's Cloister Inn opened and failed in 1926. After extensive remodeling, it reopened as the Boca Raton Hotel and Club in 1930.*

A short way down the coast is **Deerfield Beach,** a town named for
the large number of deer that once congregated nearby. The 1923
**Historic Butler House** (380 East Hillsboro Road, 305–429–0378),
built from a plan in the *Woman's Home Companion,* contains the
original furnishings and a collection of clothing dating from the
1920s. A 1920 **Old Schoolhouse** (296 Northeast Second Street,
305–427–1050) and the 1937 **Pioneer House** (Northeast Third
Street and Sixth Avenue, 305–427–1050) are preserved, complete
with original furnishings, from the days when this was a vegetable
and pineapple shipping center.

## FORT LAUDERDALE

Named for another of the string of 1830s forts that protected
settlers from Seminole attack, Fort Lauderdale nevertheless was
not incorporated until 1911, when it had a population of about
200. It began its spectacular growth during the 1920s boom, and its
"finger" canals date from that time. Today, Fort Lauderdale is a
thriving city and resort town of more than 150,000 residents, with
its own new **Museum of Art** (1 East Las Olas Boulevard, 305–525–
5500), featuring an extraordinary collection of ethnographic art
from pre-Columbian Mesoamerica, North America, the South
Seas, and West Africa. The collection of Dutch and Flemish art is
also strong, as is the assemblage of modern painting.

One of the few remaining oceanfront estates in southern Florida, the **Bonnet House** (900 North Birch Road, 305–563–5393),
also known as the Bartlett Estate, was built by the painter and art
collector Frederick Clay Bartlett about 1920. Situated on thirty-five
acres, the house and studio reflect the individuality of their owner.

The oldest section of town lies along the banks of New River.
The **Stranahan House** (Las Olas Boulevard at New River Tunnel,
305–524–4736) was opened as a general store in 1901 by Frank
Stranahan, who had arrived in the area as a trader in 1897. Later,
he converted the two-story verandahed frame cottage into a residence for his bride. It has been restored and furnished to reflect its
use as a home in the 1910s.

Farther west along the river are a cluster of buildings from the
old downtown. The **Fort Lauderdale Historical Museum** (219
Southwest Second Avenue, 305–463–4431) contains an eclectic
group of local-history materials, including a scale model of the old
fort palisade; clothing of the Seminole and early Fort Lauderdale
settlers; and a miscellany of dolls, toys, and other artifacts. The
**Discovery Center** (231 Southwest Second Avenue, 305–462–

4116), a "hands-on" science museum, is housed in the former **New River Inn,** built as a hotel by local contractor E. T. King in 1905. The complex also includes the **King-Cromartie House,** built by King in 1907. A two-story heart-pine frame home, it in no way resembles the hollow cinderblock construction that King helped pioneer. The house is restored and contains King's original furnishings. Behind the King-Cromartie House is the **First Schoolhouse,** a replica of the one-room pine school building raised near here in 1899; Stranahan's wife, Ivy, was the first teacher.

## GREATER MIAMI

In 1896 Miami was incorporated as a city, with a population of about 1,500 souls. Just the year before, the enterprising Julia S. Tuttle—who bought land on the Miami River years before the first Everglades drainage projects were initiated—sent a bouquet of Miami-area orange blossoms to Henry Flagler at Palm Beach. This happened to be the year of the great freeze that destroyed 90 percent of the then more-northerly citrus crop, damaging Flagler's railroad profits and spoiling the image of sunny Florida so important to Flagler's resorts at Saint Augustine and Palm Beach. He immediately decided to extend his railroad to Miami. In July of the following year, the city was incorporated.

The city mushroomed to 30,000 by 1920, when the great real-estate boom set in. Planter John S. Collins and his partner, financier Carl F. Fisher, had taken the 1,600 acres of mangrove swamp just east of Miami and turned it into Miami Beach, a slightly lesser version of Palm Beach. Will Rogers would soon quip, "Carl drained off the water moccasins . . . and replaced them with hotels and New York prices." Between 1920 and 1926 the population more than tripled; real-estate values soared precariously. In 1926 bust followed boom: Materials could not be transported to the sites, financial backers became nervous, and a devastating hurricane sent them howling in fright. Miami had an early taste of the Great Depression, but several of the communities begun in the 1920s boom bear testimony to Floridian aspirations.

George Merrick's **Coral Gables** and aviator-turned-builder Glenn Curtiss's **Opa-locka** are still magnificent examples of the full range of dreams. The former is an elegant planned community, with residential and commercial buildings meticulously laid out in a landscaped setting with a Moorish-Spanish theme. Some local monuments, such as the **Biltmore Hotel** (1200 Anastasia Avenue), display a more restrained elegance. Opa-locka, to the north, took a

set-designer's approach to reality, with minareted and turreted Moorish style buildings. Even the streets were laid out in Moorish crescent patterns. The best surviving examples of the community are the **Opa-locka City Hall** (777 Sharazad Boulevard) and the **Opa-locka Railroad Station** (Ali Baba Avenue).

Miami may have entered the depression early, but it was also early to dig out, largely because of tourism; it was the only major city to experience another housing boom during the depression. The 1926 bust had put the Mediterranean Revival architectural styles into disrepute—they were thoroughly identified with the boom—and by 1936, some style was needed for the whole community springing up on the southern edge of Miami Beach. Thus was born the more modern, streamlined style known as Miami Art Deco. Thanks to preservation efforts, more than 800 of these remarkable hotels and commercial and private buildings, with their pastels, portholes, and smooth corners, remain in the **Art Deco Historic District** located between Sixth and Twenty-third streets and from Ocean Drive to Lennox Avenue in Miami Beach.

## Cloister of the Monastery of St. Bernard de Clairvaux

This twelfth-century Cistercian cloister from the province of Segovia in Spain is the oldest structure of European origin in the United States, having been originally built in 1141, incorporating some stones from an even earlier church. William Randolph Hearst bought the cloister for his California mansion at San Simeon and had the stones shipped to New York in 10,751 crates. U.S. Customs had orders to remove the straw packing materials from each, since they were conceivably contaminated with hoof-and-mouth disease. Regrettably, reassembly numbers were marked on the crates, not the stones, so by the time the operation was finished, the would-be cloister was a mass of misidentified blocks and columns. Hearst washed his hands of the whole affair, but the gorgeous transitional Romanesque-Gothic cloister and chapter house were eventually and painstakingly reconstructed here, where they now house an Episcopal church.

LOCATION: 16711 West Dixie Highway, North Miami. HOURS: 10–5 Monday–Saturday, 12–5 Sunday. FEE: Yes. TELEPHONE: 305–945–1462.

OPPOSITE: *Inspired by* The One Thousand and One Tales from the Arabian Nights, *developer Glenn Curtiss built Moorish fantasies in the planned city of Opa-locka, near Miami.*

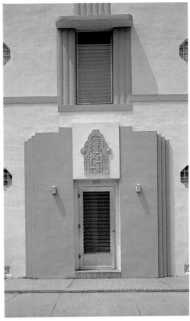

Miami is one of the best places in the United States to see Art Deco architecture, which developed in the late 1920s, influenced by the 1925 Paris Exposition des Arts Decoratifs. Art Deco was extensively employed in the Miami boom of the 1930s, when developers wanted new-looking buildings. More than 800 are preserved in Miami's Art Deco Historic District.

The **Bass Museum of Art** (2121 Park Avenue, Miami Beach, 305–673–7530) began as the private collection of Mr. and Mrs. John Bass, which they donated to the city of Miami Beach in 1964. The collection, housed in a 1930 Art Deco building, focuses on European painting, sculpture, and decorative arts from the thirteenth to the twentieth centuries.

## Historical Museum of Southern Florida

Housed in the Metro-Dade Cultural Center, this fine museum has exhibits that range from prehistoric Indian artifacts to a trolley that carried prospective buyers to Coral Gables in the 1920s. The emphasis is on experience of the past, so events are often portrayed through the eyes of an important participant, such as Ralph Middleton Munroe, the photographer, botanist, yachtsman, and pioneer of Biscayne Bay. Among the highlights of the collection is a rare double elephant folio edition of John James Audubon's *Birds of America,* some of the studies for which were done during the great naturalist's visit to southern Florida in 1831–1832.

LOCATION: 101 West Flagler Street. HOURS: 10–5 Monday–Wednesday, 10–9 Thursday, 10–5 Friday–Saturday, 12–5 Sunday. FEE: Yes. TELEPHONE: 305–375–1492.

*James Deering's Villa Vizcaya, the most elaborate house in Florida, nestled in hummock forests along Biscayne Bay.*

*Design elements of formal Italian hill gardens are combined with plants native to southern Florida in Villa Vizcaya's ten acres of formal gardens.* OVERLEAF: *Villa Vizcaya. During construction, Deering frequently asked his designer, Paul Chalfin, "Must we be so grand?"*

## Vizcaya Museum and Gardens

The Villa Vizcaya, begun in 1914 and completed in 1922 at a cost of $15 million, is the grandest mansion in Florida and an outstanding example of the Mediterranean Revival style. Loosely derived from Venetian villas, it faces Biscayne Bay; its seventy rooms are stuffed with rare European antiquities and constructed using such borrowed details as a carved ceiling from a Venice palazzo and marble-framed doors from the Torlonia Palace in Rome.

International Harvester heir James Deering and his insistent, indefatigable decorator-designer Paul Chalfin traveled all over Europe acquiring the furnishings and ornaments for the home. The magnificent formal gardens—vaguely Italian but using indigenous Florida plantings—are by Diego Suarez, as is the stone boat that forms a breakwater. The house is now open as a museum, containing the collection of decorative arts assembled by Deering and Chalfin. Across the street, in a building that once served as part of the villa's mock Italian farm town, is the **Claire Mendel Collection,** a small but interesting assemblage of pre-Modern European painting.

LOCATION: 3251 South Miami Avenue. HOURS: 9:30–5 Daily. FEE: Yes. TELEPHONE: 305–579–2813.

## Miccosukee Indian Village

A detour west on the Tamiami Trail (Route 41) from downtown Miami into the Everglades leads to a reconstructed village of the Miccosukee, inhabited by descendants of the Miccosukee Seminole, who melted into the Everglades at the conclusion of the Second Seminole War and were never defeated or removed. Tribespeople have assembled village exhibits around traditional chickee (palm-thatched) houses and raised dwellings.

LOCATION: Route 41, twenty-five miles west of Miami. HOURS: 9–5 Daily. FEE: Yes. TELEPHONE: 305–223–8388.

## Barnacle State Historic Site

One of the earliest settlers of Coconut Grove, just south of down-town Miami, was Ralph Middleton Munroe, who visited the Bis-cayne Bay area as early as 1877 and, like so many others, brought his ailing wife here to recuperate in 1881. His wife and sister-in-law both died, but New Yorker Munroe continued wintering in Florida until 1891, when he took up permanent residence here and built the simple but elegant home that would be named "The Barnacle." In 1908, when Munroe remarried and started a second family, the bungalow was jacked up and a lower floor added under it. This wood-frame house, with its verandah on three sides and an ingen-ious natural air-conditioning system, is among the finest vernacular structures in Florida. Though the once-lonely home is now sur-rounded by modern residences, the original furnishings and the many photographs by Munroe displayed in the house are remind-ers of the pioneer era. A disciple of Emersonian transcendentalism, Munroe was self-reliant not only in the building of his own home but also in boat design: His shallow-draft sailing boats brought him fame as a naval architect, and one of his creations is on display here.

LOCATION: 3485 Main Highway, Coconut Grove. HOURS: 9–4 Thursday–Monday. FEE: Yes. TELEPHONE: 305–448–9445.

## Gold Coast Railroad Museum

This museum has a fine collection of rolling stock, including two oil-burning locomotives that originally belonged to Flagler's Flor-ida East Coast Railroad; one still functions and the other is being

OPPOSITE: *Villa Vizcaya was designed by young architect F. Burrall Hoffman to be a perfect setting for the decorative objects collected by Deering and Chalfin in Europe.*

restored. There is also one of the famous observation cars from the "California Zephyr" and U.S. Car No. 1, also known as the "Ferdinand Magellan," an elaborate Pullman car.

LOCATION: 12450 Southwest 152nd Street, at Southwest 124th Avenue. HOURS: 10–3 Monday–Friday, 10–5 Saturday–Sunday. FEE: Yes. TELEPHONE: 305–253–0063.

## HOMESTEAD AND FLORIDA CITY

Thirty miles south of downtown Miami, along Route 1, these two towns are sandwiched between the Everglades and Biscayne National Park, serving as gateways to both. Homestead was built as a railroad workers' town when Flagler drove his railway south to the Florida Keys. Some of the early structures from the 1910s and 1920s survive on Krome Avenue between Flagler Avenue and North Fourth Street. The **Florida Pioneer Museum** (826 North Krome Avenue, 305–246–9531) in Florida City consists of the 1904 Florida East Coast Railroad depot and stationmaster's home and a furnished caboose. The waiting room and business office have been restored and the house contains interpretive exhibits.

# T H E   F L O R I D A   K E Y S

## KEY WEST

Key West prospered while the rest of southern Florida languished. Perched on an eight-square-mile island one hundred miles from the mainland between the Atlantic Ocean and the Gulf of Mexico, it was positioned to become the salvage center for the sailing ships that piled up on the reefs. Beginning in the 1830s—after Commodore David Porter and his famous West Indies Squadron had harried and chased the buccaneers who had long controlled the area—Key West grew quickly. By the 1890s Key West had 18,000 residents, including not only the "wreckers" (salvagers) but also sponge fishermen, Cuban cigar makers, and military personnel.

The name Key West derives from the Spanish phrase *cayo hueso*, meaning "bone key" and reportedly deriving from piles of

OPPOSITE: *Key West developed a distinctive style of vernacular architecture, the Conch house, which adapted elements from the Bahamas, New Orleans, and New England.*

human bones found here by early visitors. It has a population and an architecture that are uniquely mixed. Both more or less washed up on shore from the four quarters of the compass: The wreckers were usually Cockney Englishmen coming from the Bahamas or departing from Florida after the American victory in the Revolutionary War; then, too, there were seafaring settlers from New England, Southerners from Virginia and the Carolinas, emigrants from New Orleans, and Cubans fleeing from (or plotting) revolution in their native land less than 100 miles to the south. In 1886, a disastrous fire destroyed half the town, including the cigar district. The city was quickly rebuilt, but most of the cigar business relocated to the mainland at Tampa. "Flagler's Folly"—the remarkable Overseas Extension of the Florida East Coast Railroad—reached Key West via a string of arched bridge spans in 1912, covering 25 miles on land and 75 miles on water. (The arched bridges spanning the major channels between the keys on Route 1 are the original railroad bridges.) The engineering feat also increased tourism.

The **Key West Historic District** at the western end of the island encompasses 3,100 buildings and 190 blocks, and its structures tell, in architectural terms, the whole history of the island. Particularly remarkable are the "Conch" houses—one-and-a-half- to two-and-a-half-story frame vernacular buildings, built with a variety of ornament during the nineteenth-century heyday of Key West. The wooden structures were built with dovetail joints—even after the invention of the balloon frame—to give greater stability in hurricanes; windows have thick-louvered shutters and roofs have hatchways to improve air circulation; and cisterns sit under or near the houses, collecting rainwater from the pitched roof. Otherwise, detail runs from wrought-iron Creole porch railings and gingerbread Victorian ornamentation to worked wood taken from salvaged ships and incorporated into the house design. **Caroline Street** offers a selection of Conch houses, as well as other types of architecture. One of the best examples is the **Dr. Joseph Y. Porter House** (429 Caroline Street, private), an 1838 double-verandahed frame house with Bahaman and Yankee influence.

Another fine house is known as the **Audubon House** (205 Whitehead Street at Greene Street, 305–294–2116). Built in the first half of the nineteenth century for prominent Key West wrecker and harbor pilot Captain John H. Geiger, the large, stately

OPPOSITE: *Southernmost House, a private residence at the base of South and Duval streets in Key West.*

house was the first to be restored on the island. John James Audubon used two flowering trees he found growing on the grounds of the Audubon House as backgrounds for his portrayals of the white-crowned pigeon and the gray kingbird, and the house was dedicated in honor of his visit to Key West. The museum houses a collection of original Audubon engravings, plus a fine, eclectic collection of eighteenth- and nineteenth-century furnishings typical of the period when the naturalist visited the island in 1832.

Nearby is a museum devoted entirely to the booty of a latter-day wrecker, the **Mel Fisher Maritime Heritage Society** (200 Greene Street, 305–296–9936). Since 1972, Fisher has been salvaging the Spanish treasure galleon *Nuestra Señora de Atocha*, a vessel that sank off the Marquesas in 1622, and its sister ship, the *Santa Margarita*. A part of the fabulous collection of gold coins, chains, cups, and old cannon that he recovered is displayed here.

The **Wrecker's Museum** (322 Duval Street, 305–294–9502) is housed in an old Conch house constructed of Dade County pine in 1829. It displays photographs and memorabilia of the wrecking business on Key West as well as other local-history material. The **Key West Lighthouse Museum** (938 Whitehead Street, 305–294–0012) affords a fine view of all of Key West from its 110-foot tower, right in the middle of town. It was erected here in 1847, after an earlier and more exposed 1825 light was swept away in a storm. A museum contains artifacts of Florida lighthouses.

The **Ernest Hemingway House** (907 Whitehead Street, 305–294–1575) was built between 1849 and 1851 by a prominent merchant. The novelist bought the house in 1931 and lived here on and off until 1940, working on *For Whom the Bell Tolls* and *A Farewell to Arms*. Begun in 1845, the trapezoidal **Fort Zachary Taylor** (Southard Street, 305–292–6713), with walls varying from five to eight feet in thickness, was built to defend what was then Florida's largest city. It was held by Union forces throughout the Civil War. A museum contains a fine collection of cannon.

The **East Martello Gallery and Museum** (3501 South Roosevelt Boulevard, 305–296–3913) is housed in an 1862 fortress that was built to protect the city's southern flank. A city art gallery is here, along with a local-history collection that includes memorabilia from Key West's once-vibrant sponge and cigar industries.

OPPOSITE: *Gateposts of decorative fruit baskets, above, at the Artist House, built in 1900. Twin entrances, below, at the side of the Southernmost House.*

*The moat surrounding Fort Jefferson, half a mile in length, swarms with sharks and barracuda.* OPPOSITE: *The massive, hexagonal fort covers most of Garden Key.*

## FORT JEFFERSON

Sixty-eight miles west of Key West in the isolated Dry Tortugas—accessible only by boat or seaplane—is the largest of America's nineteenth-century coastal fortifications. Built to protect and control gulf shipping lanes, the mammoth hexagonal masonry fort has walls eight feet thick and fifty feet high and a perimeter of almost half a mile. Begun in 1846, it continued to be built for more than thirty years; by the time the fort was finished, the new rifled cannon had rendered it obsolete. During and after the Civil War it was used as a prison, its most noted inmates being the so-called Lincoln Conspirators, four men who had been convicted of conspiring with John Wilkes Booth to assassinate President Lincoln. The cell of Dr. Samuel Mudd—a physician who was imprisoned for setting the assassin's broken leg, though the doctor had not known the crime his patient committed—can still be seen. Mudd was released after he tended to the 270 men struck down by yellow fever in an 1867 epidemic at the fort.

LOCATION: Garden Key, Dry Tortugas. HOURS: 8–Dusk Daily. FEE: None. TELEPHONE: 305–247–6211.

# THE WEST COAST

## NAPLES

Another southwestern city that has grown exponentially since World War II, Naples is also the gateway to Tamiami Trail and Alligator Alley, the two routes through the Everglades to East Coast cities. (Tamiami stands for Tampa–Miami.) The **Collier County Museum** (3301 Tamiami Trail East, 813–774–8476), which exhibits local-history artifacts, includes an especially fine collection of the shell tools and ornaments of the Calusa; a diorama of a Spanish shipwreck, with actual cannonballs, coins, and olive jars; assorted Seminole and Seminole War materials, including trade items like beeswax, furs, and alligator skins; and memorabilia of the cattle-ranching period. Outside the museum is "Old Number 2," a steam locomotive that once ran local routes for a cypress-logging firm. A re-created Seminole village may be toured, as well as ongoing excavations by staff archaeologists.

## KORESHAN STATE HISTORIC SITE

Chicagoan Cyrus R. Teed led his followers to this place in 1894, preaching a gospel that included communal ownership, reincarnation, celibacy, and the notion that the sun was really inside the earth, with all life gathered on the walls of the sphere. The members of the Koreshan Unity were excellent farmers, but the 10 million adherents that Teed predicted would flock to the community never appeared. The founder himself, supposed to be immortal, perished in 1908. Twelve of the original community's frame vernacular buildings have been restored on the site.

LOCATION: Route 41 and Corkscrew Road, Estero. HOURS: 8–Dusk Daily. FEE: Yes. TELEPHONE: 813–992–0311.

## FORT MYERS

Just as its leading citizen, Thomas Edison, predicted, Fort Myers has blossomed from a sleepy cow town to become one of the fastest-growing metropolitan areas in the United States. The **Edison Winter Home** (2350 McGregor Boulevard, 813–334–3614), an 1886

OPPOSITE: *Since the 1880s, Florida developers have striven to give Florida an Italian flavor. Here, contemporary canal-front houses in Naples strike a Venetian note.*

prefabricated frame house, is actually two houses connected by a breezeway. Edison had it built to his specifications in Maine, then shipped by schooner to Fort Myers, where the pieces were assembled. The home and laboratory are much as Edison left them when he died after spending thirty-three winters here. Among the research he did here was his quest for a synthetic rubber. The specimens of local and exotic plants he assembled in his search have now grown into a lush botanical garden. The museum contains the largest collection of Edison memorabilia in the world, including the inventor's car and a huge collection of Edison phonographs.

The **Fort Myers Historical Museum** (2300 Peck Street, 813–332–5955) is a good local-history museum with a varied collection. The turn-of-the-century private railway car "Esperanza" has been restored. Exhibits of Calusa and Seminole Indian artifacts include the shell and stone implements of the former and clothing and a twenty-foot dugout canoe from the latter. Models, photos, and artifacts depict the cattle industry, important in the second half of the nineteenth century, and there is an exhibit devoted to Cyrus Teed's utopian Koreshan community. There is also an excellent collection of depression and art glass.

*A banyan tree in the tropical garden surrounding the Edison Winter Home in Fort Myers.*

*More than 170 Edison phonographs are on display in the Edison Museum, including these models with their festive morning glory horns.*

## THE JOHN & MABLE RINGLING MUSEUM OF ART

At the northern edge of Sarasota, the Circus Galleries, the mansion Ca' d'Zan, and the Asolo Theater form one of the great flamboyant complexes in a state devoted to flamboyance. John Ringling, the aggressive promoter of the circus he started with his brothers during the 1880s, spent part of his fortune on a magnificent collection of European art, primarily acquired after World War I. The Baroque collection is especially fine, with special strength in the Italian Baroque and many outstanding works by Peter Paul Rubens. There is also a solid collection of Spanish paintings.

All this is housed in an Italian Renaissance–type villa that looks modest only in comparison to the adjacent **Ca' d'Zan** ("House of John" in Venetian dialect), with details reminiscent of the Doge's Palace in Venice. Built in 1924–1926 at a cost of $1.5 million, the thirty-two-room mansion is now open to the public, displaying a profusion of decorative arts and furniture ranging from a chandelier from the Waldorf-Astoria in New York to rare tapestries to a

*The formal garden of the John & Mable Ringling Museum of Art contains a collection of Classical and Renaissance sculpture. This important museum established Sarasota as the cultural capital of Florida.* OPPOSITE: *Sarasota's Ca'd'Zan, built by circus magnate John Ringling between 1924 and 1926 for his wife, Mable, was designed by Dwight James Baum to resemble the Doge's Palace in Venice.*

working aeolian organ. Also on the spacious, beautifully landscaped grounds is the **Asolo Theater,** whose interior consists of a 1797 Italian court playhouse that had originally been installed in a castle in Asolo, Italy.

LOCATION: 5401 Bayshore Road. HOURS: 10–6 Monday–Wednesday, 10–10 Thursday, 10–6 Friday–Sunday. FEE: Yes. TELEPHONE: 813–355–5101.

## BRADENTON

The city of Bradenton contains two museums of interest. The **South Florida Museum** (201 Tenth Street West, 813–746–4132) contains a miscellany of historical exhibits, including a replica of explorer Hernando de Soto's home and chapel, dioramas of prehistoric Indian life, and a collection of Civil War memorabilia.

The **Manatee Village Historical Park** (604 Fifteenth Street East, 813–749–7165) assembles a collection of historic buildings from around the country, all restored and furnished. There's a vernacular "Cracker" house from 1912, typical of the style in this area; an 1887 high-steepled Methodist church; the 1860 Manatee County courthouse, a wood-frame building that is the oldest courthouse still standing in the state; and the 1903 Wiggins General Store, still on its original site.

### De Soto National Memorial

On the western edge of Bradenton at the mouth of the Manatee River, the park, possibly the spot of de Soto's 1539 landing, commemorates his four-year journey through the southeastern United States. Costumed interpreters give living history demonstrations of how de Soto's men would have lived and fought, including musket firing using sixteenth-century black-powder weapons known as harquebuses, and sixteenth-century crossbows. A nature trail has informational signs on the flora and fauna of this part of Florida.

LOCATION: Seventy-fifth Street NW. HOURS: 8–5:30 Daily. FEE: Yes. TELEPHONE: 813–792–0458.

Southwest of town on a group of five keys is **Fort De Soto Park** (Pinellas Bayway, 813–462–3347), a nature sanctuary that includes the fort built in 1898 to defend the entrance to Tampa Bay. Mullet Key was important in the early history of the state: It was here that Ponce de León landed in 1521, only to be driven off by the Tocobaga Indians bearing the wound from which he died.

# GAMBLE PLANTATION STATE HISTORIC SITE

The Gamble Plantation, the oldest building on the West Coast of Florida, was built for Major Robert Gamble over a six-year period in the 1840s. The mansion was made entirely of tabby, a lime-and-oyster-shell amalgam, giving it a solid, fortresslike appearance. Gamble, a Virginian, had taken up 3,500 acres in what is now Manatee County to grow sugarcane. Judah P. Benjamin, secretary of state of the Confederacy, hid here after the end of the war, before fleeing to Cuba and then England.

The home is magnificently restored, with a fine collection of period antiques, and is open for guided tours only. Also on the grounds is a furnished 1890s frame farmhouse.

LOCATION: 3708 Patten Avenue, Ellenton, four miles northeast of Bradenton. HOURS: 9–4 Thursday–Monday. FEE: Yes. TELEPHONE: 813–722–1017.

# SAINT PETERSBURG

With over a quarter-million inhabitants and a million visitors per year, Saint Petersburg is the mecca of West Coast sunseekers and retirees. Situated on Pinellas peninsula on the west side of Tampa Bay, with beaches on three sides and subtropical keys nearby, it is, as an eighteenth-century British chart maker once put it, "a pretty good place for a settlement."

Nevertheless, it remained sparsely settled for about 120 years, until Hamilton Disston, who had just bought a sizable chunk of central Florida, founded Disston City (now Gulfport) on the peninsula's southern tip. In 1887, Russian émigré Peter Demens and two partners ran their Orange Belt Railroad to Disston City. They named one of the stops along the way Saint Petersburg in honor of Demens's hometown.

Saint Petersburg had grown from 30 to about 300 inhabitants when Henry Plant took advantage of Demens's losses in the citrus

*Saint Petersburg's Don CeSar Hotel fronts the Gulf of Mexico. Its distinctive pastel color is named "Don CeSar Rouge."*

freeze to take over the Orange Belt Railroad in 1893. Several real-estate booms later, the city found itself a virtual capital for retirees—who lined the famous and now dismantled ranks of "green benches"—and the most popular location for baseball spring-training camps. During World War II, it was a center for troop training, and the county airport was converted into a training base for airmen. After the war, the area continued to be prominent in aerospace, and other industries have since arrived.

The **St. Petersburg Historical Museum** (335 Second Avenue NE, 813–894–1052) shows what the city looked like in its earlier days, with photos and memorabilia devoted to spring training, the green benches, the Benoist airboat, and the like. The **Haas Museum Complex** (3511 Second Avenue South, 813–327–1437) concentrates on earlier historic structures, displaying a furnished blacksmith's shop, a "Cracker" kitchen, a barbershop, a reconstructed Atlantic Coast Line train depot with a 1926 caboose, the 1850s Lowe House, and an archetypal Florida bungalow. The **Salvador Dali Museum** (1000 Third Street South, 813–823–3767) contains the world's largest collection of the famous surrealist's paintings and other artwork spanning his entire career.

## HERITAGE PARK

In the middle of the Pinellas peninsula, in the town of Largo, is an extensive museum and village of twenty historic structures gathered from around the county. All but two of them are furnished with antiques appropriate to the period. The oldest house is a pioneer log house of 1852, built by a militia captain who had served in the Seminole Wars. Most of the buildings date from the turn of the century, when the Plant System railroads brought the first influx of settlers. There are a gazebo, a bandstand, a barn, a train depot, and a caboose, among many other structures, arranged in a village setting. The museum contains local-history exhibits dating as far back as the Tocobaga Indian period, contemporaneous with the first Spanish landings in the area in 1528. A 400-year-old Spanish sword is among the artifacts displayed, along with a full-scale replica of the Benoist Airlines plane that ran the first scheduled air service in America, between Tampa and Saint Petersburg, in 1914.

LOCATION: 11909 125th Street North, Largo. HOURS: 10–4 Tuesday–Saturday, 1–4 Sunday. FEE: None. TELEPHONE: 813–462–3474.

## TARPON SPRINGS

This town was founded in 1876 by a few hardy settlers who thought that the tarpon spawned in Spring Bayou just east of town and named the place accordingly. Hamilton Disston bought almost all the local territory with his 4-million-acre purchase of 1881 and erected the Gulf Coast's first resort hotel here. It was not until 1905, however, with the arrival of a whole flotilla of Greek sponge fishermen from Key West, that the town took on its present character. The old **sponge dock area** on Athens and Hope streets contains many early-twentieth-century bungalows that were stuccoed over by the Greek settlers on their arrival. The **Universalist Church** (Grand Avenue and Read Street, 813–937–4682) houses a collection of symbolic religious paintings by American painter George Inness, Jr., the son of the great landscape painter, who had a house here in the first quarter of the twentieth century.

## TAMPA

Located at the head of Tampa Bay across from Saint Petersburg, and far more commercially oriented than its neighbor, Tampa is the third largest city in Florida, with a population of over 280,000. The name means "stick of fire" in the Calusa Indian tongue. A log

*A Tampa landmark, the Moorish-inspired Tampa Bay Hotel, built by railroad and hotel promoter Henry Plant in 1891.*

fort was established here as early as 1824, and its protection encouraged some settlement in the area, despite the Seminole threat.
Nevertheless, there was no city to speak of until Henry Plant
brought his railroad to town in 1884.

Two years later, Cuban cigar makers led by Don Vincente
Ybor migrated from fire-ravaged Key West to Tampa, establishing
**Ybor City,** a part of Tampa that still preserves its Hispanic flavor.
Roughly bounded by Nebraska Avenue, Twenty-second Street,
Fifth Avenue, and Columbus Drive, the area has much the look
today that it had around the turn of the century, when 20,000
workers rolled cigars in the great factories. The **Ybor City State
Museum** (1818 Ninth Avenue, 813–247–6323) tells the story of the
immigrants with exhibits on cigar making, memorabilia of the
area's important role during the Cuban wars of independence, and
period rooms. The museum is located in the 1923 Ferlita Bakery
and preserves the bakery's original 1896 brick oven.

Henry Plant was not content merely to build a railroad to
Tampa. Like his rival Flagler on the East Coast, Plant created
resort hotels, the most flamboyant of which still stands in Tampa.
The 1891 **Tampa Bay Hotel** (401 West Kennedy Boulevard) is a
wonderland of six minarets, four cupolas, three domes, keyhole
arches, ballrooms, and whatever the carriage trade could want.
The quarter-mile-long building cost $3 million, the furniture an-
other $500,000, but its effect on the area's popularity almost made
good Plant's vow to "turn this sandheap into the Champs-Elysées,
the Hillsborough [River] into a Seine." The **Henry B. Plant Museum** (813–254–1891) occupies the south wing of the hotel, which is
now a part of the University of Tampa. Some of the original
furnishings and decorations of the fantasy Moorish hotel are preserved here, along with collections of English and French antiques.
A replica of Plant's own private train is also part of the museum.

The **Tampa Museum of Art** (601 Doyle Carlton Drive, 813–
223–8130) has a collection of Greco-Roman antiquities that is particularly strong in Southern Italian and Attic vases.

# LAKE WALES

Although turpentine distillers and citrus growers had previously
inhabited the area, the town of Lake Wales really sprang up in
1911, at the junction of two railways. The depot was the first
building in Lake Wales. Its 1928 successor is now the **Lake Wales**

**Museum and Cultural Center** (325 South Scenic Highway, 813–676–5443), a pink Spanish Revival Atlantic Coast Line depot containing photographs, textiles, and a large collection of local citrus labels. A 1916 executive Pullman car is being restored, and a 1944 diesel locomotive is on display.

## The Bok Tower Gardens

Between 1889 and 1919 Edward Bok brought the *Ladies' Home Journal* to the pinnacle of the American magazine world; following his retirement, he won the Pulitzer Prize for his autobiography, *The Americanization of Edward Bok*. In 1929 he created this 128-acre sanctuary of gardens with a 205-foot-tall tower. The tower itself stands on the highest point in peninsular Florida; its fifty-seven-bell carillon is famous, and the ironwork by Samuel Yellin is outstanding. The landscaped gardens were designed by Frederick Law Olmsted, Jr.

LOCATION: Off Route 17A, three miles north of Lake Wales. HOURS: 8–5 Daily. FEE: Yes. TELEPHONE: 813–676–1408.

*Bok Tower, dedicated in 1929 by President Calvin Coolidge.*

## Notes on Architecture

### FRENCH COLONIAL

MADAM JOHN'S LEGACY, LA

Built largely in the Mississippi Valley, French Colonial structures followed models developed in the French West Indies. The main floor was one full story above the ground and was ringed by a full-length porch, or galerie, which allowed the main rooms to be insulated from both the damp earth and the sun. A prominent hipped roof, extending over the galerie, provided shade. The interior rooms were cooled by breezes passing through French windows with double casements.

### GEORGIAN

Beginning in Boston as early as 1686, and only much later elsewhere, the design of houses became balanced about a central axis, with only careful, stripped detail. A few large houses incorporated double-story pilasters. Sash windows with rectilinear panes replaced casements. Hipped roofs accentuated the balanced and strict proportions inherited from Italy and Holland via England and Scotland.

### FEDERAL

CHIEF VANN HOUSE, GA

The post-Revolutionary style sometimes called "Federal" was more flexible and delicate than the more formal Georgian. The Federal style was rooted in archaeological discoveries at Pompeii and Herculaneum in Italy in the 1750s, as well as in contemporary French interior planning principles. In the south, the proponents of the Federal style followed the lead of Thomas Jefferson, using exclusively Roman rather than Greek models. Southern Federal buildings are commonly built of red brick, with massive white porticos and, frequently, a fan-shaped window in the pediment.

### GREEK REVIVAL

UNIVERSITY OF GEORGIA CHAPEL, GA

The Greek Revival manifested itself in severe, stripped, rectilinear proportions, occasionally a set of columns or pilasters, and even, in a few instances, Greek-temple form. It combined Greek and Roman forms—low pitched pediments, simple moldings, rounded arches, and shallow domes—and was used in official buildings and many private houses.

### PLANTATION PLAIN

This style was the prominent vernacular style in the Deep South before King Cotton brought the wealth to make more ambitious houses. It is essentially an advance on the dogtrot cabin, still constructed with a wood frame, with a one-room-deep second story and a one-story porch on the back. The porches improved ventilation by making it possible to have rooms with windows on three sides.

### GOTHIC REVIVAL

After about 1830 darker colors, asymmetry, broken skylines, verticality, and the pointed arch began to appear. New machinery produced carved and pierced trim along the eaves. Roofs became steep and gabled; porches became more spacious. Oriel and bay windows were common and there was greater use of stained glass.

## ITALIANATE

HAY HOUSE, GA

The Italianate style began to appear in the 1840s, both in a formal, balanced "palazzo" style and in a picturesque "villa" style. Both had round-headed windows and arcaded porches. Commercial structures were often made of cast iron, with a ground floor of large arcaded windows and smaller windows on each successive rising story.

## QUEEN ANNE

The Queen Anne style emphasized contrasts of form, texture, and color. Large encircling verandahs, tall chimneys, turrets, towers, and a multitude of textures are typical of the style. The ground floor might be of stone or brick, the upper floors of stucco, shingle, or clapboard. Specially shaped bricks and plaques were used for decoration. Panels of stained glass outlined or filled the windows. The steep roofs were gabled or hipped, and other elements, such as pediments, Venetian windows, and front and corner bay windows, were typical.

## RENAISSANCE REVIVAL OR BEAUX ARTS

NEW CAPITOL, MS

In the 1880s and 1890s, American architects who had studied at the Ecole des Beaux Arts in Paris brought a new Renaissance Revival to the United States. Sometimes used in urban mansions, but generally reserved for public and academic buildings, it borrowed from three centuries of Renaissance detail—much of it French—and·put together picturesque combinations from widely differing periods.

## ECLECTIC PERIOD REVIVALS

RINGLING HOUSE, FL

During the first decades of the twentieth century, revivals of diverse architectural styles became popular in the United States, particularly for residential buildings. Architects designed Swiss chalets, half-timbered Tudor houses, and Norman chateaux with equal enthusiasm. Many of these houses were modeled on rural structures and constructed in suburban settings. In the South, particularly in Florida, many buildings were designed to suit the tropical climate using idealized Hispanic or Moorish styles, or sometimes combinations of the two.

## ART DECO

THE CARLYLE, FL

The late 1920s saw the development of a new architectural style, Art Deco, influenced by the Paris Exposition des Arts Decoratifs of 1925. It is marked by linear, hard edged, or angular composition, frequently achieved by the use of set-backs in the building facade. These buildings were ornamented with stylized decoration executed in the same material as the building itself or in various metals, colored glass bricks, or mosaic tiles. A popular style and relatively inexpensive to build, Art Deco became identified with the Miami boom of the 1930s when developers spurned the Mediterranean revival style that was identified with the Florida real estate bust of the 1920s.

# I  N  D  E  X

464

PHOTO CREDITS

**Cover:** Balthazar Korab, Troy, MI ; **Half-title Page:** Van Jones Martin, Savannah ; **Frontispiece:** Wendell Metzen/Southern Stock Photos; **Page 12:** Ed Malles, Winter Park, FL ; **18:** Paul Rocheleau/© 1988 Rebus Inc., *Old New Orleans* by Vance Muse, Oxmoor House Inc.; **21, 24–25:** Chicago Historical Society; **27:** © 1988 Rebus Inc.; **28:** LA State Museum ; **30, 33:** Paul Rocheleau/© 1988 Rebus Inc.; **34, 38 (left):** Karen Radkai/© 1988 Rebus Inc., *Old New Orleans* by Vance Muse, Oxmoor House Inc.; **38 (right):** Paul Rocheleau/© 1988 Rebus Inc.; **39, 40:** Karen Radkai/© 1988 Rebus Inc.; **42, 45:** Paul Rocheleau/© 1988 Rebus Inc.; **46:** John Neubauer, Arlington, VA; **48:** Giraudon/Art Resource; Musée d'Orsay, Paris; **51 (top):** David King Gleason/*Plantation Homes of LA and the Natchez Area,* © 1982 LSU Press ; **51 (bottom):** Karen Radkai/© 1988 Rebus Inc.; **52:** Nat Park Service; **54:** New Orleans Museum of Art: Gift of Wm. E. Groves; **56–57:** Jan White/LA State Museum; **60:** Paul Rocheleau/© 1988 Rebus Inc.; **62, 63:** Pat Canova, Miami; **65:** Thomas S. England/*National Geographic Traveler*; **68, 71:** David King Gleason, Baton Rouge, LA; **74:** Michael Freeman; **75, 77 (top):** David King Gleason; **77 (bottom):** Michael Freeman; **78–79:** David King Gleason; **82:** LA Office of Tourism; **85:** LA State Museum; **86:** Tina Freeman, New Orleans; **88:** Hickey-Robertson/*Southern Accents*; **89:** Tina Freeman; **93, 94:** Paul Rocheleau/© 1988 Rebus Inc., *Plantations of the Old South* by Henry Wiencek, Oxmoor House Inc.; **101 (top):** B.A.Cohen, Shreveport, LA; **101 (bottom), 102, 103, 105:** Kirk R. Tuck/*Early American Life*; **108:** LSU/Shreveport Archives; **110:** Ed Castle/*Poverty Point: A Culture of the Lower MS Valley* by Jon L. Gibson, Baton Rouge, LA: LA Office of Cultural Dev., 1985; **111:** John Guillet, Natchitoches, LA; **112:** Jonathan Wallen, Yonkers, NY; **115:** Hillel Burger/Peabody Museum, Harvard U. ; **120, 121:** John Rogers/*Southern Accents* and Rosemont, Woodville, MS; **122:** Nathan Benn/Woodfin Camp; **126:** Matt Bradley, Little Rock, AR; **128–129:** Balthazar Korab ; **130:** Michael Freeman; **132, 133 (top):** David King Gleason; **133 (bottom):** Library of Congress; **134:** David King Gleason/*The Great Houses of Natchez* by Mary Warren Miller and Ronald W. Miller, © 1986 University Press of MS ; **136:** Balthazar Korab ; **138:** John Lewis Stage/Image Bank; **144–145, 146:** Michael Freeman; **147:** The Beverley R. Robinson Collection, US Naval Academy Museum; **150:** Matt Bradley; **152:** Jonathan Wallen; **157:** Matt Bradley; **158, 161, 162:** Jonathan Wallen; **163:** Beauvoir, Biloxi, MS ; **164:** Jonathan Wallen; **168, 169:** Paul Rocheleau/© 1988 Rebus Inc.; **173:** MS Dept of Archives and History; **174:** Martin J. Dain/Magnum; **178:** Jonathan Wallen; **181:** Hillel Burger/Peabody Museum, Harvard U. ; **184:** Wadsworth Atheneum, Hartford, CT; **189:** Wendell Metzen/Southern Stock Photos; **192–193:** Ed Malles/Photo Options; **194, 195, 196:** Jonathan Wallen; **197:** Marsha Perry/Photo Options; **198:** Ed Malles/Photo Options; **201:** Ed Malles; **203:** William Stanley Hoole Special Collections Library, University of Alabama ; **205:** Balthazar Korab ; **207:** Ed Malles; **208–209:** Paul Rocheleau/© 1988 Rebus Inc.; **211:** Bruce Davidson/Magnum; **212:** Bud Hunter, Birmingham, AL; **214, 216:** Ed Malles; **218, 219:** Jonathan Wallen; **221 (left):** the National Geographic Society/White House Historical Association, Washington DC; **221 (right):** Collection of Cousins Properties Inc, Marietta, GA; **222:** Library of Congress; **223:** Jonathan Wallen; **225:** Bud Hunter; **226:** Birmingham Museum of Art; **230:** Linda Lottman/Photo Options; **233:** Jim Tuten/Southern Stock Photos; **237, 239, 242:** Ed Malles; **244:** Pat Canova; **247:** The Henry Francis du Pont Winterthur Museum; **250–251:** Van Jones Martin; **255:** William A. Bake, Savannah, GA; **257, 259, 260, 262, 263:** Van Jones Martin; **264–265:** William S. Weems/Woodfin Camp ; **266–267:** David Muench, Santa Barbara, CA; **270:** James H. Carmichael Jr./Image Bank; **274–275:** Raymond G. Barnes/Click Chicago ; **277:** Van Jones Martin; **279:** David Muench; **281:** Pat Canova; **283:** Michael Philip Manheim/Photo Options; **284, 286, 289:** Jonathan Wallen; **293:** George N. Barnard/Kean Archives, Philadelphia; **294:** Van Jones Martin; **296:** Paul Rocheleau; **297:** Van Jones Martin; **301, 302, 305, 306, 309:** Jonathan Wallen; **311, 312:** David Muench; **314, 315:** David King Gleason/*Antebellum Homes of Georgia,* © 1987 LSU Press; **316, 316–317:** Jonathan Wallen; **318:** David King Gleason; **321:** William A. Bake/National Park Service, Ocmulgee National Monument; **324, 325:** Jonathan Wallen; **329:** The Kobal Collection/Super Stock Int ; **332, 333:** Jonathan Wallen; **334, 335:** David King Gleason; **336:** William A. Bake/National Park Service, Ocmulgee National Monument; **338, 343, 344:** Jonathan Wallen; **347:** David King Gleason; **349, 350:** Jonathan Wallen; **353:** New York Public Library, Prints Division; **357:** Pat Canova; **358:** Charles E. Bennett, Wash, DC/*Settlement of FL,* © 1968 University of FL Press; **360–361:** James Valentine/Thaell & Associates, Tallahassee, FL; **362:** Milo Stewart/FL Dept of Commerce, Div of Tourism; **366:** Jonathan Wallen; **368:** David Muench; **369:** Jonathan Wallen; **370:** Courtesy of Charles E. Bennett ; **374:** Steven Brooke, Miami; **377:** FL Dept of Commerce, Div of Tourism; **381:** Steven Brooke; **383:** Charles E. Bennett; **385:** Erik Kvalsvik, Baltimore; **388:** Steven Brooke; **392–393:** Library of Congress; **395 (top):** Thomas McLendon/FL Dept of Commerce, Div of Tourism; **395 (bottom):** Charles McNulty/Click Chicago; **399:** Paul J. Crowley/Collier County Museum, Naples, FL; **400:** Luis Villota/Stock Market; **403:** FL State Archives; **406–407:** Tim Thompson, Bainbridge Island, WA; **408:** Henry M. Flagler Museum, Palm Beach, FL; **412:** NASA; **415:** Theodore Flagg/Charles Hosmer Morse Museum of American Art, Winter Park, FL; **418, 419:** Steve Hogben, Atlanta; **420:** Michael Philip Manheim/Stock Market; **424:** Randy Taylor/Compix; **426 (top):** David J. Kaminsky, Savannah; **426 (bottom):** Hiroyuki Matsumoto/Black Star; **427 (top left):** Lanny Provo/Sharp Shooters; **427 (top right, bottom right):** David J. Kaminsky; **428:** Marc Vaughn/Sharp Shooters; **429:** Laura Hinshaw/Southern Stock Photos; **430–431:** Nathan Benn/Woodfin Camp ; **432:** Mike Barrs/Sharp Shooters; **434:** Al Satterwhite/Image Bank; **436:** Randy Duchaine/Stock Market; **439:** Michael L. Carlebach, Miami, FL; **440:** Matt Bradley; **441:** Jeff Williams/Sharp Shooters; **442:** James Blank/Stock Market; **444:** Baron Wolman/Woodfin Camp ; **445:** Dick Deutsch, Ft. Lauderdale, FL ; **446:** Baron Wolman, Mill Valley, CA; **447:** Jürgen Vogt/Image Bank; **449:** Karen Kent/Stock Market; **451:** University of S FL Library, Special Collections ; **453:** Derek Fell, Gardenville, PA; **454 (top left):** Michael Freeman; **454 (top right):** David King Gleason; **454 (bottom), 455 (top left, top center):** Jonathan Wallen; **455 (bottom center):** Baron Wolman; **455 (right):** David J. Kaminsky; **Back Cover:** Jonathan Wallen

The editors gratefully acknowledge the assistance of Ann J. Campbell, Ferris Cook, Ann ffolliott, Amy Hughes, Kevin Lewis, Kerri Lamers, Carol A. McKeown, Klaske Pebenga, Martha Schulman, Catherine Shea Tangney, Linda Venator, and Patricia Woodruff.